T&T Clark Studies in Systematic Theology

Edited by

John Webster, King's College,
University of Aberdeen, UK

Ian A. McFarland, Candler School of Theology,
Emory University, USA

Ivor Davidson, University of Otago,
New Zealand

t & t clark

ISAAK A. DORNER

The Triune God and the Gospel of Salvation

Jonathan Norgate

t&t clark

Published by T&T Clark
A Continuum imprint
The Tower Building   80 Maiden Lane
11 York Road   Suite 704, New York
London SE1 7NX   NY 10038

www.continuumbooks.com

British Library Cataloguing-in-Publication Data
A catalogue record for this book is available from the British Library

ISBN-13: HB: 978-0-567-26647-7

Typeset by Newgen Imaging Systems Pvt Ltd, Chennai, India
Printed in Great Britain by the MPG Books Group, Bodmin and King's Lynn

CONTENTS

ACKNOWLEDGEMENTS

Sitting quietly in libraries, enduring long stretches of gothic German script, and trying to decipher Isaak August Dorner's labyrinthine prose have brought all kinds of challenges during the production of this work, and without the help and encouragement of many others, I would have crumpled under the strain.

I would like first to thank Professor John Webster who, after luring me into reading Dorner's *System of Christian Doctrine*, and successfully convincing me of its abiding value, provided the best support and guidance I could have hoped for. Always available to untangle Dorner's arguments, help me clarify my own thoughts, and provide gentle prodding to loosen up some of my own tortuously long sentences, he has modelled patient, insightful and respectful Christian scholarship, for which I am immensely grateful.

The community of teachers and postgraduate students in the Divinity School at the University of Aberdeen provided the perfect setting for this work. I would like to thank in particular: Andrew Stobart, Ben Reynolds, Chris Asprey, Simon Gathercole, David Gibson, Brian Lugioyo, Ro Mody and Rob Price. Thanks to Phil Ziegler and Steve Holmes for a probing and constructive examination of the thesis on which this book is based. Thanks to Richard Harvey at All Nations Christian College for much valued guidance and encouragement.

Thanks also go to Professor George Pattison for providing me with the reference to Dorner by Søren Kierkegaard.

Thanks go to the *Arts and Humanities Research Council* for its financial support for this project, as well as its generous travel grant for a three month research period at Tübingen University.

Thanks go to the staff at the various libraries in which this book has been completed: the Queen Mother Library and Special Collections, University of Aberdeen; the University Library and the Faculty Library of the Department of Theology, University of Tübingen; the University of Cambridge library; and latterly, the staff and library at All Nations Christian College, Ware.

During the period of research I have also had the privilege of being a member and elder of High Church, Hilton, Aberdeen, and more recently on the staff of Christ Church, Fulwood, Sheffield. Many thanks to Peter Dickson and Paul Williams for their ministry and support.

I would like to express profound gratitude to my family. My mother, Sandra and her husband Steve. To Rachel, Georgina and Maisie. To Robin and Anna.

I would like to give my deepest thanks to my wife, Zoë, who has provided me with the unchanging – *immutable* – support during what has at times seemed like an interminably long process of study. She has given me time and space to think. She has also given birth during the course of this research to our precious children, Max and Poppy, who have given us so much joy – as well as countless sleepless nights – and delight.

Finally, I would like to thank my father, Chris Norgate and brother-in-law, Paul Matthews, both of whom died during the production of this work. I wish they had been here to witness the end of the project, but in their quiet, strong, consistent way they lived the life of faith about which Isaak Dorner wrote. It is to their memory that this book is dedicated.

ABBREVIATIONS

I. A. Dorner's writings will be cited with the following abbreviations:

English Translations

Christian Ethics System of Christian Ethics, 1887.

History of Development History of the Development of the Doctrine of the Person of Christ, Div. I, Vol. I; Div. I, Vol. II; Div. II, Vol. I; Div. II, Vol. II; Div. II, Vol. III, 1876–1884. E.g. History of Development, Div. I, Vol. I, p. 233

Protestant History History of Protestant Theology, Particularly in Germany, 1871.

SCD A System of Christian Doctrine, Vols. I–IV, 1880–1882. Only cited with abbreviation, volume, page number: E.g. SCD, I, p. 12

Original German

Briefwechsel Briefwechsel zwischen H. L. Martensen und I. A. Dorner. 1839–1881. 2 Bände, 1888. E.g. Briefwechsel, I, p. 234

Entwicklungsgeschichte Entwicklungsgeshichte der Lehre von der Person Christi von den ältesten Zeiten bis auf die neusten. 1st Edition, 1839. 2nd Edition in 2 Volumes, 1845–1856. Unless stated, 2nd Edition cited.

SCG System der Christlichen Glaubenslehre, Zweite Auflage, Erster Band, 1886, Zweiter Band I. Hälfte & II Hälfte, 1887.
Only cited with abbreviation, volume, page number: E.g. SCG, I, p. 12, II.i., p. 44

Sittenlehre System der Christlichen Sittenlehre, 1885.

INTRODUCTION

This book is an investigation into the relationship between the doctrine of God and the doctrines pertaining to salvation in the theology of Isaak Dorner (1809–1884).[1]

> Thetic (Systematic) Theology is that part of the entire system of Theology which has to solve the problem presented by Christian faith itself – the exhibition of Christianity as truth. It embraces both the Christian Doctrine of God and His acts, or the Doctrines of Faith (Dogmatics), and the Doctrine of Morals (Ethics). But the point of unity from which both Dogmatics and Ethics start as their immediate source of knowledge, is Christian experience or Christian Faith. The aim, or the problem, is to bring the immediate and matter-of-fact certainty, which faith possesses of its contents, to scientific cognition, or to the consciousness of the internal coherence and the objective verification of those contents.[2]

With this proposition Isaak A. Dorner opens his *System of Christian Doctrine*, a work which was completed towards the end of his life (1879–1881[3]) during which time he occupied the professorial chair in Berlin previously held by Friedrich Schleiermacher. In the proposition (seeking to establish the *encylopaedic* position of systematic theology), Dorner lays out a threefold description of systematic theology as that discipline

   i. concerned with the *demonstration* of the truth of Christianity;
  ii. occupied with the doctrine of *God* and his *acts*;
 iii. having as its starting point and immediate source Christian *faith*.

---

[1] For a full biography see the entry on 'Isaak Dorner' in *Theologische Realenzyklopädia*, ed. G. Kranse (Berlin: Alter de Gruyter, 1977) or J. Bobertag, *Isaak August Dorner, Sein Leben und seine Lehre* (Gütersloh: G. Bertelsmann, 1906), pp. 9–93.

[2] I. A. Dorner, *A System of Christian Doctrine*, Vol. I, trans. Alfred Cave and J. S. Banks (Edinburgh: T & T Clark, 1880), p. 17. Hereafter, *SCD*, I, p. 17, etc.

[3] The first edition of Dorner's original German *System der Christlichen Glaubenslehre* was published in two volumes between 1879–1881. It was begun during a period of considerable illness, P. Kleinert, *Zum Gedächtniß Isaak August Dorner's* (Berlin: Dobberte & Schleiermacher, 1884), p. 22.

With these elements we have the foundational principles which inform the course and content of his exposition.[4]

First, we hear that systematic theology has as its immediate concern the demonstration of the truthfulness of the Christian faith. This assessment finds its focus, however, not in the *genera* of truth claims to which the host of Christian doctrines pertain but in the particular idea that Jesus Christ is the God-man. This leads Dorner to arrange his system into two parts: *Fundamental* or *Apologetic* Doctrine (§15–70) and *Specific* Doctrine (§71–155).

The first part – *Fundamental* Doctrine – is concerned with the task of demonstrating the certainty of the 'fact'[5] of Jesus Christ's godhumanity. This demonstration of certainty (described as 'scientific apprehension'[6]) is not found in a defence of the reliability of the ecclesiastical witnesses (of Scripture or Church[7]), since these are sources which provide *only* historical and, therefore, contingent proof. Instead, what is sought is verification of this fundamental idea by an appeal to the *contents* of faith which, when apprehended, are said to provide sufficient material for the depiction of the Christian confession about Christ's godhumanity as *necessarily true*.

---

[4] Karl Barth identified all three terms of the title of Dorner's dogmatics as integral to his theological project: 'Christian, doctrine, faith', *Protestant Theology in the Nineteenth Century*, New Edition (London: SCM, 2001), p. 564.

[5] *SCD*, I, p. 177.

[6] Ibid.

[7] Dorner's reluctance to appeal to Scripture or ecclesiastical authority as the source of religious certainty is not a mark of distrust in the veracity of those sources *per se*, but represents his conclusion that certainty of belief is *beyond* the limited capacity of historical sources since, he argues, they rest on the 'testimony and credibility of men' (Ibid. p. 109) and as such, can be doubted or disputed. The anxiety surrounding the suitability of the biblical sources to provide certainty, without excluding their place in the formation of faith and its contents (Ibid. p. 170), is Dorner's means of responding to the developments of the higher-critical scholarship of the nineteenth century. By his arrangement, he is seeking to maintain the Scripture as a norm for the construction of dogmatic or thetic theology (against those who were disputing its authority as an adequate source) but calling attention to its *secondary* or supporting place in the production of certainty to the *primary* role of *faith's contents* to which it is merely (though importantly) a historical witness. The connection between the higher-criticism movement and Dorner's theological project have been made by John M. Drickamer in 'Higher Criticism and the Incarnation in the Thought of I. A. Dorner' in *Concordia Theological Quarterly*, Vol. 43, No. 3 (June, 1979). However, we suggest that Drickamer overplays the extent to which Dorner's final account emerges as it does because he wants to be 'true...to what he considered the reliable results of modern science and historiography' (Ibid. p. 205). While there is, undoubtedly, evidence of the influence of contemporary biblical scholarship in Dorner's account (cf. his interest in the question of the '*self-consciousness* of Jesus', *SCD*, III, p. 167), Dorner's (often sparing) use of Scripture in the course of his exposition does not display an overwhelming dependence on the developments of contemporary scholarship.

This leads to the second important feature of the opening proposition, concerning the place of the Christian doctrine of God and his acts. In Dorner's sketch of his dogmatic method, he affirms this doctrine's central place and organizing function:

> The ultimate fact [in faith's contents] is the Christian idea of God. *A Jove principium*. From that idea as the ultimate unity and truth, all the declarations of faith, and all Christian truths, are to be immediately and mediately derived.[8]

The doctrine of God – and specifically the *Christian* doctrine of God (Dorner appeals to Schleiermacher's requirement that 'all positions must have a Christian character'[9]) – is counted the centrepiece of the systematic enterprise because it alone supplies the resources to account for the necessity of the incarnation. This is because the Christian idea of God itself – first received by Christian faith in Christ – *contains the source of its own verification* (and in turn the verification of Christ's godhumanity as necessary and not contingent on the entrance of sin to the world[10]):

> [T]he Christian idea of God, which, once apprehended by religious certainty in faith, becomes the material of the gnosis which learns the internal necessity of its material.[11]

However, that the doctrine of God is central not merely for its apologetic capacities becomes clear in the extent to which it also operates as the 'regulative influence'[12] on all doctrinal content, so that the *form* of God's being – which Dorner concludes is necessarily triune and as such proper ethical being – is that which orders the nature of his acts and the being and acts of the creation (including the content of both the divine acts of salvation and their human reception by saving faith). This heavy investment in the controlling influence of the doctrine of God, and the attendant interest in

---

[8] *SCD*, I, p. 170.
[9] Ibid. p. 182. This homage is, however, also accompanied with a not untypical critique of Schleiermacher who, Dorner, argues, failed to *christianize* sufficiently the doctrine of God in his treatment of the physical divine attributes, which he failed to place in any 'internal relation' to the moral attributes (Ibid.). It also does not prevent Dorner from pursuing a method of exposition which moves from the general or 'universal consciousness of God' (Ibid. p. 170) to the specifically Christian since the verification of the Christian idea includes the 'complement' of 'rational thought, restored to a normal state' (Ibid. p. 170). Dorner's is a rational approach, and not strictly speaking, an appeal to rationality.
[10] Ibid. p. 178.
[11] Ibid. p. 170.
[12] *SCD*, II, p. 359.

preserving and consolidating the specifically Christian idea of God's triunity represents Dorner's major contribution to the history of nineteenth century dogmatics (although he is, unsurprisingly, also singled out for his contributions to the development of Christology[13] and the doctrine of immutability which occupies a relatively short, though, vital part of his doctrine of God in the *System*[14]).[15] Yet it is not uncommon for Dorner's place in that history to be overlooked, when the story of modern theology *skips* from Schleiermacher to Ritschl.[16] However, in his handling of the major loci of Christian doctrine, he demonstrates himself an innovative and independent theologian who operates within the sphere of insights gathered from various strands of ecclesiastical – or philosophical – tradition (e.g. Schleiermacher's account of faith or Schelling's interest in God as 'eternally personal'[17]) without being a *derivative* thinker.

Isaak Dorner, the son of a Lutheran minister, studied at Tübingen between 1827 and 1832, being appointed Assistant Professor in 1838. As a contemporary of D. F. Strauss and Eduard Zeller, he was taught by F. C. Baur whose Christology prompted Dorner to make his first significant contribution to theological discourse of the day. In two lengthy articles Dorner set out for the first time the key features of his doctrine of Jesus Christ as *central individual*. In these articles, entitled 'Über die Entwicklungsgeschichte der Christologie',[18] Dorner critiqued the genus-Christology of Baur (and

---

[13] He is described by Ernst Günther as the christologian par excellence in the nineteenth century, *Die Entwicklung der Lehre von der Person Christi im XIX Jahrhundert* (Tübingen: Mohr, 1911), p. 235.

[14] Much interest in Dorner has focused on his account of divine immutability, possibly because of the influence which Karl Barth announces it has on his own account (cf. *Church Dogmatics*, Vol. II. The Doctrine of God, Part I [Edinburgh: T & T Clark, 1957], p. 493. However, Dorner's major development of this doctrine comes not in the System but in two long essays in *Tübinger Zeitschrift für Theologie* (1/1836 & 4/1835), translated and republished in English as *Divine Immutability*, trans. Robert R. Williams and Claude Welch (Minneapolis: Fortress Press, 1994). For an introduction to the background to Dorner's doctrine and its reception see the 'Introduction' by R. Williams.

[15] The importance of Dorner's interest in the doctrine of Trinity as the means to resolve the problem of divine transcendence and immanence was noted by D. Kirn in his entry on Dorner in the 1898 edition of Hauck, D. A., ed. *Realencyklopädia für Protestantische Theologie und Kirche*, p. 805. Wolfhart Pannenberg identifies Dorner as the 'most important champion of an essential Trinity in Protestant theology during the second half of the 19th century', *Systematic Theology*, Vol. 1, trans. Geoffrey W. Bromiley (Edinburgh: T & T Clark, 1991), p. 295.

[16] One such example of this historical abridgement is in Greschat Martin (ed.), *Theologen des Protestantismus im 19 und 20 Jahrhunderts*, 2 Vols (Stuttgart: Kohlhammer, 1978).

[17] *SCD*, I, p. 406.

[18] Isaak Dorner, 'Über die Entwicklungsgeschichte der Christologie, besonders in den neuern Zeiten. Eine historisch-kritische Abhandlung', *Tübinger Zeitschrift für Theologie*, 1835 Vol. 4: pp. 81–204 and 1836 Vol. 1: pp. 96–240.

Strauss) and argued that humanity could find realization in *one* individual and that this possibility had been reached in Jesus Christ. These articles would form the basis of the 'masterful'[19] history of Christology, first published in 1839, and revised and expanded between 1845 and 1856. This remains an unparalleled historico-theological investigation of the development of Christology.[20]

The history of Christology was also a testament to Dorner's churchmanship. As a sustained account and analysis of ecclesial doctrinal development it reflected a keen interest in locating theological discourse within church tradition. (Not all of Dorner's contemporaries shared this commitment.[21]) After advancing from Tübingen to academic posts (and accompanying appointment controversies[22]) in Kiel, Könisburg, Bonn and Göttingen, and being awarded the prestigious professorship in Berlin, Dorner was appointed Prussian Chief Church Councillor. He was an active advocate of further co-operation between Lutheran and Reformed churches begun with the Prussian Union of 1817. At the time of his death in 1884, Dorner had attained the pre-eminent professorial chair and achieved leadership in the church. Yet any influence which he may have had in theological circles was largely diminished by this time. Indeed, his major systematic theology – *System der Christlichen Glaubenslehre* – published first in 1879–1880, has been described as mirroring the spirit not of the decade in which it first appeared but of the 1840s.[23] The latter part of the

---

[19] Ragnar Holte, *Die Vermittlungstheologie: Ihre theologischen Grundbegriffe kritisch Untersucht* (Upsalla: Almquist & Wiksells, 1965), p. 114.

[20] Colin Brown, *Jesus in European Protestant Thought 1778–1860* (Grand Rapids: Baker, 1985), p. 267.

[21] Dorner's biographer, Bobertag, comments on Dorner's greater interest in the church than his contemporary Richard Rothe, see Bobertag, J. *Isaak August Dorner: Sein Leben und seine Lehre, mit besonderer Berücksichtigung seiner bleibenden Bedeutung für Theologie und Kirche* (Gütersloh: G. Bertelsmann, 1906), p. 34. Ambivalence towards the life of the church was not an unusual phenomenon, and informed later reconstructions of nineteenth-century theology. Claude Welch has noted Otto Pfleiderer's withering assessment of Dorner's interest in what he describes as the 'endless frictions of the actual world' (*The Development of Theology in Germany since Kant* [London: S. Sonnenschein, 1890], p. 374), Claude Welch, *Protestant Thought in the Nineteenth Century, 1799–1870*, Vol. I (New Haven & London: Yale University Press, 1972), p. 21.

[22] Horton Harris records the process by which Dorner was appointed assistant professor at Tübingen – in which a clinching factor according to F. C. Baur was the bad hearing of the other candidate! In addition to this factor, the appointment process of this teaching post, and others at the time, was part of a much wider conflict within the German church between those from the pietist, hegelian or schleiermachian camps, *The Tübingen School* (Oxford: Clarendon Press, 1975), pp. 40–43. It would appear that Dorner was perceived as the candidate more sympathetic to the pietist cause.

[23] Emanuel Hirsch, *Geschichte der neuern evangelischen Theologie* (Gütersloh: C. Bertelsmann Verlag, 1951), p. 211.

nineteenth century belonged not to Dorner and his theological method. Most obviously this position belonged to the rising influence of Albrecht Ritschl and a school which sought a new approach to Christian dogma (described by Barth as a turn towards an 'antimetaphysical'[24] moralism). It is, then, not surprising that Dorner's place in the development of modern German theology is often overlooked.[25] It is perhaps with Barth that Dorner's reputation begun its rehabilitation (both through Barth's theological biography in *Protestant Theology of the Nineteenth Century*[26] and in his open dependence on Dorner's doctrine of immutability in *Church Dogmatics* II.1[27]).

We need only look at Dorner's treatment of the place of faith (and the third element in the opening proposition given above) in the construction of dogmatics – as the principle of union which he calls attention to in his opening proposition – *to see* an example of how he combines innovation with a continuity with (one strain of) tradition, namely Schleiermacher's turn to faith as the 'fundamental postulate'[28] of the dogmatic system.

> [F]aith cannot be called the verifier of Christianity; the verifying power lies in objective Christianity, as it is revealed by Christ, and is attested by Scripture, and in the last resort in God...[F]aith is not the principle of the existence of Christianity (*principium essendi*)...faith is only the subjective *principium cognoscendi* of Christianity.[29]

Thus, while Dorner holds that it is the *contents* of faith (principally God as revealed in and by Christ) which is the basis of scientific knowledge (and not faith itself[30]), faith remains the principal means of immediately apprehending these contents as true, even if their verification arrives only with the demonstration of the content's truth (with the resources provided by that content). The intention is to demonstrate an inviolable connection between believer and God in which God's priority is maintained (and the

---

[24] Karl Barth, *Protestant Theology in the Nineteenth Century* (London: SCM, 2001), p. 641.

[25] Cf. Martin Greschat (ed.) *Theologen des Protestantismus im 19 und 20 Jahrhunderts*, 2 Vols (Stuttgart: Kohlhammer, 1978). This leaps in its coverage from Baur (1792–1860) and Richard Rothe (1799–1867) to Albrecht Ritschl (1822–1889). This is not exceptional.

[26] Karl Barth, *Protestant Theology in the Nineteenth Century* (London: SCM Press, 2001), pp. 563–573.

[27] Karl Barth, *Church Dogmatics* II.1 (Edinburgh: T & T Clark, 1957), p. 493 ff.

[28] *SCD*, I, p. 172.

[29] Ibid. p. 169.

[30] Contra Schleiermacher who, according to Dorner, makes the faith or the 'pious and Christian state of the subject the sole contents of Christian doctrine', Ibid. p. 172.

certainty of the belief) without reducing the participation of the believer in the apprehension of the truth.[31]

In these three principles, then, we have the skeleton of Dorner's dogmatic method, and the trace of his purposes for systematic theology. We see how he is concerned to delineate a relation between the believer and God in which the exposition of *doctrine* both stems from and also confirms the instincts of *faith*. We suggest that his handling of this material marks him out as a theologian of considerable significance, deserving recognition as both an inventive dogmatician in his own right and as a figure not to be underestimated in the development of modern theology.

We noted the centrality of the Christian idea of God to his project[32], and it is this part which forms the centre of our thesis, specifically the way in which Dorner uses the doctrine of God to inform and direct the content of his account of the doctrine of salvation. There have been major studies on the place and coherence of his doctrine of God, most notably in Christine Axt-Piscalar's *Der Grund des Glaubens*, who seeks to lay out the relation between that doctrine and his account of faith (which she argues is highly problematic);[33] and Jörg Rothermundt's *Personale Synthese*, in which he seeks to mark out the organizing power of Dorner's commitment to the concept of God as Absolute Personality.[34]

We wish, however, to examine in detail the place which the doctrine of God has in the development of Dorner's soteriology. We do not have an interest in the *genetic* makeup of Dorner's account (although we do refer to his self-acknowledged use or rejection of ideas associated with other theologians or philosophers[35]). For an exhaustive account of the way in

---

[31] Michael Hüttenhoff has provided an exhaustive account of Dorner's account of faith as an epistemological category in *Erkenntnistheorie und Dogmatik* (Bielfeld: Luther-Verlag, 1991), pp. 35–47.

[32] Dorner's *preoccupation* with the doctrine of God formed part of his son's memorial reflection on his father's contribution to theology, Prof. Dr. Dorner, 'Dem Andenken von Dr. I. A. Dorner' in *Theologische Studien und Kritiken*, Erster Band (1885), p. 425.

[33] Christina Axt-Piscalar, *Der Grund des Glaubens* (Tübingen: Mohr-Siebeck, 1990), p. 174 ff.

[34] Jörg Rothermundt, *Personale Synthese* (Göttingen: Vandenhoek & Ruprecht, 1968), p. 235 ff. The decisive importance of the concept of personality to Dorner was noted by P. Kleinert in his thanksgiving address to the faculty of Berlin at its memorial service for Dorner, *Zum Gedächtniß Isaak August Dorner's* (Berlin: Dobberte & Schleiermacher, 1884), p. 10.

[35] Dorner displays a consistent interest in the *development* of doctrine, and how ideas which have begun within the philosophical arena may be harnessed for the service of Christian theology. This is of course evidenced by his magisterial *History of the Development of the Doctrine of the Person of Christ*, in which we see not only his interest in the way in which doctrine has *developed*, but also how he and the theology of his era stands as an integral part.

which Dorner's response to the controversies surrounding Baur informed the development of his theological standpoint, see Thomas Koppehl's *Der wissenschaftliche Standpunkt der Theologie Isaak August Dorners;*[36] or for how he stands in relation to his contemporaries in German theology, see Ragner Holte's *Die Vermittlungstheologie.*[37] Our purposes are focused instead on Dorner's *dogmatic conduct,* and the way in which he uses the resources of his doctrine of God – especially God's triunity, ethical constitution and aseity – to inform and order his exposition of the doctrines related to salvation. We have already noted that his System is divided into two parts, with the *Fundamental* or *Apologetic* intended to display the certainty of the Christian faith by demonstrating the *necessity* of Jesus Christ's godhumanity. This arrangement means that those doctrines which pertain to the actual historical occurrence of Christ's incarnation are treated in the second part as *Specific* Doctrine. Accordingly, our analysis will assess the impact of this arrangement on the success of Dorner's exposition of the Gospel. However, while we will be concerned with the question of how Dorner posits the necessity of incarnation in relation to the acts of salvation, turning attention to the question of the systemic issues involved in Dorner's supralapsarianism, this will not be the dominating point of interest (not least because the questions surrounding the relationship between theories of Christ's necessary incarnation and the status of the atonement in the eternal purposes of God are well rehearsed[38]). Rather, we wish to measure the extent to which key aspects of his account of God's essential being play out in the explication of God's relation to the world, culminating in the work of atonement. This will lead us to focus on the way in which Dorner's undernoted account of divine *aseity* provides highly constructive grounds for his depiction of the *union* of God and humanity in Jesus Christ without detriment to the *distinction* of natures. Furthermore, his account of the ethical mode of God's being will provide not merely the background but the fundamental material for his account of the doctrine of atonement (as will the details of his doctrine of justification). What we intend to depict is the way in which the doctrine of God is the theological linchpin in Dorner's account of the Gospel of salvation (although, as we shall suggest, it is not without problems, particularly in Dorner's use – or *underuse* – of the doctrine of the Holy Spirit to explicate the divine relation to and ethical flourishing of humanity).

To this end we will survey those doctrines which lead up to and include Dorner's treatment of Jesus Christ's personal work of reconciliation and its

---

[36] Thomas Koppehl, *Der wissenschaftliche Standpunkt der Theologie des Isaak August Dorners* (Berlin: Walter de Gruyter, 1997), p. 21 ff.

[37] Ragnar Holte, *Die Vermittlungstheologie* (Uppsala: Almquist & Wiksells, 1965), pp. 9–21, esp. p. 19.

[38] Cf. Lewis B. Smedes, *The Incarnation: Trends in Modern Anglican Thought* (Amsterdam: Kampen, 1953), p. 135.

reception by the Christian believer through faith: The Doctrine of God; The Doctrine of the Economic Trinity; The Doctrines of the Creature and the Unity of God and Humanity; The Doctrine of Sin; The Doctrine of Jesus Christ; The Doctrines of the Atonement and Justification by Faith.

We have limited our account to these areas (by excluding from our study a consideration of the doctrines of the Church and Eschatology) because our desire to evaluate Dorner's use of the doctrine of God in salvation would not be noticeably enhanced by additional material. Furthermore, our interest in Dorner falls firmly on the way in which he manipulates the theological capital of his doctrine of God in the service of his account of the doctrine of the atonement which he describes as the 'sacred shrine of humanity'.[39] With this as our purpose we suggest that Dorner's treatment will show him not only as a *trinitarian* theologian of considerable significance, but an *evangelical* theologian whose account of the Gospel of Jesus Christ displays the earnest endeavour of a dogmatician seeking the consistent (if not always successful) connection between the triune God and the cross of Christ.

[39] *SCD*, III, p. 107.

1

THE DOCTRINE OF GOD

Introduction

In *A System of Christian Doctrine* Isaak Dorner opens his positive exposition of the doctrine of the Holy Tri-Unity (§31) by setting out the principal features which his account has, up to that stage, delivered and which he will go on to elucidate:

> The doctrine of the Divine Attributes leads back to the Trinity as it were to its underlying truth. In order to be the actual and Absolute Primary Life, Knowledge, and Goodness, the Godhead must be thought as Self-originating and Self-conscious, just as He must be thought as voluntary Love. This is only possible by the Godhead's eternally distinguishing Himself from Himself, and always returning to Himself from His other Self, that is, by God's being triune.
>
> [T]he eternal result of the eternal Self-discrimination of God from Himself, together with the equally eternal re-entrance into Himself, is the *Organism of the Absolute divine Personality*, so that only he truly thinks the personal God, who does not deny the triune God, the guarantee of Absolute Personality.[1]

Dorner is arguing that the Christian idea of a triune God is that to which a general idea of God (which has been set out in his earlier analysis of the divine attributes[2]) leads. Moreover, he contends that a revitalized account of God's triunity will rejuvenate contemporary modes of thinking about the 'concept of God generally'.[3]

Dorner's definition of God as Absolute Personality displays a shift away from conceptualizing God as Absolute Substance (which he suggests has

---

[1] I. A. Dorner, *A System of Christian Doctrine*, Vol. I, trans. Alfred Cave (Edinburgh: T&T Clark, 1880), p. 412. Hereafter, *SCD*, I.

[2] Ibid. §17–27, pp. 212–343.

[3] Ibid. p. 413.

dominated ecclesial theology since the fourth century, undermining the link between the Christian idea of God and the Christian ethical personality[4]). It is also intended to aid the understanding of how God is both the cause of His own essential triune Being, and the cause of a world which is *united* but not *identified* with this self-constituting divine essence. He proceeds to articulate how this definition supports the suggestion that the apprehension by faith of this idea of God as Absolute Personality has scientific certainty, and as such manifests the *priority* of the objective content over its reception. The project pursues the foundations of faith in the Christian idea of God rather than what he sees as the weaker certainty provided by the theological model which perceives in *faith itself* the principle which secures the foundation of the Christian idea of God. This is linked to a concern to display the truth of the *ethical* constitution of the Christian Personality by faith:

> [T]he *evangelical principle of faith* is by no means sure itself apart from the Trinity, [thus] the conscious, new, and godlike Personality only finds its objective and Absolute foundation in God as the triune.
>
> Our aim must be that the Trinity legitimate itself to believing apprehension as the objective foundation in God of the Christian Personality, and especially of that which is peculiarly evangelical.[5]

Dorner is concerned to see a reawakening of the doctrine of the Trinity in Christian dogmatics, both in order to secure for the Christian Personality a foundation outside itself, and to ensure that this Personality matures into greater conformity with the God who *freely conforms* Himself to His essential Being as triune. Dorner sees the evangelical principle of faith (won in the Reformation) as that which sees 'free agency [coalescing] with the morally necessary, and the necessary with the free, forming a vivacious unity',[6] and this principle may be seen to be founded in the God who, apprehended as triune, is the unity of freedom and necessity. The key to this lies with the *ethical* definition of God. Before we move on to a detailed analysis of this, we ought to observe the place of Jesus Christ in Dorner's dogmatic configuration. He describes the 'union of the divine and the human, of which Christ is the principle, [as] the fundamental idea in Christianity'.[7] This means that the Christian idea of God is apprehended by *faith in Christ*. As the 'theanthropic Personality', Christ is the 'objective basis of our communion with God' because in Him dwells the 'fulness

---

4 Ibid. p. 419.
5 Ibid. p. 417.
6 Ibid. p. 418.
7 Ibid. p. 28.

11

of Godhead'.[8] The pursuit of a doctrine of the triune God for the sake of evangelical piety is therefore a pursuit both informed by and seeking to inform the doctrine of the Person of Christ. With this we see that Dorner's is a project which seeks to secure the link between faith and God through the mediation of Christ. His concern is not only to demonstrate the *necessity* of the Christian idea of God apprehended by faith, but to do this so that it leads to an understanding of the incarnation of the God-man as that which may be apprehended with scientific certainty.[9] It is the act of the God whose essence as Love, when ethically conceived, shows 'internal tendency to communicative love'[10] without detriment to His essential Being. We will investigate the question of God's relation to the world and the incarnation in subsequent chapters. For the moment, it will suffice for us to note the intimate connections in Dorner's system between the three *loci* of faith, Christ and Trinity.

This brings us to the primary purpose for this chapter. Since our overall project is to demonstrate the centrality of the doctrine of God to the wider exposition of the gospel of salvation, as we lay out the details of his account (and our critique) we will make note of those points in his doctrine of God which inform and prepare the ground for his soteriology. Throughout our project, we will focus on how Dorner's theological account is ordered according to the terms of his doctrine of God. For example, in the introduction to his account of evil he comments:

> The Christian idea of God, as treated of in the First Part, must preserve its fundamental position because of the regulative influence it exerts in reference to all the principal doctrines, securing in this way systematic coherence.[11]

The doctrine of God is, therefore, decisive in the way in which it functions as a dogmatic control for the wider project. We will set out its central features in the present chapter, preparing for our representation of its controlling role in the overall course of Dorner's account up to and including the doctrine of atonement.

---

[8] *SCD*, I, p. 415.

[9] Dorner conceived the task of developing scientifically the *objectivity* of Christ as the God-man from the principle of faith as the most pressing task and responsibility of theology in his day. He expresses this point in a letter to Martensen and, in agreement with him, offered the dualism of contemporary philosophy and theology as the alternative which needed to be refuted, *Briefwechsel zwischen H. L. Martensen und I. A. Dorner, 1839–1881, Erster Band* (Berlin: H. Reuter's Verlagsbuchandlung, 1888), p. 19. Hereafter, *Briefwechsel*, I.

[10] *SCD*, I, p. 444.

[11] *SCD*, II, p. 359.

This chapter will be divided into two parts. We will look first at the *General* Doctrine and second at the *Christian* Doctrine, reflecting the fundamental distinction in Dorner's account.[12] Before we begin our survey, however, we shall comment on how Dorner situates his dogmatic exposition as that which has an apologetic function.

I. The Doctrine of Faith and Fundamental or Apologetic Theology

Dorner places his account of the doctrine of God at the start of his system of Christian Faith. It is, however, preceded by a lengthy prolegomena in which he explicates a doctrine of faith which will satisfy the epistemological demands occasioned by the presentation of the Christian confession as truth. In his opening discussion of the place which dogmatics has within the wider classification of the theological sciences (the theological encyclopaedia), he suggests its primary purpose is apologetic: 'to solve the problem presented by Christian faith itself – the exhibition of Christianity as *truth*'.[13] We have noted in our introduction that his intention for the doctrine of God is to seek a foundation for faith via the demonstration of the necessity of its object, and that this is intended to provide security for the believer consonant with the character of this object.[14] This concern is intended to demonstrate its necessity not only for the believer but for the general enquirer also. Systematic theology has, then, a *public* function and is not exhausted by its significance for the believer.

Dorner identifies the Christian doctrine of faith (rather than ecclesial authority or Scripture) as that which offers the most satisfactory basis upon which to *begin* this project. It is not our intention to provide a detailed account of his argument. This he sets out in the eccentrically entitled 'Pisteology'[15] (§2–12), coming between the discussion of the 'Encyclopaedic

---

[12] He divides the account into three sections: (1) General; (2) God as immanent Trinity; (3) God as Economic Trinity.

[13] *SCD*, I, p. 17.

[14] Ibid. p. 179.

[15] M. Hüttenhoff has identified only two examples of the term 'Pisteology' in use before Dorner: in W. T. Krug, *Pisteologie oder Glaube, Aberglaube und Unglaube sowohl an sich als im Verhältnisse zu Staat und Kirche betrachtet* (Leipzig: Baumgärtner, 1825), to whom Dorner himself refers in his *Geschichte der protestantischen Theologie* (München: Gotta'schen Buchhandlung, 1867), p. 748; and in P. Marheineke's *Die Grundlehren der christlichen Dogmatik als Wissenschaft*, (Berlin: Dunker & Humblot, 1827), p. 71. However, Hüttenhoff admits to being unable to determine whether Dorner adopted these terms or whether he formed them himself, Michael Hüttenhoff, *Erkenntnistheorie und Dogmatik* (Bielfeld: Luther-Verlag, 1991), p. 46. Hereafter, *Erkenntnistheorie*.

Position of Christian Doctrine' (§1) and the formal start of the *System of Christian Faith* (§15 ff.) with forbiddingly complex argumentation[16]. Such analysis has already constituted a significant part of the critical assessment of Dorner's theological project.[17] We do want to note however that Dorner's 'pisteological' scheme is part of an agenda which leads him to arrange the various doctrines of the Christian faith according to a two-tiered structure, of *Fundamental* (§15–70) and *Specific* Christian doctrines (§71–155).[18] This separation displays the central concern to foreground the apologetic purpose of dogmatics.

This is manifest in the very structure of his system. While faith represents the starting point of the theological quest for certainty, it is not faith itself but the object of faith (or faith's 'objective contents'[19]) which provides the basis of scientific certainty. This 'certainty' is attained when the *actual* revelation of the person of Jesus Christ as the God-man is demonstrated to be necessarily true. The aim, therefore, of Fundamental or Apologetic theology is the 'demonstration of the necessity of Jesus'.[20]

This agenda sees the first part of the *System* being concerned to display the truthfulness of the Christian proclamation concerning the Godhumanity of Jesus by displaying its consistency with the natures both of God and man.

It is not as Jesus' soteriological aspect coheres with the needs of the sinful world that his truth will primarily be demonstrated (though there is here an appropriate match). Rather, it is the extent to which the *idea* of the God-man, actualized in Jesus, conforms to the necessary idea that God and man are not mutually exclusive. Rather, God and man lean towards each other; the divinely constituted world is that which is capable of receiving and bearing the divine, without detriment either to the distinct integrity of God or world. Certitude will be found in the demonstration of the complementarity of the *form* of the God-man with its *foundational idea*:

> [W]e are not in a position to formulate the necessity of sin, and to make sin the basis of the necessity of the manifestation of Christ, which would thus never receive scientific verification, resting as it

---

[16] The speculative complexity of Dorner's *System* was noted by Adolf Jülicher as a block to his understanding, *Die Religionswissenschaft der Gegenwart in Selbstdarstellung*, Band 4, 1928, p. 11.

[17] Most notable are Christine Axt-Piscalar, *Der Grund des Glaubens* (Tübingen: J. C. B. Mohr/Paul Siebeck, 1990) (hereafter, *Grund*) and Hüttenhoff, *Erkenntnistheorie*.

[18] This arrangement is unique to Dorner, but in Alexander Schweizer's *Die Christliche Glaubenslehre* (Leipzig: Hirzel, 1877), he too treats and designates as a second and separate part 'der spezifisch christliche Glaube' (those doctrines which pertain to sin and salvation).

[19] *SCD*, I, p. 168.

[20] Ibid. p. 177.

would upon something casual, something born of human caprice. If, on the other hand, quite apart from sin, and because of the nature both of God and man, the possibility of the union of those two natures in the incarnation has been recognised, we have convinced ourselves that this two-fold nature offers no opposition to the incarnation, but calls for it and tends towards it; in that case, the *form* of the incarnation, which has become necessary because of sin, and of which the second Part treats, will have found its *meet foundation*; whilst on the other hand, the necessity of the incarnation because of the entrance of sin, will have become manifest from a new side.(my italics)[21]

With this decisive move Dorner is constructing a project which seeks security not in the mere *description* of the content of Christian faith, but in a demonstration of the necessity of this content for faith's security. As previously noted, Dorner places the doctrine of God first in his system (after the prolegomena). He does this because while faith is that activity which apprehends its objects, faith is not *by itself* the grounds of scientific certainty (although it does carry a, lesser, religious certainty which is nonetheless sufficient for the pious believer to live without anxiety in the world[22]). Instead, Dorner claims that the 'Christian idea of God' is the 'supreme basis of Christianity',[23] and thus, the first point of call for Fundamental Theology:

[It is the] *Jove principium*. From that idea as the ultimate unity and truth, all the declarations of faith, and all Christian truths, are to be immediately and mediately derived…The Christian idea of God, which, once apprehended by religious certainty in faith, becomes the material of the gnosis which learns the internal necessity of its material – it will be exhibited as essentially true and necessary, since, on the one hand, the indissoluble association of the idea of God in general with the reasoning nature of man and on the other hand, the perfection and completion of the idea of God in the Christian idea of God are established.[24]

[21] Ibid. p. 178.
[22] 'There is no need of proof to be pious', SCD, I, p. 210.
[23] Ibid. p. 170. Dorner's conviction concerning the central place of the doctrine of God within the wider dogmatic agenda also finds expression in his account of other religions. Thus, in his historical reconstruction of early christology, he concludes (in connection with the struggle between gnosticism and the Church Fathers) that 'every religion is what it is through its concept of God', Isaak Dorner, *History of the Development of the Doctrine of the Person of Christ*, Division First: First Four Centuries, Div. I, Vol. I, trans. W. L. Alexander (Edinburgh: T & T Clark, 1861), p. 224. Hereafter, *History of Development*, Div. I, Vol. I.
[24] SCD, I, p. 170.

15

The 'declarations of faith' are 'derived', not self-constituting, and hang on one central idea which comes to be recognized as necessary in two stages. First, with the initial apprehension of faith comes *religious* certainty, which he will later describe in terms of bringing a 'congruity of the consciousness of Christian faith with thought (Denken[25])'.[26] Secondly, with the subsequent apprehension of this faith's contents as necessary comes *scientific* certainty and a conformity with 'the reasoning nature of man'[27] ('the very development of the divine idea afforded by empirical piety cannot scientifically exist, unless it reaches the point where the reason must apprehend that the knowledge of God is divinely knit to the reason (Vernunft[28]) as such'[29]). Dorner identifies the Christian idea of God as the key to this movement towards verification. Central to the progress of this argument is establishing the connection between the general and specific ideas of God, to which we now turn.

a. The Connection between the General and Specific Ideas of God

First, we note Dorner's reference to the exhibition of the truth of the Christian declarations of faith in the 'indissoluble *association* of the idea of God in general with the reasoning nature of man' and 'the perfection and completion of the idea of God in the Christian idea of God'.[30] With this notion of an association between the general and the specific ideas of God, Dorner displays the *public* nature of his project. Since his intention is apologetic, his concern is to demonstrate how the Christian idea of God both completes *and* surpasses general non-Christian ideas of God.

> [If] the Christian concept of God shows itself the goal of the whole process of critical survey, a process which finds its resting place in none of the extra-Christian religions…the superiority of the latter to all extra-Christian religions…will have been shown.[31]

Dorner justifies this order because of its dialectical service to the demonstration of the Christian idea of God. There is also a theological justification. Dorner is seeking a connection between the first and second creations. At the close of his survey of the divine attributes and proofs he affirms that the

---

[25] I. A. Dorner, *System der Christlichen Glaubenslehre*, Erster Band, Grundlegung oder Apologetik, Zweite Auflage (Berlin: Wilhelm Hertz, 1886), p. 197. Hereafter, *SCG*, I.
[26] *SCD*, I, p. 210.
[27] Ibid. p. 170.
[28] *SCG*, I, p. 196.
[29] *SCD*, I, p. 210.
[30] Ibid. p. 170.
[31] Ibid. p. 249.

'knowledge' which is given with the 'first creation' is not destroyed but 'preserved in Christianity'.[32] While the general account may be 'insufficient for the satisfaction of the Christian consciousness and apprehension', it remains a 'point of junction'[33] between the humanity of the first creation and the humanity of the second creation. Referring to Scriptural passages which he claims in support of this view (John 1.3, Rom. 1.20 & Acts 17.29) – though without any detailed exegesis – he dismisses those theological projects which emerge after Schleiermacher that give only what is 'specifically Christian' and as a consequence 'omit much which belongs to the complete inheritance of the Christian'.[34] This move coheres with his concern to exhibit the necessity of the union of the God-man as that to which the first creation order was always heading for its fulfilment. To deny the status of the general would weaken the claim that the first creation, represented dogmatically as the 'general', was leaning towards the second creation occasioned by the incarnation.

This does not mean that Dorner sees no limitations in the general. Rather, these limitations are built into his account, and their exposure a reason to begin with them: 'It is not silence upon this pre-Christian apprehension, but its correct guidance and animation, which shows its defects, and arouses the conscious apprehension that without Christ the world would be a fragment.'[35]

Dorner proceeds from general to specific. However, he maintains that the *existence* of God may not be treated separately from a consideration of the *essence* of God. In his general account, he treats attributes together with proofs.[36] Additionally, he treats the proofs not as separate but as coalescing together as one argument.[37] We shall look later at how he does this. For now, we want to note a consistency in this method not properly recognized by Christine Axt-Piscalar in her assessment of Dorner's approach. Axt-Piscalar speaks of the arrangement as methodologically speculative and ambivalent with regards to the relationship between general and specific doctrine:

1. 'Daß Dorner sich nicht davon überzeugen kann, "die Gotteslehre mit der Trinitateslehre zu beginnen", hängt mit seinem spekulativen Interesse

---

[32] Ibid. p. 338. fn.
[33] Ibid. p. 338.
[34] Ibid. p. 338. fn.
[35] Ibid. p. 338. fn.
[36] The innovativeness of Dorner's decision to treat these two together was noted by a successor to his Chair in Berlin, Julius Kaftan, *Dogmatik* (Freiburg: Mohr Siebeck, 1897), p. 156.
[37] Jörg Rothermundt, *Personale Synthese: Isaak August Dorners dogmatische Methode* (Göttingen: Vandenhoek & Ruprecht, 1968), p. 145 Hereafter, *Synthese*. Dorner's reconstitution of the *proofs* has been singled out for the richness of its resulting doctrine of God, Jan Rohls, *Philosophie und Theologie in Geschichte und Gegenwart* (Tübingen: Mohr Siebeck, 2002), p. 490.

zusammen, den christlichen Gottesgedanken als vernünftigen, ja als einen den Gottesbegriff der Vernunft erst vollenden zu erweisen.'[38]

2. 'Da jedoch der spezifisch christliche und zugleich der für die Vernunft höchste Gottesbegriff nur mit der Trinitätslehre erreicht ist, welche die Vollgestalt des Wesens Gottes ausdrückt, handelt er in einem zweiten Schritt im Anschluß an die immanente Trinitätslehre…Darin kommt die Ambivalenz zum Ausdruck, die aus seiner Zuordnung von allgemeiner Gotteslehre und Trinitätslehre resultiert.'[39]

We suggest that on the first point Axt-Piscalar has failed to account properly for the *internal* relationship between the general and specific, conceptualized as first and second creations. Dorner is precisely *not* speculative, because the general has a preparatory status for the specific, both because of the divine preservation of the first creation with or by the second, and because the first creation serves a purpose given to it of exhibiting inadequacy which finds resolution in the specific idea of the Christian God. On the second point, by describing the interdependent role which Dorner gives to general and specific doctrine as 'ambivalent' (so that the Trinity cannot be looked at in abstraction from the Being, Essence, and Attributes of God discussed in the general account, but the Essence of God can only be thought properly as Trinitarian) fails again to regard the significance of the first in relation to the second creation. It is not ambivalence, but an attitude of dependence, which the insight of the second creation affords to the first.

We suggest the more pressing problem is the absence of a discussion on how the first creation is affected by sin. This absence arises, of course, because fundamental doctrine does not allow reference to the effects of contingent human action. Dorner's system avoids speculation on the specific point of the relationship between the general and specific ideas of God, *but only because he has made the wider speculative point* of seeking certainty by separating 'necessary' and 'contingent' doctrines. This is problematic because he does not make clear how the *evangel* itself (and the revelation of God as *Saviour*) provides either the impulse or resources to make this distinction. Jorg Rothermundt makes the key observation that Dorner has partially *forgotten* the evangelical principle that humanity does not possess a holy essence before he encounters God.[40]

b. The Problem of Foundations

The second point concerns the problem of discerning where exactly Dorner situates the foundation for the Christian faith. We have previously noted

---

[38] Axt-Piscalar, *Grund*, p. 195 f.
[39] Ibid. p. 201.
[40] Rothermundt, *Synthese*, p. 148.

that the doctrines of faith, Christ *and* Trinity are the three key elements in this question.

Axt-Piscalar has argued that Dorner is inconsistent in commending first the 'evangelischen Glaubensprinzips' and then the 'Trinitätslehre' as the 'Konstruktionsprinzip' with which theology operates.[41] Faith is regarded by Dorner himself, however, as the foundation principle only insofar as it is the *means* by which the Christian truth is received. Elsewhere, he describes it as the '*Vermittlungspunkt*…, durch welchen das Wissen und Lieben Gottes, worin er sich selbst offenbart, zum menschlichen Wissen wie von der eigenen Erlösung so von Gott und seiner Liebe' (my italics).[42] Faith is certain, but 'not the principle of the existence of Christianity (principium essendi), just as little are the Holy Scriptures and the Church'.[43] Faith receives and seeks certainty in its objective content, which is the proper foundation. Axt-Piscalar's analysis requires an opposition between faith and the objects of faith. Yet rather than the ground being either faith *or* Trinity, it is for Dorner both/and, in which the objective doctrines apprehended with religious certainty *in* faith, acquire the status of knowledge and are recognized as the true foundations *from* faith. This is the import of Dorner's dual contention that Jesus Christ is the 'fundamental idea in Christianity',[44] and the 'Christian idea of God' is the 'supreme basis of Christianity'.[45]

The key is to see that, for Dorner, the Christian idea of God is revealed in the Godhumanity of Christ as that which *always intends* to bring this union into existence. It is an intention in full conformity with the divine essence predisposed to perfect fellowship with the human essence:

> [If] because of the nature both of God and man, the possibility of the union of those two natures in the incarnation has been recognised, we have convinced ourselves that this two-fold nature offers no opposition to the incarnation, but calls for it and tends towards it.[46]

Christ may be described as the 'fundamental idea in Christianity' because it is in him that this 'fellowship' of God and man is perfectly instantiated (and through which humanity may have fellowship with God). Furthermore, the Christian idea of God is the 'supreme basis of Christianity' because it lies in

---

[41] Axt-Piscalar, *Grund*, p. 174.
[42] Isaak Dorner, *Gesammelte Schriften aus dem Gebiet der systematischen Theologie, Exegese und Geschichte* (Berlin: Wilhelm Hertz, 1883), p. 76.
[43] *SCD*, I, p. 169.
[44] Ibid. p. 28.
[45] Ibid. p. 170.
[46] Ibid. p. 178.

God's essential being to bring this union to effect:

> In the last resort, therefore, it is in the true idea of God that the veri-
> fication of the world and of man, and especially of revelation and the
> fundamental Christian facts, as to their possibility and necessity, is to
> be sought.[47]

The interest in revitalizing the Christian doctrine of God is, therefore, intended to secure the truthfulness of the Christian proclamation concerning the God-man. This is achieved by beginning with the *true idea of God*.

All this means, of course, that Dorner's is a system which seeks to demonstrate the certainty of the divine economic operation by displaying its conformity with the immanent divine essence.

This brings us to an appropriate place at which to assess *how* Dorner configures his *general* doctrine of God. This will mean seeing how he prepares for the subsequent demonstration of the truth of the *Christian* idea of God, which is itself the grounds for demonstrating the necessity (and certainty) of the incarnation.

II. The Doctrine of God: The General

Dorner begins with the general idea of God before proceeding to the specific. He treats together the divine proofs and attributes, making this move because 'there is no idea of a thing apart from its essential characteristics'.[48] He rejects their separation because, he argues, only with a demonstration of the *essence* of God is the *being* of God fully confirmed:

> Before, therefore, the essential and constituent elements of the funda-
> mental idea are gained, the existence of God is at any rate non-proven.
> Thus it follows that the proof for the divine existence and the proof
> for the essential and constituent attributes are not two proofs, but are
> one and indivisible, and can only attain completeness side by side. The
> proof for the existence of God has only been plenarily completed with
> the proof for these attributes.[49]

---

[47] *SCD*, I, p. 180.
[48] Ibid. p. 190.
[49] Ibid. Axt-Piscalar observes that with this Dorner follows Hegel who, in the 'Science of Logic', argues that the essence of a thing cannot be understood without the awareness of its attributes, and that the essence is understood as existent with its defined attributes, G. W. F. Hegel, *Wissenschaft der Logik*, Bde. I u. II, quoted in Axt-Piscalar, *Grund*, p. 198.

His argument against separation leads him to treat the proofs together. Although he treats the traditional proofs in a definite order, he regards them as interdependent:

1. Ontological;
2. Cosmological;
3. Teleological;
4. Moral.

In keeping with Dorner's insistence on their basic unity, we will seek to show their interdependence. Furthermore, we note that Dorner speaks of the need to discern a single 'principle existent in God which arranges and governs'[50] the attributes (which have, contra Schleiermacher,[51] objective existence[52]):

> If we had knowledge of such a principle in God, by which He is Himself Absolutely supreme, that principle might be called the all-governing principle, the divine essence, of that which is innermost and highest in God, and contradistinguished from the attributes as the things governed, which are made use of as the material and media of the principle or essence.[53]

This single, divine principle is the triune God. Dorner later confirms that the doctrine of the divine attributes 'leads back to the Trinity'.[54] We will later detail how he understands this 'governing' occurring. Here we want only to note that Dorner's system, at the general stage, is preparing for the appearance of the specific,[55] consonant with his conclusions that the triune God is properly conceived as Absolute Personality.

---

[50] *SCD*, I, p. 202.

[51] Ibid. p. 199. Schleiermacher advances the idea that the attributes denote 'not something special in God' but only something 'special in the manner in which the feeling of absolute dependence is to be related to Him', Friedrich Schleiermacher, *The Christian Faith*, eds. H. R. Mackintosh & J. S. Stewart, (Edinburgh: T & T Clark, 1976), p. 194. The attributes are indicative not of God in Himself but His apprehension.

[52] Interestingly, in relation to the subjectivity attributable to Schleiermacher's project, Dorner suggests in a letter to Martensen, that he thinks that Schleiermacher's theological subjectivity does, in fact, have its grounds in the objective Person of Christ (on account of his having received this representation of Christ from the Church) but fails to recognize or systematize this in his theological product, *Briefwechsel*, I, p. 2.

[53] *SCD*, I, p. 202.

[54] Ibid. p. 412.

[55] Axt-Piscalar refers to the fact that Dorner 'hat die Trinitätslehre in seinem System ihren Ort im Anschluß an jene', *Grund*, p. 176.

Dorner contends that the general account will not itself supply the full personality of God, but will prepare for it. This is not to say that *any* general idea of God will lead to the Christian:

> It is not every representation of God that possibly exists which can serve to verify the Christian revelation, but only that representation of God that possibly exists which the complete System of Christian faith has to form and defend.[56]

This arrangement explains the terms and scope of Dorner's apologetic intentions. Dorner himself recognizes that his account will not satisfy every rational enquirer. It does not intend to do this. The project is intended to display the way in which the Christian revelation coheres with, by completing, the general idea of God which finds its completion in the Christian idea of God. It is a question which accompanies the exposition of the divine proof to which we now turn.

a. The Divine Proof

Dorner contends that there is merely *one* divine proof which is to be considered under its different aspects or elements: Ontological, Cosmological, Teleological, and Moral. This means that he treats them as interconnected parts of one whole argument. Each one *alone* is insufficient to bring proof, but has value when brought into connection with the whole. For this reason, we shall first comment briefly on the way in which they are interrelated, and then go on to discuss the particular qualities (and limitations) of each.

1. The Interconnectedness of the Proofs

Dorner's cumulative approach means that each proof or element has only a limited function within the wider scheme. Each proof requires supplementation from another. The Ontological element, for example, furnishes the idea of God's necessary existence. Yet it needs to be supplemented by the Cosmological element to lead towards a characterization of God as *living*. While the Ontological proof helps to establish existence, it is the Cosmological proof which opens up the possibility that God may be described in non-static terms as the eternal cause of Himself.

Moreover, these notions need to be refined by the Teleological element. This element alone offers the grounds for this God, conceived as living or *Life*, to be seen as distinct and not conjoined with the world. The final element has two stages, Juridical and Moral, and is the culmination of the overall proof and as such is the element which most immediately prepares

[56] *SCD*, I, p. 180.

the ground for Dorner's specific account of God. These stages show how God must be conceived as *Spirit* so as to emphasize God as the *Good* without detriment to His freedom.

However, while his approach leads Dorner to posit the necessary existence of a moving, distinct and good God, it is not an end in itself. Rather, these proposals, belonging to a general account, are merely preparatory. An appeal to proofs is insufficient, though productive, since there are insufficient resources to demonstrate how the attributes discerned through each element (necessary existence, vitality, distinctness, goodness) properly cohere in God. It is from here that Dorner presents the *Christian* idea of God as the means of resolving the problem. We shall come to the details of this presentation after we have made an assessment of each element.

2. The Elements of the Divine Proof

i. The ontological element

Dorner opens his treatment of this element by first speaking of its *inadequacy*. This does not mean, however, it need be entirely rejected.[57] In his survey of the history of the proof, he argues that Anselm presented a 'clear outline of this proof' by asserting that 'being is not inseparable from [its] thought'.[58] Insufficient ground was given, however, for demonstrating this particular thought's necessity. Dorner seeks to resolve this by positing the wider notion that the existence of God is necessary for *thought* itself to be rational (a point on which he is both indebted[59] to Kant and in conflict[60]). This is the case, he argues, because God's existence alone provides the grounds for human thought to become *definite*, since only when man can posit another distinct from himself can he be sure of himself *and* his rational thought:

> It is not open, we say, to the rational thinker to avow an Absolute or not – he must avow it. The Absolute so coincides with the roots of rational thought, with its possibility, that without it that which is one's own mentality (die eigene Geistigkeit) must cease. It is already manifest generally, that without the Absolute there is no longer anything infinite for men, and also an absence of knowledge of the finite as

---

[57] *SCD*, I, p. 215.

[58] Ibid. p. 215.

[59] He acknowledges Kant's supposition that 'consciousness which has got rid of the thought of absolute Being would become prey to an endless Atomicism and dissolution', Ibid. p. 227.

[60] Thus, while Kant acknowledged the regulative property of the idea of God for rational thought, the existence of God remains a 'problematic, not a constituent concept' (Ibid. p. 221).

such; for apart from opposition to the infinite, even the finite as such cannot be known. Thus understanding at most might remain, but not reason.[61]

However, though this notion has the advantage of positing the idea of God's necessary existence, alone it can lead to the *confusion* of humanity and God (as Dorner witnesses in Hegel's use of the Ontological proof[62]). Although a proof may allow for God's existence, what is not given is the idea of a necessary *distinction* between the God who exists and the humanity whose rational thought is secured by this existence.

This possibility leads to the Cosmological element. We will assess his treatment after we consider briefly his interpretation and use of those attributes which accompany the Ontological element. They are organized into four groups:

1. Unity;
2. Solity;[63]
3. Simplicity;
4. Infinity.

With these attributes Dorner is preparing the ground for what will be his controlling definition of God as distinct from, though leading towards, the world: the Absolute Personality.

He conceives the divine Unity as that which speaks of God as the 'original and only possibility of everything, *but not all*' (my italics);[64] the definition of God as Absolute *Being* need not mean that God is *all* being.[65] This

---

[61] *SCD*, I, p. 227. Here he is again distinguishing himself from Kant, from whom he takes the regulative notion that the idea of God is indispensable to every intelligent consideration of things, but which does not carry with it the resources to posit this God as actually existent but merely necessary for our thought to be rational. Dorner takes the first point, and contends the second which leads, he argues, merely to sceptical despair of 'the cognizability of truth in general' (Ibid. p. 224).

[62] Ibid. p. 225.

[63] 'Solity' is the rather eccentric translation given by Dorner's translators for 'Einzigkeit'. It is so eccentric that, according to the Oxford English Dictionary, it finds here its only usage: 'SOLITY. rare – 1882, Cave & Banks tr. Dorner's *System of Christian Faith*, p. 201'.

[64] *SCD*, I, p. 230.

[65] There is confusion on this point in Dorner's exposition. While he maintains here that God is not 'all', he later says in a summary of his account, 'We have previously regarded God as the original Being or Essence – indeed as the original *All* of being' (my italics), p. 319. This latter statement is picked up by William G. T. Shedd in *Dogmatic Theology*, Third Edition (Phillipsburg: Presbyterian and Reformed Publishing Company, 2003) as evidence that Dorner has fallen into the error of 'confounding the infinite with

he connects to the attribute of Simplicity, according to which God may be described as a 'definite Being' (This does not, however, exclude *plurality from Unity*).[66]

He goes on to explain that God's definiteness manifests itself in an *intensive* relation to space and time. This means that God's particularity does not bring Him merely *above* time and space, which would make Him finite 'because He would be excluded from them'.[67] Rather, He is immanent *within* time and space without being captive to them. God is free from time and space, since He is definite. Yet this does not mean He is *only* distinct from time and space, but that He is free to relate to them in different ways.[68]

With this glossing of these attributes (only briefly delineated here), Dorner is getting ready for his Christian idea of God as *definite* Being, who stands in a positive but not exhausting relation to time and space, and who, crucially, has a plurality in His unity. It is a preparatory exploration which will find its completion in the doctrine of Trinity.

ii. The cosmological element

The Ontological element is, therefore, profitable insofar as a link may be made between human rational thought and the necessary existence of God. It cannot, however, by itself prevent a confusion of God and world (as Hegel used to his advantage). Neither does it inhibit the characterization of God's Being as anything other than *static*. It lacks a concept of divine *movement*, or of the divine capacity to exist in a posture of *relatedness* without detriment to His own constancy. Dorner suggests these are features which may be supplied, at least in a provisional form, by the Cosmological element.

> The Cosmological argument, together with the relation of Causality upon which it rests, promises to enrich absolute Being with a new definition. Indeed, it promises to conduct us beyond the indeterminateness which the Ontological argument could not of itself yet surmount.[69]

the all', which leads to pantheism (p. 176). We suggest that Dorner has either been careless in his summary or assumes that his earlier account provides the context in which he can refer to 'All' without implying *everything*. What can be said, however, is that in accordance with his proposition that the conclusions of the *general* idea only find their completion in the *specific*, and thus he allows that the definition of God as Absolute Being does indeed threaten to break out into pantheism and stand in competition with the idea of God as Absolute Personality until it is 'resolved by means of that idea of God which is specifically Christian', *SCD*, I, p. 319.

[66] *SCD*, I, p. 235.
[67] Ibid. p. 240.
[68] Ibid. p. 243.
[69] Ibid. p. 254.

The Cosmological element brings to the proceedings the 'concept of *the absolute Cause*'.[70] It serves an advantageous purpose in establishing both a *distinction* between God and world as Cause and effect, and introducing the concept of divine 'agency'[71] or activity. God is the 'cause of the world'[72] rather than merely undifferentiated 'absolute Essence'.[73]

However, rather than merely reading the Cosmological element as the search for a First Cause for the caused world (a task for which, Dorner argues, it is ultimately ill equipped[74]), it finds fuller value in a revised form. Therefore, rather than operating with the Cause-caused scheme which 'applies inconclusively to the relation between God and world',[75] Dorner applies the terms of the Cosmological proof to the preliminary conclusions of the previous Ontological proof, and to the 'divine sphere itself'.[76] (In this conflation of elements, we begin to see what it means for Dorner to have only *one* divine proof.)

This move marks the beginning of a decisive and consistent engagement (as we shall see) with the doctrine of God's aseity. It comes from redirecting the concept of causality to the idea of God, generated by the Ontological element, as absolute and necessary Being. The result of this is:

a. God, according to the Ontological proof, is 'actually and absolutely existent, absolutely in Himself realized Potentiality (*Potenz*), *actus purissimus*'.[77]
b. God, as actually and absolutely existing, *retains* potentiality or causality eternally, since it cannot 'have ceased in action in the realization of Deity'.[78]

The God who, in the Ontological element, was found to be necessary Absolute Being may also, with the aid of the Cosmological element, be seen to be the 'perennial and eternal *cause of His absolute reality*, and not merely the past and contingent cause' (my italics).[79] God is realized potentiality, and as such the eternal cause of His absolute reality: 'He is at once originator and originated.'[80]

---

[70] *SCD*, I, p. 254.
[71] Ibid. p. 248.
[72] Ibid. p. 248.
[73] Ibid. p. 248.
[74] The Cosmological argument is inadequate because it 'presupposes the world as a certain being, in order to derive God as the cause of the world'. Ibid. p. 255. However, the world is not certain and therefore neither is the cosmological syllogism.
[75] Ibid. p. 256.
[76] Ibid. p. 256.
[77] Ibid. p. 256.
[78] Ibid. p. 256.
[79] Ibid. p. 256.
[80] Ibid. p. 257.

According to this representation of the Cosmological element, God's aseity means that He is not *static* Being, since He is self-constituted eternally by the movement from Cause to Caused, or Originator to Originated. This leads Dorner to propose that God be defined not merely as Absolute Causality (which the traditional proof implied) but as *Life* (§21). God's is a 'double-sided causality…a circular motion of originating that is at the same time originated.'[81]

However, though this notion of God as Life represents an advance on the representation of God as static, undifferentiated Being, it is inadequate since it is considered only under the category of *causation*. As such, it is not yet capable of displaying the divine Life as attained on the basis of His own freedom to act in *conformity* with His necessary being. While causation is a category which brings the concept of movement, it brings nothing *but* movement. A consequence of this is that the *world* may be posited as the place in which God moves in an eternally restless motion of causation, with the principle of causation represented as a force *over* God to which He is subject (which Dorner describes as a 'physical category'[82]). The problem finds partial amelioration with the Teleological element.

iii. The physico-teleological element

Dorner is highly sceptical of the weight given to this proof, and it is this very scepticism which he uses to continue his process of refining his argument for the existence of a *particular* God. He describes as the 'customary form' of the proof the idea that since the universe is perfect and harmonious, there may be presupposed a First Cause who 'orders in an intelligent manner, who has made the world according to the ideas of purpose and beauty'.[83]

He sees, however, no such straightforward reason to infer from the world a designer ('nature shows us no all-embracing purpose upon which we could rely: it is rather a cycle of rising and setting'[84]). However, the teleological proof has value in drawing attention to what the world is *not*. It stands in contrast to a God who, unlike the world, may be said to be a 'perfect organism, in which there can be nothing superfluous or casual'.[85] With this contrast comes the principle, so highly sought after by Dorner, of a distinction between God and world. He has, of course, arrived at the notion by altering the empirical disposition of most uses of the teleological proof.[86]

---

[81] Ibid. p. 257.
[82] Ibid. p. 261.
[83] Ibid. p. 264.
[84] Ibid. p. 266. There is, then, no reference in Dorner's treatment to the notion of a natural *vestigia trinitatis*.
[85] Ibid. p. 268.
[86] On this point, we are reminded of Dorner's aversion to those accounts of Christian doctrine which he sees resting upon merely 'empirical and reflective manner' (Ibid.

Instead, he advances by a progress of negation, and does so by making two key moves.

First, since he has now proposed the principle of a distinction between world and God, he develops the idea of God as the 'absolutely *harmonious* Life'.[87] God's Life may no longer be confused with that of the world (which was still possible under the terms of the Cosmological element[88]). Second, the world's incompleteness takes us to God who *is* complete ('the primary Forms of things, and primary ideas of Adaptation and Beauty, must be in God'[89]) and leads him away from the conception of God determined merely by a physical category, such as causation.

Instead, we are preparing for the necessary transition to what he calls the *'spiritual sphere'*.[90] The cumulative conclusions of the Ontological, Cosmological, and Teleological proofs lead to a declaration concerning God as the 'One Absolute'[91] in whom are gathered 'the ideas of Order and Measure, of Adaptation and Beauty, which are all moments of the idea of Harmony'.[92] These definitions fail, however, to reveal the fullness of the 'absolute Life of God'[93] because an 'absolute purpose'[94] to which they each conform has not yet been discerned. God's Life, if it is to be thought absolutely harmonious, does not have possession of these ideas only insofar as they exist momentarily, but as they are consistently and continually present to the particular divine being. Absolute purpose is, therefore, that which speaks of God's *Self*-possession. Divine order, measure, adaptation and beauty do not exist for anything other than God's own sake. Neither are they dependent for their coherence on anything outside God's own Self-determination. In this regard, absolute purpose pertains to God's *spiritual* essence: the merely physical is that which has something other than itself to account for its constitution or effect. Spirit is that which is 'always its own motive power'.[95] The teleological proof does not deliver this principle. Dorner turns therefore to the final and highest element of the one proof: the *moral* proof. Dorner contends it has the resources – supported by the cumulative argument of the previous elements – to prepare *most* adequately for the demonstration of the truth of the Christian idea of God.

---

p. 168), since, he argues, they too are incapable of moving to a state of certainty or distinction between faith and its contents.

[87] *SCD*, I, p. 269.
[88] Ibid. p. 261.
[89] Ibid. p. 271.
[90] Ibid. p. 276.
[91] Ibid. p. 269.
[92] Ibid. p. 269.
[93] Ibid. p. 275.
[94] Ibid. p. 275.
[95] Ibid. p. 287.

iv. The moral element

The final element is laid out in three stages. As we have already noted, the teleological proof pushes Dorner to seek out an absolute principle in God. In the first section of this final proof (§23 on the 'Transition from the Physico-teleological Argument to the Idea of Right and to the Spiritual Sphere'), Dorner lays out in more detail what is at stake in this process.

The teleological element had brought attention to the *finite* nature of worldly order, measure, adaptation and beauty. What this finitude, this mutability, brought into view was an 'essential difference from the Absolute',[96] and Dorner infers from this difference two concepts which both ensure the *appropriateness* of finite nature's finitude and also pertain to the constitution of God's appropriate and living infinitude: the ideas of Right (das Recht) and Justice (die Gerechtigkeit). Each of these he utilizes in the course of the two subsequent parts of the element under the rubrics of the 'Juridical Argument' (§24) and the 'Moral Argument' (§26 & 27). Dorner begins the account by referring to how these two concepts pertain to finite nature. We will look at each in turn.

First, Justice is that which 'opposes'[97] the natural by bringing it to its proper end. It is that divine attribute which ensures the natural sphere retain its proper identity as finite (and we will see in Chapter 3 how this feeds into Dorner's account of death before the Fall). It brings the natural to an appropriate completion:

> Justice effects necessary subordination, and by means of the spiritual vindicates the determinateness of the natural as one aspect of the natural.[98]

Justice is that which preserves appropriateness. According to the 'Juridical Argument' God Himself may be defined as *absolute* Justice:

> Justice is the Self-preserving Honour of God as the absolute, the ideal, and the actuating norm and guard of all worthy bestowal.[99]

In the natural sphere, Justice preserves the identity of the finite. For God Himself Justice is the Self-*preserving* identity of the infinite God. Justice is not an attribute *external* to God but internal to His immanent being. In God there is the 'norm' but also a 'standard of judgement in conformity with this

[96] Ibid. p. 276.
[97] Ibid. p. 276.
[98] Ibid. p. 293.
[99] Ibid. p. 286.

29

norm'.[100] Justice is that which describes God's Self-identity or as Dorner calls it that 'zeal of Self-preservation':[101]

> He is Himself that norm, He is equally the energetic Will which effectuates and establishes that norm, and therefore Himself.[102]

Justice is not the arbitrary or ineluctable effecting of the divine essence, but God's Self-preserving of that essence.

Second, Right is that which pertains to the *content* of things and which is *protected* by Justice. It is, for example, the *right* of the finite to be finite, and this is preserved by Justice in its preserving finitude.

> It is Right, and the order which establishes and guards the worth of everything, which is executed in the merely finite world by its passing away, in order that nothing should transgress its idea…this boundary, Right, is guardian of boundaries between different things, and between finite and infinite, and will show itself the turning point leading from nature to spirit.[103]

The finite world is *rightly* finite, and in this is the basis of the transition from nature to spirit. As the *guardian of boundaries* the natural sphere is allowed by Right to stand as *no more than* natural, in distinction from the infinite or spiritual. This part of the moral element helps to clarify the point that the distinction between God and world is, if anything, merely a *respecting* of particular spheres.

Justice preserves appropriateness and Right is that which *is* appropriate. In the natural world, the world's *rightful finitude* is demonstrated by its mutability and decay. The limitations of the world, brought into focus by the teleological element, are appropriate to that sphere, and mark the point of distinction with the *rightful* infinitude of God. Right therefore is the point at which a distinction may be made between one thing and another and, most crucially, between nature and spirit.

This brings the argument to its decisive stage. Up to this point Dorner has used the energy of the teleological element to define how Justice and Right relate to the finite world in *contrast* to the divine (even though, as we have seen, in the Juridical Argument he has already begun to define God's being as both normative and Self-conforming). In §25, he comes to a transitional section. He lays out how the dual concepts of Justice and Right, as applied simply to God, pertain to the 'idea of an absolute end'[104] as opposed to the

---

[100] *SCD*, I, p. 294.
[101] Ibid. p. 295.
[102] Ibid. p. 295.
[103] Ibid. p. 277.
[104] Ibid. p. 303.

'mere finite ends'[105] which have been the main occupation of the proofs up to this point.

The need for an *absolute end* arises because neither the concepts of Justice nor Right in themselves provide complete explanation of the 'proper contents of the spiritual world'.[106] While Justice is a spiritual end in itself since it secures what is appropriate, it is not the *absolute* end because it depends on something other than itself:

> Its own absolute right and its necessity it derives from a positive and absolute end, *which it protects, but which it does not create, but which must rather be given to it together with its whole empire.*[107]

Right too is dependent:

> *Right generally presupposes things of worth to be already given, whether finite or infinite,* which it arranges and manages justly, and for the sake of which it exists.[108]

What is lacking is an absolute end to which Justice and Right may be said to pertain and gain their derivative, though definite, significance. The possibility of a definition of this absolute end lies in the *ethical* definition of God as

> [T]he Good simply, and that not merely as law, or as potential good, but as perfect and existent good.[109]

The ethical idea of God as the Good is the culmination of Dorner's attempt to reach a stage of certainty concerning the 'absolute reality in the absolute Essence'.[110] As we observed of the previous elements, what was lacking was the idea of an Absolute Purpose or an Absolute End. Dorner comments:

> The fact that Life and Fulness of Might and Order and Design and Beauty exist, has merely a *conditional* important. (my italics)[111]

---

[105] Ibid. p. 303.
[106] Ibid. p. 304.
[107] Ibid. p. 304.
[108] Ibid. p. 304.
[109] Ibid. p. 305.
[110] Ibid. p. 308.
[111] Ibid. p. 308.

ISAAK A. DORNER

It is with the ethical idea (albeit in its general definition) that the 'absolutely highest thought'[112] is given:

> [O]pposed…to everything else, by virtue of its internal worth and its necessity, a necessity infinitely higher than any in the physical sphere, and able to claim the highest honour.[113]

The ethical idea of God as the Good holds this high status. The Good is necessary because an 'end absolutely worthy'[114] is needed to secure the exigencies of rational thought and moral human life (Dorner acknowledges Kant's proposal that the ethical is not discretionary for the rational subject but a duty.[115]). Yet this is not merely necessary for rational thought and as such only ever potential. This would mean that something *other* than the absolutely worthy would exist outside of the absolute Being, namely the *thought* of the absolutely worthy (and on this point we recall Dorner's insistence concerning the ontological element that the existence of God is necessary for rational thought[116]):

> [T]he ethical cannot be mere subjective product of human thought, for the necessity for thinking it precedes the thought, and is not made by the thought.[117]

The necessity of God's absolute goodness is, for Dorner, secured by this proposition. However, a more earnest problem arises which will ultimately lead him to propose the Christian idea as its only adequate solution.

The problem concerns the extent to which God as the Good is not merely necessary but also *Self*-willed. It is a problem which pertains to whether God can be described as Personality (in free possession of His necessary Being) or as Substance (subject either to His necessity or arbitrarily free to be whatever He chooses):

> If God were only fatalistically and compulsorily determined in His Being by the law of the ethical, or were He immediately at one therewith without conscious will, He would merely be a necessitated ethical substance, and not the God who is the prototype of holiness, whose image we ought to be.[118]

[112] *SCD*, I, p. 308.
[113] Ibid. p. 308.
[114] Ibid. p. 311.
[115] Ibid. p. 311.
[116] Cf. Ibid. p. 227.
[117] Ibid. p. 312.
[118] Ibid. p. 315.

THE DOCTRINE OF GOD

This is the key question for Dorner, and the reason why the moral element, though highly suggestive in its general form, requires the Christian idea of God. God as the Good will be successfully defined only when this Goodness is both that which is necessary *and* freely willed. Goodness must be *consciously willed* in order for it to be fully possessed by God Himself; but it must be *necessary* to God's essential being in order for it to be more than merely one among many options available for God to be Himself. God is Good by necessity, but freely so. These are the terms on which God may be defined not merely as Substance but Absolute Personality (since He demonstrates both 'Self-consciousness and Self-determination'[119]). Dorner contends that the moral element in its general form is unable to bring these concepts of necessity and freedom together. What they lack (even though they are part of the proof) is a principle of unity by which their coherence and commensurability can be demonstrated. What the proof furnishes is *obscured* knowledge of God as 'positively good'.[120]

This represents the culmination of Dorner's account of the divine proof, and provides for him the decisive factor in explaining that the Christian idea of God alone will complete the picture of how necessity and freedom coinhere in God.

The argument has brought Dorner to the stage at which he begins to connect his definition of God with the definition of the Christian personality, and in doing so provides an outline of its objective verification. This is because evangelical faith is that which *freely obeys* the good of the moral order displayed in God's revealed essential being. This conjunction occurs because God is the One who freely obeys Himself as the Good; and with this a consonance between the (believer's) Subjective apprehension and the (divine) Objective content is secured.[121] It is also the grounds for the description, to which the divine proof has been heading, of God as Absolute Personality. This is possible because Dorner connects to the Moral element the attributes of Intelligence and Wisdom since the notion that God lives in free conformity with Himself invokes the idea of God's Self-consciousness, since it is only as He *knows* Himself that He can live in synchronicity with Himself. This brings the attendant observation that God as Absolute Knowledge is such 'apart from the world'.[122] Ethically conceived, His distinction is maintained, and as Absolute Knowledge He may be defined in terms of Personality rather than Substance.

---

[119] Ibid. p. 319. '[I]f Self-consciousness and Self-determination are associated [with God's internal Being], Personality is demanded for the concept of God', Ibid. p. 340.

[120] Ibid. p. 319.

[121] This is a consonance which must be discerned in order for the believer to fulfil his moral imperative to conform properly to who God is as ethical essence, Ibid. p. 307.

[122] Ibid. p. 337.

Dorner concludes his general account of the doctrine of God, therefore, with the idea that God's essential Being is best defined as ethical and, as such, as Absolute Personality. It functions for him as a 'point of junction'[123] for the Christian apprehension of God. This brings us to a suitable position from which to survey the next turn in his exposition, and how he develops the notions laid out in this general proof.

III. The Doctrine of God: The Specific

a. Transition from General to Specific

At the close of the general doctrine of God, Dorner suggests that principles have been affirmed which represent a *'point of junction'*[124] with Christianity itself. This has both a positive and negative aspect. It is positive because certain positive truths have been 'established'.[125] It is negative because an 'apprehension of the defects'[126] has emerged of the general account. Chief among these positive truths is the principle of God's distinction from the world (attained finally in 'thinking God as the ethical Absolute'[127]). This distinction means that the idea of God's *'Transcendence'*[128] is reached (and the 'pancosmistic form of Pantheism'[129] discarded).

However, just as the ethical element was seen to require a principle which will demonstrate how God is both the cause *and* end of His Goodness, so too is a principle required to demonstrate how God's transcendence is compatible with His immanent presence in the world. Indeed, such an undertaking is necessary for the vitality of the ethical definition of God (and the concept of Personality):

> God cannot be at the same time absolutely good and yet desire existence and goodness exclusively for His own advantage, excluding by His idea the possibility of another sharing His Being and Goodness.[130]

Dorner contends that such an explanatory or unifying principle is found in the *specifically Christian Doctrine of God*. This alone will show that 'God is not merely distinct from the world, but also distinguishes Himself from it and it from Himself…and by means of this absolute inalienable Self-mastery

---

[123] *SCD*, I, p. 338.
[124] Ibid. p. 338.
[125] Ibid. p. 338.
[126] Ibid. p. 338.
[127] Ibid. p. 339.
[128] Ibid. p. 339.
[129] Ibid. p. 339.
[130] Ibid. p. 342.

of God, this doctrine opens the prospect that God can communicate Himself to the world without Self-detriment.'[131]

b. The Positive Exposition of the Christian God

Dorner opens his account of the specific doctrine of God with detailed examinations of the Old and New Testament sources (§28) followed by an extended account of the ecclesiastical development of the doctrine (§29–30). At the end of these surveys, he offers his own contribution. It connects with the findings and failings of the earlier general account:

> The Doctrine of the Divine Attributes leads back to the Trinity as it were to its underlying truth. In order to be the actual and absolute Primary Life, Knowledge, and Goodness, the Godhead must be thought as Self-originating and Self-conscious, just as He must be thought as voluntary Love. This is only possible by the Godhead's eternally distinguishing Himself from Himself, and always returning to Himself from His other Self, that is, by God's being triune.[132]

The Christian idea of God as triune is that which most ably fits the demands uncovered and unresolved by the general idea. The idea of God's immanent triunity furnishes the principles of unity *and* difference. These are principles which are needed for the general idea of God to gain coherence and stability.

As we shall see, the way in which Dorner configures the Christian doctrine is heavily reliant on the particular way in which he has ordered his general doctrine. The culmination of his positive exposition sees the Trinity defined primarily in terms of its *ethical* constitution. However, before he reaches that point, he proceeds by attending to the two means which he identifies as having occupied the most ground in ecclesial definitions of triunity: 'the so-called physical and logical syntheses of the Triunity'.[133] We will look at each of these in turn.

Before we do this however, it is worth recalling that central to Dorner's doctrinal ambition is the concern to see a correspondence between the Christian idea of God and the idea of the *Christian personality*. The union of 'free agency' and 'moral necessity'[134] which he discerns as normative to the Christian personality requires an 'eternal necessity in God Himself'.[135]

---

[131] Ibid. p. 343.
[132] Ibid. p. 412.
[133] Ibid. p. 418.
[134] Ibid. p. 418.
[135] Ibid. p. 418.

This will be, for Dorner, the *secure* and *objective* grounds for the verification of Christian faith.

Furthermore, the concern for a demonstration of the union of freedom and necessity in the Godhead is a concern to demonstrate how Jesus Christ himself may be asserted to be the Son of God (itself contributing to the confidence of the Christian personality). The persistence of eternal distinctions *and* unity in God is necessary to secure the proposition that Jesus is the God-man, to maintain that the 'unity of God is quite consistent with such distinctions'.[136] These are the concerns with which Dorner begins his positive account.

1. Physical[137]

The Physical Definition recalls the notion which emerged from the Cosmological element of the divine proof. The concept of God's necessary being, won in the Ontological element, is developed so that He is both the eternal cause of His Absolute reality *and* the caused. Yet what was lacking in the general definition were the resources to show how this movement is achieved without an endless 'theogonic series' in which a 'third produces a fourth, and so on':[138]

> [T]he unity of the Godhead is only permanently assured, in so far as the living effect or the life effected eternally finds its way back to the first efficient cause, and serves the end of eternally establishing God Himself as effect.[139]

Dorner suggests that the danger of an endless restlessness in the divine essence is resolved by positing a *third* principle which will bring cause and caused into a *definite* relation:

> [T]his reference of the effect to the cause only exists by means of the mediation of a *third*, which preserves as well as unites them in diversity.
>
> This principle of union in the organism of the absolute Life we call the Holy Spirit, to whom even a physical importance attaches.[140]

---

[136] *SCD*, I, p. 415.

[137] Dorner's use of this term refers to what we might call the *mechanics* of the dynamics internal to the triune Godhead. Thus, the physical definition is that which displays the *way* in the triune relation is constituted as such. It will, however, only be with the *ethical* definition that the full explanation of how and why this relation obtains.

[138] *SCD*, I, p. 420.

[139] Ibid. p. 420.

[140] Ibid. p. 421.

The Holy Spirit is identified, therefore, as that element through whom divine Unity is produced. Dorner speaks of 'physical importance' because the *effect* of this mediation is the constitution of God as Organism or Life. *Physical* is here not posited in opposition to *spiritual*. Rather, it is consonant with spirit because it stands in a state of free cooperation with the other two principles and not against or over them. It is both the mark and mediator of their free mutual relations. This third principle *constitutes* the Organism, yet does so 'together with the other two' for 'God could not part Himself unless He were sure of the principle of union'.[141]

2. Logical

The Physical definition refers to causation or origination, and posits the Holy Spirit as the key to the resolution of the problem identified in the general account. The Logical definition pertains to the idea that God is 'self-conscious'.[142] Again, the Holy Spirit holds the key. The idea of divine Self-consciousness is said to depend on an 'antithesis of subject and object, of thinker and thought'.[143] It is, however, an antithesis which requires a principle which will bring unity out of the dialectic of Self-distinguishing or Self-diremption. Dorner proposes the Holy Spirit as this principle. An eternal mediator who issues forth in God as His free capacity to have complete knowledge of Himself:

> Only by the thinking and determining Godhead, who is in both, knowing His own Essence in what is different to Himself, in what is thought and determined, is Self-consciousness constituted in God. But for that end a third and equally real principle of union is necessary in God, the Holy Spirit, to whom Paul (1 Cor. 2.11) ascribes exclusive dignity in the Self-knowledge of God in His depths.[144]

As with the Physical definition, it is a configuration which depends on the introduction of a third principle. This is consistently identified by Dorner as the Holy Spirit. He is that divine principle by whom the two other principles or 'forms of Being of the Godhead'[145] have consciousness of the unity or 'community'[146] of their essence. The Christian idea of a triunity is taking shape as the means of resolving the problems which emerged in the general account.

---

[141] Ibid. p. 421.
[142] Ibid. p. 422.
[143] Ibid. p. 422.
[144] Ibid. p. 425.
[145] Ibid. p. 425.
[146] Ibid. p. 425.

3. Ethical

Dorner refers to the definition of God as the primary ethical essence in the final and crowning element of the divine proof (§26). He recalls the inability of the general definition to account satisfactorily for the *way* in which God was to be thought as the Good. The problem was how God could be both the product of volition *and* determined; how could God be *free* to be what He *must* be?

Dorner sets out his understanding of how the Christian idea of God alone is capable of resolving this dilemma by making two very important moves, both of which hang on the idea of divine triunity.

First, he argues that both God's willing of goodness, and the goodness which God wills, may be supposed 'at the same time' because God 'has no *mere simple* form of being' (my italics).[147] Rather, the divine being must be posited as a *diverse being* in order to apprehend how freedom and necessity relate in a constructive way. The problem of *two* principles will not be resolved if God's simplicity is thought only in terms of an absolute (or a kind of numerical) *oneness*. The second significant move he makes is contending that, in order to show how such a diverse being may be seen to resolve the problem, we must *start* in our dogmatic exposition '*at the ethically necessary, not from the free*'.[148]

On the first point, we see Dorner presenting the idea of *diversity* as that which is explicable as triunity. It brings, however, binitarian overtones. In speaking of two principles coexisting *at the same time*, it might be said that a simple concurrence of two principles is sufficient to adequately explain their complementarity. However, it is not an insuperable problem because Dorner's intentions are to move beyond mere complementarity to mutual engagement. It is the second point, therefore, which proves more problematic. Dorner's contention that the account must start with the ethically necessary is proposed undefended. For the sake of dogmatic exposition, it might be said to provide a *helpful* starting point, since it provides the opportunity to recognize the *fixedness* of the good in God before explaining how it is a *Self*-fixedness. (Dorner himself refers to the non-arbitrariness of the ethical and how it inheres in the 'circumference of the divine Being'.[149]) Yet if Dorner is to argue for a mutuality in the relations of necessity and freedom, to speak of a necessary ordering of the exposition is either to privilege necessity or itself be an arbitrary act.[150] A more adequate justification

---

[147] *SCD*, I, p. 432.

[148] Ibid. p. 432.

[149] Ibid. p. 432.

[150] Robert R. Williams has also expressed concern about the grounds for Dorner's privileging or positing the 'primacy of ethical necessity over freedom', 'I. A. Dorner: The Ethical Immutability of God' in *Journal of the American Academy of Religion*, Vol. 54,

might have necessity coming first for formal reasons since it will be demonstrated that there is material interdependence (though not identification) with freedom.

This issue raises significant concerns about Dorner's *method*, because his doctrine of God as triune emerges as the resolution of *problems* (e.g. of the physical, logical and ethical loci). Instead of *beginning* with the Trinity, and working out the internal relations thereafter, his method threatens to *import* to the positive doctrine an agenda fixed by the terms and conditions of what is seen as problematical.

A consequence of this is that he is exposed to the charge that he treats the doctrine of God not primarily in terms of how God *saves*, but how God *solves* the problems of His own Being. It is a question which repeatedly recurs in Dorner's system. His agenda often seems to underplay the weight of the soteriological content of the Christian faith for the sake of positing its necessary truthfulness. It is a question which arises in his treatments of anthropology (Chapter 3), incarnation (Chapter 5) and atonement (Chapter 6). We will see in each of these areas the particular ways in which he is vulnerable. In the present chapter we will address problems with his account, as identified by Christine Axt-Piscalar, after we have laid out more fully the details of Dorner's account. We continue now, therefore, with the conclusions of his ethical definition of God.

Dorner orders his account of the ethical definition according to the traditional order of the divine Hypostases:

1. The Father is identified as the principle of necessity, in whom 'necessarily good Being, Goodness and Holiness are based';[151]
2. The Son is identified as the principle of freedom, who is the 'instrument for (God's) ethical Self-production so to ensure His absolute ethical Personality and His living Love';[152]

No.4, p. 736. Robert Williams sees it as Dorner *undercutting* 'his own emphasis on divine will and freedom', Robert R. Williams, 'Schelling and Dorner on Divine Immutability' in *Journal of the American Academy of Religion*, Vol. 53, No. 2 (June 1985), p. 247. On this latter observation, however, we would want to question whether Dorner emphasizes freedom and then pulls back from following through in his intentions by appealing to ethical necessity. Rather, in his appeal to the complementarity of freedom/necessity, we see an insufficient justification for Dorner's *beginning* his exposition with necessity.

[151] SCD, I, p. 433.
[152] Ibid. p. 434. We suggest that Piotr J. Malysz gives a misplaced reading of the Son's relationship to the Father by stating that the Son '*imposes* the ethical necessity on the Father' (my italics), Piotr J. Malysz, 'Hegel's Conception of God and its Application by Isaak Dorner to the Problem of Divine Immutability' in *Pro Ecclesia*, Vol. XV, No. 4

3. The Holy Spirit is the principle of unity, by whose agency the 'self volition of the free is eternally effected in the necessary, and that of the necessary in the free, as absolute, self-conscious, free love is effected'.[153]

Again the Holy Spirit plays a major part in resolving the problem presented
by the idea of the ethical essence of God, and affords Dorner the opportunity to posit the idea of God as Absolute Personality. This is because
he has established that God is Absolute Self-consciousness, Absolute Self-
determination and, as the Unity of ethical necessity and freedom, is Self-love
since the impulse to Unity manifests the interest of God to live in internal
fellowship:

> [L]ove is the unity of ethical necessity and freedom because it wills the
> ethically necessary as such, that is, with consciousness and absolute
> desire.[154]

Dorner infers from this ontology of love the definition of God as 'eternally
absolute Personality'.[155] As Father, Son and Holy Spirit He eternally effects
(by the agency of the Holy Spirit) the free obedience (by the agency of the
Son) to ethical necessity (by the agency of the Father):

> [T]he self-volition of the free is eternally effected in the necessary, and
> that of the necessary in the free, that is to say, *absolute*, self-conscious,
> free Love is effected.[156]

With this, Dorner contends that the theological verification for the Christian
personality has arrived:

> What else is the godlike personality of the sons of God but the con-
> scious union of the free with the ethically necessary as the absolutely
> worthy and deserving love? The necessity of the ethical for religion is
> theologically verified by the fact that God, the ethically necessary is,
> according to His Essence, content with nothing less than Self-conscious
> and free desire after the good, and that He straightaway requires the
> form of this freedom as the only worthy means of the realization of
> the good.[157]

(Fall 2006), p. 468. The relation is *free* and as such it is merely the *corresponding*
response to the Father's necessity.

[153] *SCD*, I, p. 437.
[154] Ibid. p. 437.
[155] Ibid. p. 437.
[156] Ibid. p. 437.
[157] Ibid. p. 446.

The search for correspondence between the Christian personality and the Christian God is thus resolved with the ethically defined representation of God as the freely willed Good or 'holy Love'.[158]

Now that we have provided an outline of the account, we will conclude this section with a detailed analysis of the major critique offered by Axt-Piscalar. She identifies problems in all three of Dorner's definitions of triunity. We will briefly lay out each in turn, before laying out our response.

First, Axt-Piscalar suggests that the Physical Definition is subordinationist. Dorner's interpretation of causation sets caused *over against* cause, and means that the definition of the Trinity has its focus on the *first* moment of that relation. What emerges is a subordinationist conception, with Father against Son, with the Spirit actually functioning as the dominant principle in bringing union between these two opposing elements: 'somit die Person des Vaters gegenüber dem Sohn und dem Geist dominant erscheint'.[159]

Second, she suggests the Logical Definition is also subordinationist, problematizing the place of the Holy Spirit for different reasons. This is because the Subject and Object are unified by a third principle, which means that there is too great a focus on the *distinction* or difference of each principle. The definition emphasizes the relationality of the Father and Son according to their *own* definition rather than their mutuality (e.g. '[B]oth [Father and Son] are dominated by the tendency to self-conscious personality'[160]). This has further deleterious consequences for the conceptualization of the Holy Spirit. No space remains for His *personal* participation in the process of unification. He becomes merely the *force* which brings resolution to the eternal dialectic of Father and Son. In the end, the Logical construction of the Trinity clings to the Father as the sole instance of Subjectivity and brings a subordinationist inclination to the relations of the three.[161]

She argues the Ethical Definition is beset with similar problems. The concepts of Necessity and Freedom are *overcome* by the Holy Spirit as the principle of Love. The same problems which beset the previous definitions afflict too this final and highest moment in Dorner's account. When combined, Axt-Piscalar argues that they lead to the unity of Father, Son and Holy Spirit being achieved *only* through the mediation of the Spirit.[162] As a consequence, the Spirit is seen as a power *external* to the Father and

---

158 Ibid. p. 444.
159 Axt-Piscalar, *Grund*, p. 179.
160 Ibid. p. 425.
161 Ibid. p. 180.
162 Ibid. p. 183. This is not a new criticism of Dorner's account. W. F. Geß in *Das Dogma von Christi Person und Werk, Entwickelt aus Christi Selbstzeugniß und den Zeugnissen der Apostel*, (Basel: Detloff, 1887), argued that an implication of Dorner's idea of

41

Son and thought either dominant or subservient to the needs of the two others.[163]

Axt-Piscalar is correct in arguing that Dorner's approach brings subordinationist tendencies and the attendant problem of externalizing the Spirit from the Father and Son whose relations He mediates (and we shall see in our final chapter on sanctification that Dorner's treatment of the Spirit is considerably underdeveloped). However, at this stage in his exposition we suggest that Axt-Piscalar has underestimated the *safeguards* which Dorner has himself imposed on these definitions. When he posits the Holy Spirit as the means by which the Father and Son are related (as Cause and Caused, Object and Subject, Necessity and Freedom), he argues that the Spirit acts in this way '*together* with the other two'.[164] It is not merely the First and Second Principles which are constituted by the eternal act of unification. The Third Principle, as the unifier, is also constituted as part of this triunity in this eternal process.[165] Indeed, the movement would not occur if the Holy Spirit were *not* a part of the essential being: 'God could not part Himself unless He were sure of the principle of union.'[166] Furthermore, Dorner appears to recognize that his definition might lead to the conclusion that the Holy Spirit is merely the *product* of the relations between Father and Son and, as such, seen as either subordinate or superior to these other two:

> 'The third is not *the mere sum*' (and subordinate) 'of the two first forms of Being of the Godhead, is *not the divine Essence as such*', (and superior) 'but one of the modes of the existence of the divine Essence, as the two others also are'.[167]

We suggest that these insertions in Dorner's account display a sufficient concern to guard against those problems flagged up by Axt-Piscalar. We note again, however, a fundamental problem with Dorner's overall method. Because he begins his dogmatic exposition of the doctrine of God at the general level in such a way as to lead on to the specific as that which provides *solutions* to the problems, the Trinity becomes a doctrine *primarily* concerned with problem solving (which is surely only one part of the force

---

Personality being ascribed to God in His unity means that God is not yet realized in the first and second forms of divine being, but 'only in the third', p. 313.

[163] Axt-Piscalar, *Grund*, p. 184.

[164] *SCD*, I, p. 421.

[165] Dorner had earlier noted in his account of the ecclesial development of the doctrine of the Trinity the need for the Spirit to be with the Father seen as the co-determining principle in order to exclude the subordination of the Spirit, Ibid. p. 384.

[166] Ibid. p. 421.

[167] Ibid. p. 425.

of the doctrine). Furthermore, according to the terms of that scheme the problems solved pertain not principally to those which attend the revelation of the triune God who *saves*, but with the problems which come with the general notion of God. The agenda for the Christian doctrine of God is set by the non-Christian, and it is this which occasions the tensions identified. We will close with an analysis of Dorner's conclusions concerning the relationship between the concepts of Absolute Personality, hypostases and attributes.

c. The Absolute Personality, Divine Hypostases and Attributes

Since the Absolute Personality is the eternally present result in the trinitarian process of the Life and Spirit of God, the Self-conscious/willing/possessing God is also present in each of the divine distinctions, that, though not of themselves and singly personal, have a share in the One Divine Personality, in their own manner.[168]

Dorner suggests that the Absolute Personality is the *result* in the trinitarian process, and as such, the hypostases are not in themselves 'personal', but in their eternal mutual relations, constitute 'one divine Personality' which 'eternally participates in a living manner in each of the members'.[169] The hypostases are personal insofar as they participate in the one Personality which together they create. For this reason Dorner refuses to designate the hypostases as 'Persons', and instead uses the term 'Modes of Being' (Seinsweisen).[170]

We observed earlier that Dorner sought in his account of the attributes a single 'divine Principle' which would 'govern' the attributes. Furthermore, we noted that this quest represented the predisposition of his general account for a *personal* rather than *substantive* definition of God.

Accordingly, his account of the Christian idea of God provides such a principle. It is the triune God defined as 'holy Love', ethically conceived, and as such the 'unification and the supreme power of all the divine attributes'.[171] This construction has the advantage of refusing to the hypostases *Self*-constituting distinction (as we noted above in our response to Axt-Piscalar). It is only *as* Trinity that God is Absolute Personality without requiring a fourth element, above the Seinswesen, to constitute the

---

[168] Ibid. P. 447.

[169] Ibid. p. 450.

[170] E. Hirsch suggests that Dorner's is the most glorious expression of this notion among his contemporaries, (Emanuel Hirsch, *Geschichte der neuern evangelischen Theologie*, Bd. 5 [Gütersloh: C. Bertelsmann Verlag, 1951], p. 382.

[171] *SCD*, I, p. 448.

Personality.[172] Yet a major problem emerges with the implication that the hypostases are *merely* elements (Momente) in the production of the *one* Personality.[173] As such each has content only as a *relation* in a process which issues forth in a divine Unity. While Dorner has gained a definition which seeks to maintain a *personal* monotheism ('the One God [is] no impersonal neuter'[174]), the extent to which it comes from a concern to reconcile apparent contradictions (revealed in the general account) means that there is less of an interest in expositing more fully the particularities (and we might say glory) of each hypostasis. It is, we suggest, a systemic weakness of Dorner's project.

We close with an evaluation of his account of the relation between the Absolute Personality and the attributes.

The definition of the 'personal triune'[175] God brings closure to Dorner's primary apologetic endeavour. It is the conclusion *required* by the provisional findings of the 'one continuous course of proof'.[176] The Christian idea of God as triune is, therefore, necessary for the proper definition of God as the 'real primary ethical Being'.[177] From this vantage point Dorner returns to a question which he asked early in his investigations. Is there a principle in God by which 'He is Himself absolutely supreme…and contradistinguished from the attributes as the things governed'[178]? Since the principle has now been established, Dorner lays out the details of its relationship with the attributes.

[The attributes] appear in a close unity, as necessarily verified and guaranteed by the absolutely supreme instance, since we shall succeed in regarding these attributes as determinations, which God as personal Love necessarily and eternally has and wills for the eternal Self-production of His own absolute ethical Personality.[179]

The divine attributes are the *determinations* of God. They *conform* to His essential, personal constitution as triune. This means that the divine attributes are absolutely conformed to the necessary divine being *and* willed

---

[172] '[T]he divine Personality is not a fourth to the three, but only exists by their means and their eternal union', Ibid. p. 450.
[173] *Briefwechsel*, I, p. 121. Dorner compares the idea of the 'drei Centra' with Martensen's notion of the 'Ichpunkte'. He asks how important it is to think of every hypothesis as personal, when Personality comes not 'durch die Hypostase für sich, sondern durch die Immanenz der andern in ihr', p. 122.
[174] Ibid. p. 448.
[175] Ibid. p. 453.
[176] Ibid. p. 454.
[177] Ibid. p. 454.
[178] Ibid. p. 202.
[179] Ibid. p. 454.

by God for His eternal Self-production and Self-preservation:

> God, who as the unity of Self-preservation and of the will to com-
> municate Himself is Love, wills Himself in all His attributes, as love
> requires.[180]

God as Love is served by His attributes. God governs His attributes. Therefore, with regard to those physical attributes (which we noted earlier) – Beauty, Harmony, Infinity, Life, Fullness of Power, Omnipotence – we must see that their working is 'dependent'[181] on their service to the production and main-tenance of the divine Personality. For example, infinity is not an attribute by which God is bound to be 'everywhere the same'.[182] Rather, God as Love is free if He 'so desires' to be present in 'one revelation'[183] such as Christ.

This is an arrangement which has occasioned a much noted account of divine immutability.[184] We wish only to note that God's essential constancy is not in competition with His capacity to be *moved* by His participation in the world (as indeed, His omniscience is not in competition with His capacity to treat the Christian with regard to the future and not the past[185]).

---

[180] Ibid. p. 456.

[181] Ibid. p. 458.

[182] Ibid. p. 458.

[183] Ibid. p. 458.

[184] While we wish to acknowledge the important place Dorner's account of immutability has in his wider project (and we will refer back to it throughout the course of our argument) since it has already been the subject of much interest (see below), our focus on it will be limited to the way in which it fits in the wider ambitions of his theological work. We do want to note, however, the identification of Dorner as a major player in the development of the doctrine in modern theology. For example, Thomas G. Wein-andy, in *Does God Suffer?* (Edinburgh: T & T Clark, 2000), remarks that Dorner 'may have been the first theologian to argue that the biblical notion of God expresses an ethical understanding of his immutability and not an ontological understanding', p. 61. The genetic contours of Dorner's doctrine of immutability have been ably traced by Robert Williams (on the relationship between Dorner and Schleiermacher) in the 'Introduction' to Isaak August Dorner, *Divine Immutability*, trans. Robert R. Williams & Claude Welch, [Minneapolis: Fortress Press, 1994], pp. 12–19) and (on the relationship between Dorner and Schelling) in 'Schelling and Dorner on Divine Immutability', in *Journal of the American Academy of Religion*, Vol. 53, No. 2 (June 1985), pp. 237–249; and Dorner's influence on Barth has been surveyed both by Robert Sherman in 'Isaak August Dorner on Divine Immutability: A Missing Link between Schleiermacher and Barth' in *The Journal of Religion*, Vol. 77, No. 3 (Jul. 1997), pp. 380–401; and Matthias Gockel in 'On the way from Schleiermacher to Barth: A critical reappraisal of Isaak August Dorner's essay on divine immutability', in *Scottish Journal of Theology*, Vol. 53, No. 4 (2000), pp. 490–510.

[185] On this point, Dorner challenges Augustine and Thomas' notion of an 'eternal present' in God's relation to time, which he says 'labours under preconceived opinions from pre-Christian time', *SCD*, I, p. 330. Rather, God's omniscience is governed by His

Indeed, it is only by allowing Himself to be 'conditioned in His action by the action of men'[186] that God *remains* immutable, that is, in conformity to His ethically defined essence. As Dorner himself notes, this understanding will have major implications for an account of the work of atonement, on which we will comment in Chapter 6. For now, it will suffice to note how Dorner's configuration of the doctrine of God allows him to posit the notion that God's economic operation does not bring a *lessening* of His essential being, but rather His immanent constitution provides the grounds for a dynamic relationship in which He *maintains* this essence: God's distinction from the world is not in competition but in consonance with His relation to the world (and for this reason, a doctrine of atonement should be capable of displaying God as Judge without detriment to His primary definition as Love). The definition of God as holy Love brings Dorner to the conclusion of his original ambitions. The Christian idea of God is that which is required for theology to proceed with integrity.

Conclusion

The methodological progression from general to specific in Dorner's project presents significant problems, since its course is so significantly impacted by the demands placed on it by the agenda peculiar to the problematics of the general doctrine. However, he makes some key moves which, for the purposes of our project, demonstrate a way of delineating the gospel of salvation as that which consistently *coheres* with the essential being of the triune Godhead and posits the gospel as meeting the demands of divine justice without detriment to the divine compassion or love. We have already noted how his assessment of divine immutability assists his understanding of the way in which God relates to the world with constancy *as* it is affected by the created world's activity. This has obvious implications for the doctrine of atonement (as we shall see in Chapter 6) and the depiction of how God remains faithful to Himself as He instantiates a saving faithfulness to the world in the death of Christ.

However, while we will come on to address those issues in subsequent chapters, we wish here to note the way in which his concern to depict the

---

essence, so that God, while not being surprised by events, relates to time as it occurs, and knows 'past *as* past and not as present' (p. 331), 'the present is alone real; what is not yet real, God cannot know as real' (p. 332). God is the source of possibility and it is on this ground that future acts are not in competition with divine omniscience or that God's omniscience is in competition with the progress of time. Indeed, it is on this basis that God relates to the world without destroying the distinction, and in relation to the Christian personality, is the basis of the scriptural notion that God forgets sin.

[186] *SCD*, I, p. 462.

eternally present triune relations as holy Love means that he has begun his account with a means of positing God as freely in control of Himself, and as such, the ethically *vital* Absolute Personality who is *prior* to His apprehension by faith. It is a representation which, we suggest, enables Dorner to depict God's relation to the world as neither impairing His self-sufficiency, nor impeding His persistent personal engagement with the world. The corollary of this is, of course, that a potential space is opened up for the creaturely sphere to be both distinct *from* and in relation *to* its Creator. We will see in the following chapter the way in which this is worked out in detail. The doctrine of God, however, provides the key to the remainder of his dogmatic project. In the subsequent delineation of the divine purposes for the world, which embrace the exigencies of sin and salvation, we suggest that Dorner's interest in depicting God as triune allows for the persistent representation of God's activity as commensurate both with His own essential being and the positing of a distinct creaturely sphere of ethical activity. We will see how central to his dogmatic purposes the doctrine of the triune God is as we proceed; and we will see that its careful representation of God as *holy* Love allows for the depiction of the attainment of salvation for the world as *consistent* with the divine essential being.

2

THE DOCTRINE OF THE ECONOMIC TRINITY AND THE CREATION OF THE WORLD

Introduction

In his treatment of the doctrine of the immanent Trinity set out in the previous chapter we observed that Dorner defines God as *holy* Love. The triune relations as those which eternally instantiate a union of the truly necessary and the free. This is the real form of the 'truly ethical', and as such divine love is holy love:

> For love is the unity of ethical necessity and freedom, because it wills the ethically necessary as such, that is, with consciousness and absolute desire.[1]

The Father is conceived as 'that which is true, necessary, and good in itself'[2]; the Son is the 'mode of God in the form of freedom'[3]; and the Holy Spirit is the divine mode who 'combines in God the ethically necessary and the free'.[4] In this eternal divine exchange, God is eternally consistent with Himself and lives in an eternally fulfilled movement of self-sufficient constancy.

Having posited this doctrine of immanent completeness, with its union of necessity and freedom, as that which is discernible in 'the traces…given in (evangelical) faith',[5] Dorner moves to an assessment of how this ethically conceived triune God lives in relation to the world. Formally considered,

---

[1] *SCD*, I, p. 437.
[2] Ibid. p. 433.
[3] Ibid. p. 434.
[4] Ibid. p. 436.
[5] Ibid. p. 427.

this treatment of the economic Trinity comes, unsurprisingly, as a sub-division of the Doctrine of God. Yet what is noteworthy is that it comes *within* the First Division of Part One of his *System*, and is therefore treated under the category of *Fundamental* Christian Doctrine. Together with the Second (The Creature, especially Man[6]) and Third Divisions (The Unity of God and Man[7]) of this First Part – which we will survey in the following chapter – Dorner constructs his account of the economic relations in terms of the way in which they cohere with the idea of God as Absolute Personality.

This next stage in the doctrine of God is not, therefore, *who* God is in His relation to the world (this he has already affirmed, as 'God is in Himself, so He also reveals Himself'[8]), but *what* God's relation is to the world. The key question is then: what *reason* can be discovered in God for the creation of the world.[9]

The dogmatic order is to this extent: *opera Dei ad intra – opera Dei ad extra*,[10] since he advances to the question of God's relation to the world on the *basis* of the conclusions arrived at concerning who He is in Himself. In the process he will attempt to ameliorate what he sees as the persistent threat to the dogmatic distinction between God and world occasioned by pantheistic and subjectivist doctrines of God.

This does not mean that the economic has had no place in the configuration of the immanent idea of God. Rather, in accordance with his apologetic desire to demonstrate as foundational the belief in the triune God, he appeals to the *trace* of Trinity[11] given in evangelical faith.[12]

This trace is not a *vestigium trinitatis* in the Augustinian sense of being an *evidence* within created reality which images the triunity of God, but rather the *object* of evangelical faith brings with it a pre-scientific apprehension of God's triality. Dorner's concern is not to uncover traces of triunity *per se*, but instead to make the link between the evangelical principle of faith and its appropriate attendant contents and presupposition, which is the doctrine of the Trinity. On this point, we suggest that Otto Weber's suggestion that Dorner developed (along with Sartorius) a speculative doctrine

---

[6] *SCD*, II, pp. 64–103.

[7] Ibid. pp. 106–294.

[8] *SCD*, I, p. 446.

[9] *SCD*, II, p. 9.

[10] Thomas Koppehl rightly observes this point, Thomas Koppehl, *Der wissenschaftliche Standpunkt der Theologie des Isaak August Dorners* (Berlin: Walter de Gruyter, 1997), p. 169. Hereafter, *Standpunkt*.

[11] '[F]aith includes traces of a divine Triality', *SCD*, I, p. 417.

[12] 'The objective persistence of eternal distinctions in God is *the necessary presupposition in faith* as regards personal communion with God. This persistence is the ground in fact, which is present and efficient in faith, that spiritual, that divine and human reality', *SCD*, I, p. 414.

of the Trinity merely from the 'basic idea that God is love'[13] misrepresents the way in which the definition of God as Love is arrived at in conjunction with and out of the apprehension of faith's contents. Therefore, it is *as* God appropriates and is appropriated by the believer in the activity of faith that the beginning and basis of the end of God's apprehension as triune is given. Love is, therefore, given as the proper definition of God in and with God's apprehension as triune (Indeed, Dorner himself criticizes Sartorius for developing his scheme from the principle of love because it does not allow for the 'distinctions in God'[14]). For one thing, Weber's analysis fails to acknowledge the importance for Dorner of describing God as *holy* Love. The adjective is not incidental since it indicates the extent to which the doctrine is certified in connection with its apprehension in the ethical content of evangelical faith.

He seeks to explain its truth by demonstrating that the idea of God (as holy Love) is only properly posited in the Christian idea of God as Trinity (according to which ethical necessity and freedom are related in a perfect eternal unity). The order is triple-layered: beginning with the traces of the Trinity in the experience of faith, it proceeds to the intellectual demonstration of the idea of God as Trinity, before moving on to an explication of the economic Trinity as that which coheres with the immanent.[15] It is the *trace* of Trinity given with evangelical faith in Christ which is the *origin* of the doctrinal investigation (and in this, an economic datum) but in the process of intellection it is the Christian idea of God (the immanent idea) which becomes itself the *basis* of faith, in order to secure the certainty of the contents and soteriological effects of that faith.[16]

On this point we differ once again from Axt-Piscalar's assessment of Dorner's project. At the close of her consideration of his doctrine of the economic Trinity, she suggests that an insoluble problem attends his schema because of his retention of the 'traditionellen Gotteslehre',[17] according to

---

[13] Otto Weber, *Foundations of Dogmatics*, trans. Darrell L. Guder, Vol. 1 (Michigan: Eerdmans, 1981), p. 375.

[14] *SCD*, I, p. 409.

[15] We are indebted on this point to observations made to slightly different ends by David Coffey who uses the triple-layered structure to explicate our knowledge of the Trinity. He differs from Dorner in beginning with 'biblical data' as the basis of the knowledge of the immanent Trinity, which in turn is the basis for the affirmation of the truthfulness of the economic Trinity, David Coffey, *Deus Trinitas: The Doctrine of the Triune God* (Oxford: Oxford University Press, 1999), p. 17.

[16] *SCD*, I, p. 417. Dorner later speaks of Sabellianism as a 'Christian mode of thought' (in spite of its limitations) because it acknowledged that the 'knowledge of the immanent Trinity must always issue from the economical Trinity, from history', *SCD*, III, p. 286. E. Günther correctly states that Dorner held that the doctrine of justification would be properly secured only with the belief in the immanent Trinity, *Die Entwicklung der Lehre von der Person Christi im XIX Jahrhundert* (Tübingen: Mohr, 1911), p. 236.

[17] Axt-Piscalar, *Grund*, p. 219.

which he does not speak of the divine essence *on the basis* of its economic expression, but the economic on the basis of the divine essence. It means that the problem of whether the creation is an act of divine necessity or chance is unresolved. Not that Dorner is simply *unsuccessful* in arranging the resources available to him, but that he is not in *possession* of the theological resources to do so. The economic operations remain *external* to the already arrived at idea of the self-sufficient absolute Personality:

> Wird unter den Bedingungen der traditionellen Gotteslehre die absolute Persönlichkeit als Schöpfungssubjekt vorausgesetzt, so gibt es zwischen den beiden Alternativen, entweder die Schöpfung als einen notwendigen Akt der Selbstentsprechung Gottes zu verstehen oder sie als zufälling zu behaupten und damit das Verhältnis Gottes zur Welt als ein dem göttlichen Wesen äußerlich bleibendes zu bestimmen, keinen Ausweg.[18]

Axt-Piscalar suggests that the solution to this problem has arrived in the theology of the twentieth century:

> Wenn sich die Theologie unseres Jahrhunderts in besonderer Weise der Verhältnisbestimmung von immanenter und ökonomisher Trinität widmet mit dem Ziel, auf die Implikationen der Geschichte Gottes mit der Welt und deren Bedeutung für sein Wesen zu reflektieren, so ist dies als Ausdruck desjenigen Problembewußtseins zu würdigen, welches sich aus der Konstellation der beschriebenen Aporien ergibt.[19]

Perhaps what Axt-Piscalar intends is displayed in the following extract from T. F. Torrance's description of the designation of God the Father as Creator: 'Creation arises, then, out of the Father's eternal love of the Son, and is activated through the free ungrudging movement of that Fatherly love in sheer grace which continues to flow freely and unceasingly toward what God has brought into being in complete differentiation from himself. This is *a truth which we have come to grasp only through the incarnation of his Love in Jesus Christ*....Because God is love, we cannot and may not try to press our thought speculatively behind that Love to what might have happened, had not the fall taken place, had not the world become disordered through evil.'[20]

We will assess later Dorner's success in overcoming the problem of creation's necessity of arbitrary existence (a point on which we find Axt-Piscalar's actual reconstruction of Dorner's conclusions a profitable aid).

---

[18] Ibid.
[19] Ibid.
[20] T. F. Torrance, *The Christian Doctrine of God, One Being Three Persons* (Edinburgh: T & T Clark, 1996), pp. 209–210 (my italics).

Here we wish only to suggest that the description of Dorner's doctrine of God as *traditional* is misleading. It fails to do justice to the complex way in which he marshals his material in order to show the *interconnected* relationship between immanent and economic, which we have described as triple-layered. Axt-Piscalar *is* correct, however, to highlight the importance to Dorner of addressing the question of creation's existence: necessary or arbitrary. As we proceed with our account we shall see how the problem holds great interest for Dorner.

For the overall purposes of our study, what we wish to display in this chapter is the way in which Dorner's particular conceptualization of God's perfection (seen in Chapter 1) means that he has the dogmatic resources to depict the divine relation with the world as indicative of both *God's* perfection, and the *world's* dependent perfectibility. God eternally maintains Himself in *determinate* movement – as the simple intra-Trinitarian ethical exchange of the divine modes of being – so that His being is *living* (without ever being indefinite), and the world enlivened. This issues forth in a creative use of the doctrine of divine *aseity* (as that which specifies not stasis but secure vivacity) in relation to the reason for the world's creation. It also allows a distinction between creation and conservation/concursus in which God's ongoing maintenance of the creature enables the preservation and not interruption of its freedom.

In this we see the marks of Dorner's attempt to trace a picture of God's relation to the world in which the intimacy of that relation – which will culminate in the incarnation – does not bring the confusion of God and world . Rather, it opens up the notion that the world has a *free capacity* to temporally instantiate the character of its creator. It is *as* God is most intimate that His distinctiveness is most keenly demonstrated (we will see in Chapter 5 that this is a central feature of his doctrine of Jesus Christ). We suggest it lies in Dorner's foundational engagement with the doctrine of the immanent Trinity that we find the valuable resources for this constructive thesis. The importance of the details of his doctrine of God may be seen, therefore, in this chapter and, as we proceed, display themselves as the central feature of Dorner's entire project, culminating in the doctrine of the world's reconciliation.

We begin the present chapter, however, with an analysis of the way in which Dorner moves from the doctrine of the immanent to the economic.

I. God's Revelation of Himself in the World

Following his treatment of the Doctrine of God in its immanent form, Dorner proceeds to the doctrine of God's relation to the world. This is divided into three sections:

1. Creation;
2. Conservation and Concursus;
3. Providence.

In preparing for these sections, he offers a chapter which marks the formal transition from the doctrine of the immanent Trinity to the doctrine of the world. In it he sets out the reason which he discerns, on the basis of the immanent idea of God, for the revelation of God in the world:

> Neither to supply a deficiency in His perfect essence, nor on account of a superabundance of which He is supposed not to be master, God, of His perfection and blessedness in love, sets forth as a really second object a world, which He calls out of non-existence into existence, that, loved and loving, it may be a relatively self-dependent image of His perfect triune nature and attributes.[21]

Dorner's concern is to obviate the notion that God is *obliged* to act either from His need for self-completion ('to supply a deficiency') or by His nature ('a superabundance'). Rather, it is precisely because He *is* Self-sufficient and in control of Himself that He brings into existence an Other which is destined to 'be God's likeness outside of God'.[22]

It was the resolution of the first part of his account that God's Self-sufficiency guards His distinction from the world. This was a conclusion which owed much to his concern to circumvent the identification of God and world. He identified this in the panentheistic notions of the theological systems (informed by Hegel) which embraced a reading of religious history in which Jesus stands as the individual who overcomes the opposition between God and humanity maintained by Israel.[23] For Dorner, God in

---

[21] *SCD*, II, p. 9.

[22] Ibid. p. 15.

[23] Falk Wagner identifies the following statement as programmatic for Hegel's post-Kantian scheme: 'Der Idee der Juden von Gott als ihren Herren und Gebieter über sie, setzt Jeus das Verhältnis Gottes zu den Menschen als eines Vaters gegen seine Kinder entgegen.' (N302), Falk Wagner, *Der Gedanke der Persönlichkeit Gottes bei Fichte und Hegel* (Gütersloh: Gütersloher Verlagshaus, 1971), p. 145. Central to its conclusions is the interest in removing the distinction between the reality of God and the reality of human existence, so that the one is necessarily bound to the other: 'Gott und das wirkliche Dasein des Menschen sollen nicht getrennt werden', Falk, Ibid. Axt-Piscalar identifies the theism of the nineteenth century as largely preoccupied with the reaction to this 'pantheism' by positing God as in Himself self-grounding, self-thinking, and self-willing absolute personality who is independent from the world, Axt-Piscalar, *Grund*, p. 209. Dorner's view that Hegel was responsible for confusing

Himself does not lack perfection[24] and is not lost in a process of becoming in the world: 'Er ist...nicht über sich hinausgehender Prozess, der sich in der Selbstmitteilung an die Welt völlig verliert.'[25]

Yet in His constitution as holy Love neither is He ineluctably abstracted from and indifferent to the world as supposed by the deistic theological tradition. This is the cash value of Dorner's ethical definition of the divine essence: 'In order to preserve His ethical Self-identity, God cannot be indifferent to history, but He remains Self-identical in His participation in the world.'[26] It is not the case that the world is the product of a 'purposeless, absolutely spontaneous will of God, which called forth a world without necessity of any kind'.[27] This would threaten the *certain* knowledge of the world, since all knowledge would be merely 'empirical', and would imply that 'it is utterly indifferent to God whether the world exists or not – a disparagement of the world contrary to Scripture'.[28]

Dorner therefore begins his account of the relation of God to the world by refocusing on God's essential being as holy Love. This is the *reason* for the divine positing of the world as a distinct object whose destiny is to be conformed to the divine image: 'Love...will exert itself to bring this second into existence. In this way we reach the absolute derivation of a world.'[29]

We shall analyse the details of the notion of the world as *imago dei* in the subsequent sections on Creation, Conservation and Concursus. For the moment we wish only to concern ourselves with the question of how Dorner justifies his opening affirmation, that Love is the reason for the creation of the world. As we shall see, it is an explanation which has occasioned considerable critique.

God and world has however been ably critiqued by Piotr Malysz, who argues that 'though human subjectivity is the medium of cognizing God (God is thinkable!), God is prior to subjectivity and to thought', Piotr J. Malysz, 'Hegel's Conception of God', p. 462.

[24] The divine perfection as that which is instantiated in the world's realization has been noted by Jörg Splett as a distinctive of Hegel's contribution to the idea of the Trinity. It is the means by which a relation may be realized with an Other in such a way as to bring about the full self-consciousness of God (since He will know Himself in distinction from another yet this Other will, in its reciprocal relation to its positer, instantiate its *identity* with its source), Jörg Splett, *Die Trinitätslehre G. W. F. Hegels* (Freiburg & München: Verlag Karl Alber, 1965), p. 144.

[25] Arthur Drews, *Die deutsche Spekulation seit Kant mit besonderer Rücksicht auf das Wesen des Absoluten und die Persönlichkeit Gottes* (Berlin: Paul Maeter,1893), p. 527.

[26] *SCD*, I, p. 460.

[27] *SCD*, II, p. 10.

[28] Ibid. p. 11.

[29] Ibid. p. 15.

a. Love as the Reason for the Creation of the World

Crucial to Dorner's exposition of Love as the reason for the creation of the world is the notion that preceding the act of creation is the *conception* of a second in the divine self-consciousness. God is posited, as ethical Absolute Personality, not only as the absolute seat of His *own* necessary being (since he conjoins the attributes of Intelligence and Wisdom to the Moral element) but also the seat of *all* possibilities:

> As formerly shown, God's Intelligence is the primary seat of all possibilities. God's *scientia necessaria* embraces not only Himself, but all possibilities; for these too reside in Him, and His self-consciousness would not be absolute unless He were conscious of Himself as the primary cause of all possibilities.[30]

The difference, however, between God's self-knowledge – which is necessary ('He Himself is *actus purissimus*, no mere potential existence'[31]) – and God's knowledge of the world ('the simply possible, as not actually existent, is distinct from him'[32]) which is merely possible – is sharply observed. This notion of a possible Second is described by Dorner as the 'world-idea'.[33] As such, it is a possibility which does not have ontological purchase in the divine essence but neither is it merely nothing. Rather, it stands *between* divine reality and nothingness: 'if not actual reality, neither is it Nothing. But it is also not God.'[34] It is known by God as another *possible* object of love, and it is the knowledge of the *non-existence* of this possible object which is the 'starting-point for God's spontaneous love'.[35] This is an important feature of Dorner's doctrine of *creatio ex nihilo*. It is *within* the Trinitarian exchange which eternally results in the Absolute Personality that the world-idea occurs eternally. This is itself the *mediator* of creation, and nothing else. The point may be clarified by reference to Colin Gunton's appeal to the significance of creation 'Trinitarianly conceived' as the 'necessary condition of the doctrine of creation out of nothing, because without it matter, or some other feature of the universe, becomes the mediator, and thus eternal'.[36] However, it is precisely at this point, and with the notion of God's *spontaneity*, that we find the most pressing problems presented to the scheme.

---

[30] Ibid. p. 13.
[31] Ibid.
[32] Ibid.
[33] Ibid. p. 15.
[34] Ibid.
[35] Ibid.
[36] Colin E. Gunton, 'The End of Causality? The Reformers and their Predecessors', in *The Doctrine of Creation*, ed. Colin E. Gunton (Edinburgh: T & T Clark, 1997), p. 74.

Dorner contends that it is therefore the world-idea's non-existence which causes God to bring the world into being. He does this because He Himself is not only love in His 'self-affirming personality' but 'loves the sentiment of love in itself'.[37] Since God *is* holy Love, holy love is a mode of being which God privileges absolutely and as such desires. He is '*Amor Amoris.*'[38] With the knowledge of a possible world in which He could love and be loved, He *exerts* Himself by bringing this world ('destined for the kingdom of love'[39]) into existence. Dorner explains that this movement is itself a demonstration of the 'humility' of divine Love which is 'drawn towards that which is poor and destitute of existence and life'[40] (and here he cites Luke 1.42, 53; and 1 Cor. 1.28) and which will be a feature of his explication of the reason for God reconciling Himself to the world.

In this description of the transition from the possible to the actual, Dorner speaks explicitly only of divine *freedom* in creation (expressed in terms of spontaneity and exertion). Yet he insists we must not mistake this for an arbitrary freedom or absolute spontaneity (*merum supremum arbitrium*). It is not 'utterly indifferent to God whether the world exists or not'.[41] Rather, because it is born of Love it is an intentional act in which the world has an aim and a purpose to love and to be loved.

Dorner is convinced that this provides a sufficient explanation for why the world was created. Jörg Rothermundt contends, however, that Dorner has failed to resolve the problem. We will set out his objections, and seek to demonstrate how Dorner's account does display a systematic consistency which Rothermundt has himself failed to observe.

b. Rothermundt's Critique of Dorner

Rothermundt correctly notes that while referring to the transition from the possible to the actual Dorner speaks only in terms of divine freedom (a point on which Axt-Piscalar curiously says the opposite: 'er *nicht zögert* den Übergang zur Welt als einen notwendigen zu beschreiben' [my italics][42]), it must be read in the context of his intention to derive the world not from a physical necessity in God, but from an ethical necessity.[43] When Dorner speaks of divine freedom as the cause of the realization of creation this is the divine freedom which is always in perfect union with divine necessity. This is in accordance with the previously determined ethical definition

---

[37] *SCD*, II, p. 14.
[38] Ibid.
[39] Ibid. p. 15.
[40] Ibid.
[41] Ibid. p. 11.
[42] Axt-Piscalar, *Grund*, p. 212.
[43] Rothermundt, *Synthese*, p. 153.

of God's essential being, and as such may also be described as 'ethischer Notwendigkeit'.[44]

To support his claim that this link must be made, Rothermundt cites Dorner's statement in the posthumously published *System der Christlichen Sittenlehre*:

> Weder aus physischer Notwendigkeit seines Wesens noch aus bloßer Willkür seiner Allmacht ist die Welt abzuleiten, sondern aus der göttlichen Freiheit, die in sich ethisch und wahre göttliche Freiheit dadurch ist, daß sie mit dem ethisch Notwendigen oder Guten geeinigt ist.[45]

While Dorner speaks of the derivation of the world from divine freedom, he speaks of an *ethical* freedom which is united with ethical necessity or the Good. If freedom is abstracted from necessity it then can be only an arbitrary act of power; but divine freedom is that which is united to ethical necessity in the inner Trinitarian relations.[46] According to Rothermundt, therefore, when Dorner speaks of creation as a spontaneous act it means that it is a necessary act, since Dorner has already posited freedom as that which is not inimical to necessity but instantiated in willing conformity. With this connection fully in place, Rothermundt contends that Dorner's account cannot resolve the problem of why the merely possible world becomes actual.[47] Although Dorner's reference to freedom must be considered with reference to the matrix of the ethical constitution of God as Absolute Personality, it is precisely because it is *the Son* who is the principle of ethical actuality that the world is not needed. Only the possibility of the world is proved (and the necessity of that thought in the divine self-consciousness) but *not* its actualization.

While the existence of the world does not contradict the ethical being of God, since this ethical being is self-sufficient, there can be no *positive* explanation for its realization. Attributing the move to create the world to love is insufficient because it fails to explain how this realized world is either a free

---

[44] Ibid. p. 151.
[45] Isaac Dorner, *System der Christlichen Sittenlehre* (Berlin: Wilhelm Hertz, 1885), p. 84. Hereafter, *Sittenlehre*.
[46] Wolf Krötke has correctly identified the *relational* dimension of this view of ethical freedom as that which appertains to the trinitarian structure of God's essential being which, in the relationship between the modes of being, loses no freedom in the exchange but has rather its freedom *instantiated* in the relation to the other: 'Ethische Freiheit is an der *Freiheit der anderen* orientiert, freilich nicht so, daß sie sich selbst an die Freiheit der enderen verliert', Wolf Krötke, *Gottes Klarheiten* (Tübingen: Mohr Siebeck, 2001), p. 209.
[47] Rothermundt, *Synthese*, p. 154.

act (since God is not obliged to create in order to complete Himself) or a necessary act (since God fulfils in Himself the free obedience to the Good in the Son). Rothermundt argues that Dorner's success in avoiding pantheism and dualism in his doctrine of the immanent Trinity comes at the expense of explaining how the world is actually derived from God. Indeed, he goes on to argue that if the reason for the creation is God's love of love, there would appear no grounds for stopping at the creation of only one world, for if He is desirous to share His Love and be loved by an Other apart from Himself, should this not give rise to the *continual* creation of worlds?[48]

The root cause of this problem, according to Rothermundt, lies in Dorner's apologetic interests. Because he is attempting a synthesis of belief and knowledge, he takes steps that he has no hope of completing. *Faith* knows ('*weiß*'[49]) that God is the personal opposite who does not need man, and *faith* knows that God is the creator. Yet *speculation* can prove nothing more about the way in which the creation is derived. Rothermundt argues that Julius Müller alone among the *Vermittlungstheologe* has grasped this point:

> Die Liebe Gottes bedarf zu ihrer Betätigung nicht der Welt, denn sie verwirklicht sich immanent in der Trinität. Die Welt ist für Gott also nicht notwendig, sondern kontingent…Die Spekulation kann also die Möglichkeit und die Sinnhaftigkeit der Schöpfung beweisen, mehr nicht. Sie darf aber auch nicht mehre beweisen, da sie sonst dem Inhalt des Glaubens widerspräche.[50]

Speculation (which here includes Dorner's attempt to infer from the doctrine of the immanent Trinity a reason for the economic act of creation) is not merely unable to supply a suitable answer to the question of why God created the world. It ought not seek further proof unless it contradicts the content of faith. According to Rothermundt, this is the most appropriate way of responding to the question. We would, however, question this use of Müller. It is part of a wider misreading of Dorner's approach.

While Müller's *fideistic* approach is fundamentally at odds with Dorner's, the kind of speculative programme which he rejects is different enough from Dorner's system to bring into question the appropriateness of Rothermundt's application of it. The speculative project which Müller opposes is one in which it is the *thinking subject* which moves the speculative programme

---

[48] Rothermundt, *Synthese*, p. 154.

[49] Ibid.

[50] Ibid. p. 156. Rothermundt cites J. Müller, *Die christliche Lehre von der Sünde*, 6 Aufl. (Stuttgart: Stuttgart, 1877), I, pp. 18–20; II, pp. 35–37, 184–191. Julius Kaftan also accuses Dorner of indulging in 'kosmologischer Spekulation' and in so doing falling outside of the Christian position which takes this issue by faith rather than speculation, Kaftan, *Dogmatik*, p. 234.

forward ('Vielmehr bewegen sie sich nur dadurch, daß das denkende Subjekt sie in Bewegung setzt'[51]) with *no* reference to the status of faith ('Aber wir sind freilich weit von dem Glauben'[52]), and does so through a process of dialectical negation without a sense of the goal of the process ('daß nun diese Bestimmungen...wie Automate sich nach ihrer innern logischen Notwendigkeit zu einem unbekannten Ziele hin zu bewegen beginnen'[53]). None of these are features of Dorner's project, since it is with the contents of faith that he begins, and proceeds, albeit with a process of logical intellection, with a careful sense of the teleological purpose of his project.[54] His is not a crudely speculative account of the type disabused in the section cited by Rothermundt, and for this reason is an unconvincing foundation for his critique that Dorner's project is necessarily unsuccessful.

We suggest that he has made a major error in not giving due weight to the way in which Dorner proposes the divine *aseity* as the *grounds* for divine action.[55] The ethical definition of God actually makes it consistent for Dorner to speak of the act of creation as an act which is more appropriately described in terms of divine freedom than necessity; and is an account of creation which displays a systematic consistency with his earlier determination of God as Absolute Personality. It is a move, furthermore, which will prove continually fruitful throughout the progress of his project, as we hope to demonstrate.

c. Response to Rothermundt's Critique

We suggest that the problem begins with Rothermundt's opening description of Dorner's project as being the search for a *proof* of the necessity of creation. By this he means a proof of the same kind that was displayed in the demonstration of the truth of the Christian doctrine of the triune God.[56] Yet this is not how Dorner describes his intentions. Rather, he calls for an 'eternal reason'[57] ('ein ewiger Grund'[58]) for the world, and speaks only of

[51] J. Müller, Vol. I, p. 18.
[52] Ibid.
[53] Ibid.
[54] Dorner had expressly distanced himself from Hegel's notion of a 'principle of negation' as the principle of movement or advance in the divine becoming, SCD, I, p. 251.
[55] This has been correctly noted by Frank Meesen: 'Während die Immanenz Gottes als Vermittlung seiner ethischen Substanz mit seiner ethischen Subjektivität sich selbst genügt, enthält sie zugleich das Moment der sich nach außen mitteilenwollenden Liebe. Auf diese Weise entsteht die Schöpfung. Sie ist Objekt seiner Selbstmitteilung und liegt in Gottes Selbstliebe als Postulat begründet', Frank Meessen, *Unveränderlichkeit und Menschwerdung Gottes* (Freiburg: Herder, 1989), p. 86.
[56] Rothermundt, *Synthese*, p. 149.
[57] SCD, II, p. 11.
[58] SGC, I, p. 450.

necessity when he rejects any theory of creation as an act of divine caprice in which there comes forth a 'world without necessity of *any kind*' (my italics).[59]

This is neither an accidental or incidental choice for Dorner. Not merely because he does not wish to evoke those theological models which posit the creation as necessary for the completion of God's being. Or as the necessary consequence of His nature, over which He has no control. Much more it displays a concern to distinguish the act of God, of which He Himself is the result, and the act of God of which the world is the result. To speak of the realization of the world *explicitly* in terms of necessity (although, as we will see, there is a *kind* of necessity in Dorner's model) will serve only to confuse the status of the two very different 'results' of the two very different types of causes. The concept of *necessity* is properly reserved to describe the divine Personality as He who must be the 'perennial and eternal cause of His absolute reality, and not merely the past and contingent cause'.[60] As God is the cause and caused, He is the ground of His own being and as such necessary; He alone is *a se*. This factor must be properly acknowledged in order to understand Dorner's intentions and how he comes to make the claim that it is *because* of and not in spite of the self-sufficiency of God that the realization has its eternal cause in God's ethical being. It is a feature which Dorner himself repeatedly asserts: 'Since God is to be conceived as all-sufficient in Himself, the world could add nothing to His perfection, because what it is it can only have from God';[61] 'In Himself He must be love and blessedness already';[62] 'God distinguishes Himself as the absolutely necessary';[63] 'God is the all-sufficient and blessed Personality';[64] 'assured through its self-sufficiency';[65] 'God alone who has eternally independent existence';[66] 'God's self-existence...remains an eternal distinction between God and the creature, and a safeguard against the danger of confounding the two';[67] 'One thing God cannot communicate, absolute self-existence or self-origination. The world remains eternally distinct from God.'[68]

For a correct understanding of his account of God's relation to the world this doctrine must be properly acknowledged. It is the conclusion of the doctrine of the immanent trinity that God is not mere potency or in need

[59] *SCD*, II, p. 10.
[60] *SCD*, I, p. 256.
[61] *SCD*, II, p. 9.
[62] Ibid. p. 11.
[63] Ibid. p. 13.
[64] Ibid.
[65] Ibid. p. 15.
[66] Ibid. p. 16.
[67] Ibid. p. 17.
[68] Ibid. p. 18.

of anything outside Himself to bring Him to perfection. Rather He is *'actus purissmus*, no mere potential existence'.[69] This is the presupposition on which he begins his account of God's relation to the world. He looks for a *reason* for its realization which is consistent with the definition of God as Absolute Personality.

This distinction seems to us very important if we are to be faithful to Dorner's own understanding of his project. That this is the key distinction would seem to be evidenced in the fact that Dorner insists that none of God's communicable attributes will be withheld from the world *apart* from 'eternally independent existence'.[70] Rothermundt makes a fundamental error when he describes the divine act of creation as the positing of a *necessary* Other ('[D]er Schluß von der Liebe Gottes auf die Welt als sein notwendiges Gegenüber'[71]), since what Dorner is proposing is precisely the *opposite* of positing a *necessary* Other, but an Other which has its cause outside of itself and as such is *not* necessary. That does not mean that the act of creating the world may not, in some sense, be described as necessary. However, this must be understood in the context of God's absolute self-sufficiency and not pertaining to His fulfilment, which has been already established.[72] Rather, the act may be described as necessary in a *relative* sense. Relative to God's essential being as holy Love. The act of creation is necessary in so far as it is an act in which God exerts Himself in full consistency with His ethical essence which is predisposed to bring the non-necessary Other into being. In this way, the act is not arbitrary, but neither is it absolutely necessary, since such a category belongs only to God Himself. The world cannot be absolutely necessary, but in its realization it is the product of an act which conforms to the ethical constitution of its enactor.

The 'eternal reason' for the world's realization lies not with God's physical essence (which would mean it was absolutely necessary in order to complete His necessary being). Rather, it lies with God's ethical essence.[73] According to this the world is created because God does *not* desire non-entity: 'in love is delight in the existence and life of a second possible object.'[74] For this reason Dorner speaks of the act of creation in terms of the divine freedom. Not

---

[69] Ibid. p. 13.

[70] Ibid. p. 16.

[71] Rothermundt, *Synthese*, p. 154.

[72] This distinction is not observed in one recent critique of Dorner's doctrine of God: 'Unfortunately Dorner interprets God's ethical actuality in such a way that entails God's creation, thus compromising divine freedom (p. 182). He seems to assume that if God's relation to creation is accidental, then his love for it is arbitrary and its existence is unimportant to him. This does not follow', Jay Wesley Richards, *The Untamed God: A Philosophical Exploration of Divine Perfection, Simplicity and Immutability* (Downers Grove: InterVarsity Press, 2003), p. 198, n. 9.

[73] *SCD*, II., p. 11.

[74] Ibid. p. 15.

that it is devoid of necessity, since it conforms to His ethical constitution; and as such, it is a non-arbitrary *free* act. For Dorner to describe it as free reflects the contingency of the world, rather than the absence of any kind of necessity.[75] By describing the divine act of creation in terms of freedom he is foregrounding the contingency of the worldly essence as that which is dependent on God for its existence, and as such is unnecessary for the completion of the divine perfection.

It might be profitable to see this move in counterpoint to the choice he made in his doctrine of God. When he set out his account of the divine Trinity as the perfect unity of necessity and freedom (§31b) he began with the concept of necessity. We suggested in chapter one that this decision appeared to be arbitrary and yet in the context of our present discussion it may be seen to be a part of a systematic consistency in Dorner's account. Although the world does not exist through itself 'but through God who alone has eternally independent existence (*Aseity*)' it is nonetheless designed 'to be the object of His perfect, unreserving love'.[76] Indeed, it is because God *is* Self-sufficient that the act of creation may be properly described as an act of divine love. This is because divine love is already 'absolutely assured through (the) all-sufficiency of its own perfection'[77] and is therefore prompted by no need of its own. Rather, it allows the world to be the scene of His perfect love and not than the scene in which His love is perfected.[78]

All this, of course, leaves open the question of whether God was free *not* to create the world. The evidence that we have amassed from Dorner's own account indicates a reluctance to speak of creation as free in the sense that God could *not* have created the world. Such a decision would have been arbitrary. While God is in Himself self-sufficient and does not need the world for His perfection, His self-constitution nevertheless leads Him to create the world. For Him to resolve not to create the world would not impinge upon His own perfection. It would however be an act with no grounds in His ethical essence, according to which God is the lover of life: 'were God to desire to keep or leave that portion of the possible...in a state of non-existence, He

---

[75] This crucial distinction is missed by Hermann Bavinck who unfairly classifies Dorner with numerous other 19 c. theologians who, he suggests, teach that 'God *must* impart reality to the idea of the world' (my italics), Herman Bavinck, *Reformed Dogmatics, Volume 2: God and Creation* (Grand Rapids: Baker, 2004), p. 432.

[76] *SCD*, I, p. 16.

[77] Ibid. p.15.

[78] Ibid. p. 16. We have been helped in seeing this feature in Dorner's account by the description of God's act of creation given by T. Weinandy. While he describes the trinitarian relations primarily in terms of relationality (which is not Dorner's model), he argues that it is only with the establishment of the self-sufficiency of God that the act of creation can be properly seen as the scene of 'beneficient and altruistic love', Thomas Weinandy, *Does God Suffer?*, p. 143.

would desire nonentity as such.'[79] Thus, it would be arbitrary because God's ethical self-constitution means He favours existence. A divine choice *not* to create the world would have no grounds since it would pertain to a desire for non-entity. This would not have purchase in the ethically determined divine essence.[80]

In positing Love as the reason for the creation of the world Dorner has explicated it as a free act (which, as Axt-Piscalar also suggests, ensures its compatibility with the 'christlich theologische Bewußtsein'[81]) without the attending implication that the ability to do otherwise constitutes it as a free act. Rather, it is because God's essence is ethical, and as such not indifferent to whether the world is or is not, that the freedom is expressed in His act of creation. It is not in the ability to create or not to create. Eleonore Stump describes this kind of 'freedom' in her discussion of Aquinas' theory of the will: 'Because the will is not a neutral capacity for choosing but a hunger for the good, which takes as good what the intellect represents as good…it is possible for a person to will freely and yet have no alternate possibility open to her.'[82] According to Dorner's own representation the act of creation may be described as both free without being arbitrary and necessary without being needed.[83]

d. Conclusion of Dorner's Account of God's Relation to the World

Dorner's use of his doctrine of aseity in establishing the contours of the divine relation to the world means that he is able to explain the world's positing as that which is *consistent* with the divine constitution without

---

[79] *SCD*, I, p. 15.

[80] Axt-Piscalar has correctly observed this feature, Axt-Piscalar, *Grund*, p. 218.

[81] Ibid.

[82] Eleonore Stump, 'Intellect, Will, and the Principle of Alternate Possibilities', in *Christian Theism and the Problems of Philosophy*, ed. M. D. Beaty (Notre Dame: University of Notre Dame, 1990), p. 278.

[83] On this point we find Axt-Piscalar's description helpful, although her subsequent conclusion, which we have discussed in the introduction to the chapter, that Dorner's account implies that the *whole* occurrence of the economic trinity remains 'äußerlich' to the 'allgenügsamen Wesen Gottes' is less convincing. By beginning with a definition of God as the self-sufficient Absolute Personality, Dorner is simply intending to clarify the proper distinction between world and God. Indeed, as we have previously suggested, since his theological method (contrary to Axt-Piscalar's assessment) is one in which he posits the doctrine of the Trinity in the context of its original instantiation in the 'traces' of faith, it is inappropriate to describe it as one which determines the way in which God is with no reference to its relation to the world. His schema is more varied than this. The *vestigia trinitatis* are found only in *faith*, not in human consciousness per se or in a universally available knowledge of the world.

detriment either to God's perfection or the world's relative independence.[84] By utilizing it in this way we see the beginnings of a pattern which, as we shall see in Chapter 5, will come into play with particular significance in his depiction of the incarnation. It is, we suggest, an aspect of Dorner's project which has been underplayed. It is a major part of his efforts to promote the priority of God without detriment either to the independent integrity of the world nor its concomitant dependence on God. God relates to the world because He is in Himself self-sufficient; and the world is free to relate to God because it depends on God. The relations are not the same, but there is consonance with God's own ethical essence in the way the world is created for *free* dependence – or obedience – to God. This is a theme which obtains continually through his system, and which we will seek to highlight.

II. The Doctrine of Creation

The act of creation has its eternal ground in divine Love. It is the realization of a Second Object which is distinct from God ('God's eternal love creates a free world, distinct from God'[85]) and yet 'destined to reflect the triune life'.[86] After proposing this, Dorner proceeds in the subsequent chapter to set out what this means for the world's constitution. It is, as the reference to 'destiny' implies ('daß sie Gottes dreieiniges Leben abzubilden *bestimmt* ist' [my italics][87]) a constitution which is firmly teleological in its content. The world created by God *is* posited in order to *become* the image of God. With this come two key features of his account: that the world is 'progressive';[88] and that the world is the intended 'image of God'.[89] We will discuss later what Dorner means when he speaks of the 'world' *tout court* as the image of God, and evaluate in Chapter 3 the relationship between *imago dei* and humanity. For the moment, we wish to observe only that the world is constituted as that which will be the creaturely correspondent of its creator. *Will* be because it is that which is 'destitute of self-existence'.[90] As such it does not and cannot exist as the *eternally present* result of the process of free obedience to the Good. This is the characteristic of God alone. Rather,

---

[84] This is the import of the following proposition (indebted to Dorner): 'God can be wholly identified with his revelation without being entirely reduced to it…[this] is the point of the doctrine of aseity', Michael Scott Horton, *Lord and Servant: A Covenant Christology*, (Westminster: John Knox Press, 2005), p. 33.

[85] *SCD*, II, p. 21.

[86] Ibid.

[87] *SCG*, I, p. 459.

[88] *SCD*, II, p. 22.

[89] Ibid. p. 47.

[90] Ibid. p. 28.

the world is to become the reflection of the divine ethical essence through a *temporal* process, which God immanently directs, in a way which is consistent with the freedom of the creaturely response to the Good. The relationship between this divine direction and human freedom is dealt with by Dorner in the sections on conservation and providence. In the section on creation, Dorner must explain how the manner of the original instantiation of the world occasions a world which will be capable of becoming the image of God. This world is there described as an 'organism',[91] and as such is constituted according to the character of its source who is the '*Organism of the Absolute Personality*'.[92] He suggests that for this to occur, the world requires diversity and unity, and in order to confirm their presence in the world Dorner says that we 'must come to a decision about the questions of the eternity of creation' and 'creation out of nothing'.[93]

a. The Eternity of Creation

The eternity of creation must not be thought to imply an endless number of 'personalities'.[94] The diversity which exists in the world is not to be thought of as *unlimited* variety. Rather, it is to be conceived as a diversity which is limited according to *its right idea*; and the key to this lies in the 'end'[95] to which the world is ordered. This *end* is the attainment to the divine image:

> The number (of spiritual personalities) is not to be considered absolutely unlimited; it is limited by the end in view. Only such spiritual personalities are created as are able by reciprocity of giving and receiving to subserve the life of love, every one having something distinct. Thus the end of God's creative love and wisdom cannot be a poor infinity of countless individuals, but only that the complement of possible individualities considered as capable of special excellence may be filled up. But while multiplicity is thus obtained in the world, i.e. a limited one, unity amid this multiplicity, despite its power of growth, is secured. As certainly as the end is a definite one, does it require a definite complement.[96]

---

[91] Ibid. p. 21.
[92] *SCD*, I, p. 412. In all of this, we see the way in which the form of his doctrine of the immanent God *informs* the structure of his account of the economic relations. The significance of the definition of God as holy Love is seen in the way that it is this paradigm which sets the agenda for all other doctrinal commitments, as we shall see in the subsequent chapters on Christology, and Atonement and Justification.
[93] *SCD*, II, p. 21.
[94] Ibid. p. 26.
[95] Ibid.
[96] Ibid.

This statement concerning the numbers who will fill heaven (the 'definite complement') indicates Dorner's view of the divine determination concerning the identity of those who will be present at the end. He, and we, will address the way in which this determination is consonant with human freedom in the final section on providence. For the moment, we wish only to note the connection between unity and variety and the discussion of the eternity of the world.

This conception of a unity amid multiplicity should not surprise us. Dorner is simply projecting on to the formation of the world the idea of infinity which he presupposed as proper to God. According to this definition, God may be said to be *infinite* but not *indefinite* (reflecting the key distinction between Infinitum and Indefinitum[97]). His infinity refers not to an *absolute* absence of limitations (which would imply an imperfection of the divine essence), but the presence of a 'moral limitation'. This is itself the very basis for His *unlimitless* as the eternally 'harmonious Life',[98] eternally self-preserving in an 'ethical self-love' which, rather than limiting God to Himself, is the very basis for His 'Self-communication and immanence in another'.[99] The world must be defined as eternal without implying an endlessness. The very diversity of the world is *preserved* because of the *limiting* which is necessary for love to find purchase in the relations between the diverse creaturely personalities.

Dorner does this by speaking of the eternity of the world in terms of two stages. The first is that which pertains to the 'form of temporal succession'.[100] The second is that which attends the attainment of perfection in the 'celestial life'[101] with the 'simultaneous presence of its elements'.[102] It is on the basis of the second of these that the world's eternal duration may be posited without presuming an endless number of personalities. Rather, the limited number of

---

[97] *SCD*, I, p. 237.

[98] Ibid. p. 270.

[99] Ibid. p. 443. This notion that there is in God not only a self-communicating element (das mittheilende), but also a self-maintaining element (das selbst-behauptunde) has been identified as corresponding to the scholastic period's distinction between *communicativum sui* (to define love) and *conservativum sui* (to define justice), George Smeaton, *The Doctrine of the Atonement* (Edinburgh: T & T Clark, 1868), p. 366.

[100] *SCD*, II, p. 32.

[101] Ibid. Dorner explicates the reasonableness of ascribing such an intended future state of being to the world in connection with the existence of the 'world of pure spirits' which are 'withdrawn in the first instance from all relation of succession, and exist in the simultaneity of all their constituent elements' (Ibid. p. 33). This is, of course, the angelic kingdom, which exists 'prior to our historical period', but is 'a lower stage of being, because the potentiality of freedom does not yet emerge independently in it' (Ibid.). Thus, while this difference between the two worlds is seismic, the principle that our world will attain a state of simultaneity is consonant with this other type of spirit world.

[102] Ibid.

personalities (derived from the first stage of the world's eternity) will exist 'perpetually'[103] in a state of 'simultaneous'[104] meeting of ends and means. On this basis will there be limitless capacity for love, and in this way the world will become the cosmical image of the divine trinity:

> The world becomes an organism of love, in which the end and its means of accomplishment are realised not in succession, but simultaneously.[105]

According to this account, the eternity of creation is a specifically end-oriented concept.

What though of time? For Dorner, following Augustine, time is that which is created *with* the world ('There is no time apart from the world'; 'Mundus non in tempore sed cum tempore factus est'.[106]), and is that *in* which ends are reached in succession (and it is precisely for this reason that Dorner rejects the view of a temporal creation[107]).

This endorsement of Augustine's attribution of the creation of time with the creation of the world leads him to make the corollary statement that 'it cannot be said that there was a time when the world was not'.[108] This means that the world is not eternal in the same way that God is eternal, since the world owes its eternity to God. Dorner insists that God was always able to create if He willed but 'He did not always will.'[109] However, while he acknowledges this feature of the divine relationship to creation, he maintains on the one hand that there is little 'religious interest' in positing a difference between the divine knowledge of the world-idea and the willing of that world-idea into existence, while on the other hand the 'interest of religion' demands the 'firm distinction of God from His creation'.[110] That is to say, what is most at stake in the discussion of the relationship between God, time and the world is not the analysis

---

[103] Ibid.

[104] Ibid.

[105] Ibid.

[106] Ibid. p. 29.

[107] 'There is no time without something contained in it. If time existed apart from the world, God must exist in time' (Ibid. p. 29). But God is 'above time in Himself' (Ibid. p. 35). Yet this non-temporality does not exclude the possibility of God's immanence in time, rather it is the very basis of His free engagement in time ('He places Himself, after the appearance of a temporal world, in a positive relation to it and time' [Ibid. p. 35]), such that His eternal freedom from space and time means that He must not have 'continually and immutably a similar relation to space and time', *SCD*, I, p. 244.

[108] Ibid. p. 30.

[109] Ibid. p. 29.

[110] Ibid. p. 34.

of how the delay in creation is concordant with the immutability of the divine essence, but rather that the fundamental distinction between God and world in all its components is asserted. This is clearly consistent with Dorner's rejection of pantheism, but it would appear threatened by his reluctance to set out in more detail how the proposition that God may be said to have not always willed the creation is consistent with the notion that His Intelligence and Will are not in disjunction. The way in which Dorner seeks to resolve this problem is by the idea that the world is that which is both 'destined to wear God's likeness'[111] but as the destined object whose actual existence hangs on God's conception of it. With this it might be said that he does offer an account of God's relation to the world and time which does not leave God uneluctably separate, though distinct, from the world, since the world is that which is in God's hands as that which He destined to create. Thus, the difference between God and world (and time) is not a contrast but a distinction which allows God to enter into a positive relation with what He has made.

Time is linear and as such is the sphere in which the perfect end of creation will be attained by the free obedience to the Good. With this we reach a key motif in Dorner's theological project. It will become especially obvious in his developmental theory of the incarnation[112] and the centrality of Christ's humanity in atonement, which we will lay out in Chapters 3 (The Doctrines of the Creature and the Unity of God and Man) and 5 (The Doctrine of Christ). The question of how the end is attained in the context of creation's eternity is spoken of both in terms of God's self-communication, and also through creaturely self-determination. We have the following statements in fairly quick succession:

> But that the world may be an ethical organism, God destines it to be an image of Himself, as well of His perfections as of His triune character, and this in such a manner that, *through His existence in it*, through His Self-communication, it may be a perfect image of Him. (my italics)[113]
>
> If at first (the world) is necessarily imperfect, in order that scope may be left for *the free-play of Self-determination*, even this is neither evil nor a contradiction, but part of the world's excellence. (my italics)[114]

---

[111] *SCD*, I, p. 34.

[112] We will attend to the connection between Creation and Christ in our next chapter on the Unity of God and Man. We will see that the End of Creation is in fact Christ: 'In Christus vollendet sich die Schöpfung', Friedrich Mildenberger, *Geschichte der deutschen evangelischen Theologie im 19. und 20. Jahrhundert* (Stuttgart: Verlag W. Kohlhammer, 1981), p. 101.

[113] *SCD*, II, p. 27.

[114] Ibid. p. 28.

The end is attained by the co-operation of the creature, in consonance with the divine projection, without detriment either to creaturely freedom or divine sovereignty.[115] The way in which Dorner works this out, as previously intimated, is given in his section on Providence. Here we wish only to make note of the fact that the eternity of creation, which is teleological in its structure, is explicated in terms of *creaturely* responsibility in attaining that end, though, not in *sustaining* that eternity. This brings us back to the key role of the divine *aseity* in maintaining the distinction between God and world, and is that upon which Dorner affirms the consistency of his account of eternal creation with traditional dogma:

> [T]he firm discrimination of God from His creation, of His eternity from theirs [is that] the latter is derived, not original.
> And this is secured by the dogmatic formula, perfectly in unison with church doctrine to the effect, that the world is that form of being which, although destined to wear God's likeness, still only comes into actual existence…through the divine conception of its non-existence, indeed, through its non-existence.[116]

This brings us to Dorner's account of the question of creation out of nothing.

b. Creation out of Nothing

The connection between the doctrine of creation out of nothing and the idea of the world as an ethical organism is not given much explanation by Dorner. However, the key to the relationship would appear to lie in the fact that an account of the world as organism will only succeed if the manner of its creation allows it to be distinguished from its creator without threatening its dependence on Him. We recall that in his account of the reason for the creation of the world, Dorner attributed decisive weight to the world-idea whose non-existence is the reason for its creation. He returns to the concept of the world-idea here, but increases its scope to include a consideration of the origin of the *matter* of the world, and in doing so differentiates the form of the world, contained in the world-idea, from the matter of the world. Since the form of the world is given in the world-idea it cannot be said to be 'nothing', yet is not yet *something* since it lacks 'not merely matter, but the realization of the form *outside* of God'.[117] The matter out of which the world is formed, however, *is* from nothing. Yet this is not nothing as potentially

---

[115] This notion of co-operation will be a crucial feature of Dorner's doctrines of Christology and salvation, as we will see in later chapters.
[116] *SCD*, II, p. 34.
[117] Ibid. p. 37.

something, but rather that which has its determination *as* nothing in the act of negation by creation: 'all that is given is Nothing, which cannot even be called a potentiality of being, inasmuch as it does not originate, but is only negatived by origination.'[118] The key here is, of course, a concern to avoid ascribing the material constitution of the world to any 'nature' in God.[119] Yet by positing this notion of creation out of nothing Dorner allows the world to be seen as actually distinct from God. However, the world, though distinct, may still be said to be dependent on God (and thus ensure the viability of His immanence in the world), not merely because its material constitution is dependent on Him, but because the form of the world is created after the image of the Image of God Himself:

> God creates the world through the Logos, and after His image, but still Logos is more correctly spoken of as the primary form *for* the future real world, not the archetypal world itself.[120]

This statement connecting the form of the world *with*, and the mediation of the creation of the world *through*, the Logos is the first time that Dorner has explicitly delineated this link in his own dogmatic reconstruction of the doctrine of creation. Yet the significance of its usage here lies not specifically in its description of what have been called the 'distinctive forms of agency in creation',[121] but principally in the grounds it supplies for ensuring that the world may be conceived in terms of a *personal* dependence on God without a confusion of either 'nature'. Indeed, even though the world-idea is that which has its provisional existence in God and is formed according to the form of the Logos, it is not the case that the form of the world is therefore a

---

[118] *SCD*, II, p. 38. As T. F. Torrance explains, 'The creation of the universe out of nothing does not mean the creation of the universe out of something that is nothing, but out of nothing at all', Thomas F. Torrance, *The Christian Doctrine of God, One Being Three Persons*, p. 207. Dorner maintains the meaning of the concept of nothing as *nihil negativum* not a *nihil ontologicum*.

[119] Dorner has previously discussed the various major proposals:
  1. The idea of the world being formed out of some 'eternal matter' (*SCD*, II, p. 35) is excluded because it is dualistic;
  2. The notion that the divine nature divides itself in order to give its form to the world is refuted because it is inconsistent with the divine immutability (which does have an ontological basis, contrary to Thomas Weinandy's reading of Dorner, Weinandy, *Does God Suffer*, p. 61);
  3. The idea that the divine nature has a 'twofold mode of existence'(*SCD*, II, p. 36), one eternal and one mutable, is rejected because it would imply a 'process of depotentiation' in the divine essence.

[120] *SCD*, II, p. 40.

[121] Colin E. Gunton, 'The End of Causality? The Reformers and their Predecessors', p. 67.

type of the divine form, but rather *merely* but *importantly* formed after the divine form. This is the weight of the circumscription of the Logos as the form *for* the world and not the *archetypal* world itself.[122]

In his account, then, of the creation out of nothing, Dorner has sought to affirm the absolute dependence of the world on God, without adding an identification of God and world. The world may be properly designated as that which has the properties conducive to its becoming a perfect ethical Organism. It is formed after the divine image (and as such has an ethical ground and telos) yet is not a mere extension of the divine essence but an Object which is dependent in such a way as not to hinder its freedom. This means that the world is posited as that which is not yet perfect at its beginning, having only the 'rudiments' of perfection. Dorner insists that such an original perfection of the world could not have been 'implanted in the world in perfectly realized unity'[123] because such a state of instant simultaneous perfection belongs only to God. Since realized perfection is attained through a process of the free obedience to the ethically necessary, which in God is eternally realized, the world must attain perfection in conditions which are suited to its status as *always-dependent* Object. For this reason the laws of temporality to which the creation is subject are best seen as the conditions in which the creaturely perfection is *attained*, at which point such temporal teleology would be supplanted by the simultaneity of non-successive succession:

> In our world teleology appears in the form of temporal succession. But this cannot be essential and necessary for the world in the abstract. On the contrary, only when perfection is arrived at does true life begin in the simultaneous presence of its elements, which, as they logically condition each other, exist perpetually in combination.[124]

God is unable, not merely unwilling, to posit an already perfect world in which there is from the start a complete unity of freedom and necessity. This would be a divine act in which the world would be merely passive and have no determinative role in its perfected constitution. The world itself must freely obey the Good and this means, for Dorner, that the notion of

---

[122] This means that the Logos is not the first and the world the second form of the divine freedom. Dorner is here simply seeking to maintain the immanent perfection of the divine essence, and reject the notion that the Logos is a potency fulfilled in creation, rather, as T. Koppehl observes, than the 'moment in the immanent trinitarian process as the object of love', T. Koppehl, *Standpunkt*, p. 172 (my translation). This means that the Logos may be said to be the archetype *for* the world, but not the archetype *of* the world.

[123] *SCD*, II, p. 27.

[124] Ibid. p. 32.

an originally perfect world is precluded, since this would exclude proper creaturely freedom (We note here that this notion of original imperfection destined towards perfection following a temporally bound process of free obedience to God is exactly the structure which obtains in Dorner's doctrine of Christology, which we will come to in Chapter 5.[125]). Thus, at the end of his treatment of the doctrine of creation, Dorner has posited a world which is wholly dependent for its existence on God and yet is constituted in order to attain perfection through a process of ethically free obedience. However, he insists that a sharp division must be made between the doctrine of creation and that of conservation, to which we turn now.

III. The Doctrine of Conservation and Concursus

The world's existence comes about apart from the co-operation of finite causality. It is otherwise with conservation. If we take away the activity of creature from the idea of conservation, it can no longer be distinguished from creation.[126]

This is a key move for Dorner and establishes the ground on which he seeks to explicate the meaning of creaturely freedom, and its relationship to the divine intentions for the world. The way in which he configures this relationship is of profound significance for the way in which he will go on to lay out the structure of the incarnation. For now we note only the place which he gives to creaturely activity in the maintenance of the world. Without this 'only a *creatio continua* is left'.[127] This dogmatic separation is intended not to

[125] Koppehl correctly observes that the key is that for God there is no lapse between thought and deed, as there is for man. It is for this reason that the incarnation occurs gradually, since the human Jesus must respond ethically in the manner befitting His creatureliness, Koppehl, *Standpunkt*, p. 177. We will set out the details of this Christological model in a subsequent chapter, but it is worth noting here that for Dorner the original imperfection of creation is not evil, rather it is a necessary presupposition of its attainment of perfection. The same can be said of Dorner's view of the gradual development of the incarnation.

[126] *SCD*, II, p. 44.

[127] Ibid. Dorner's distinguishing of *creatio ex nihilo* and *creatio continua* is one which seeks to foreground the difference between God and world. This is a feature which appears lacking in one contemporary proposal for abandoning the distinction between *creatio ex nihilo* and *continua*. Alan Torrance, in a discussion of J. Moltmann, (Alan Torrance, 'Creatio ex Nihilo and the Spatio-Temporal Dimensions, with special reference to Jürgen Moltmann and D. C. Williams', in *The Doctrine of Creation*, ed. C. E. Gunton [Edinburgh: T & T Clark, 1997]) suggests that such a distinction is based upon a false view of God's relation to time, such that it should not be thought in terms of an absolute, linear, temporal process which leads on to the divine order, but rather as that which is part of an interconnected matrix created from nothing. We would

diminish the extent to which the creation remains existent only on the basis of divine sustenance (and as such is not a deistic conception[128]): 'No doubt the energy in the act of self-conservation is every moment to be referred to the divine causality, which is conservative not merely creative.'[129]

However, Dorner's main concern is to delineate an account of conservation and concursus in which the divine and creaturely freedoms are not seen as competitive but conducive to the attainment of the end of creation in which the destiny of the world is the result of divine-creature co-operation. What distinguishes the act of creation from that of conservation is not that the latter is any less a divine act, but rather that the conditions posited by the first act bring the possibility of creaturely co-operation in the divine purposes:

> Conservation is the continuance of the divine creative will, but in such a way as to embrace what is instituted in its vitality, to employ its secondary causality as the means of its reproduction, by which of course it becomes a creaturely image of the divine self-origination (self-existence), only on the basis of God's ever-present, sustaining omnipotence.[130]

For Dorner, conservation is for God the maintenance of the conditions of worldliness in which the world co-operates in its conservation. This co-operation will express itself in ways which reflect the divine image (as in the process of reproduction which mimics the divine self-origination). The act of creation is that which, while an act of God's alone, posits a world which is intended to participate in the attainment of its perfection:

> The efficiency of secondary causes is already involved in the idea of creation, which is only completed in the institution of such causes.[131]

suggest that while this model does offer a way of ensuring that God's singular creative relationship to the world is not seen to stop with the beginning, it does not offer much explanation of the way in which creaturely freedom is maintained or expressed.

[128] Thus, while they appear as distinct sections, the divine role in creating and maintaining creation is the key link and, indeed, the very basis for the integrity of creaturely freedom. For this reason, we would suggest that Dorner's notion of conservation would acknowledge the sense in which it has been recommended to remain connected e.g. 'Schöpfung und Erhaltung sind nicht von einander zu trennen, sondern ein zusammenhängender Vorgang', 'Gewissheit durch Differenz und Konkretion: Zum Verhältnis von Schöpfung und Erlösung bei Oswald Bayer', Christian Herrmann, in *Theologische Zeitschrift*, 58 (2002), p. 115.

[129] SCD, II, p. 45.
[130] Ibid. p. 45.
[131] Ibid. p. 46.

In all of this is a concern to account for the world as the scene of crea-turely freedom in the process of attaining perfection. Commensurate with this intention is Dorner's account of the way in which the two aspects of the world – nature and spirit – may be said to relate in this process. On this point, Dorner insists that creation must be differentiated from conservation not merely in order to allow for the relative independence of the world in its progress, but also to preserve the uniquely creative act by which the origin of man is explained (and on this point an obvious connection is made with the possibility of new creative acts in the world without disruption to the conservation of the world).

The world is capable of receiving new elements of divine creativity (i.e. miracles) without threatening the integrity of the conserving element built into the world's constitution. Dorner explains that this is possible for two reasons: (1) the already existent has a receptiveness for the new; (2) the new element 'can only enter into the world for the purpose of becoming the object of conservation'.[132]Thus, Dorner predicates the possibility of new creative acts on their consistency with the original constitution and teleol-ogy of the creation. That is to say, the receptivity is that which pertains to the createdness of the world and its need for continued support for its exist-ence and the integrity of its causality; and the connection between the new and the principle of conservation indicates that the miraculous is that which conforms to the relative independence of the world and does not mean the suspension of that relative independence of the world, but is that which pertains to the ongoing dependence on the God who has instituted a world which is free in its dependence on Him.

Dorner insists that while the world as Nature pre-exists the origin of man, it is not given to Nature to be the sufficient cause of *Spirit*, which is that divinely posited aspect of man by which he is 'distinct from Nature' (by the possession of 'knowledge, will and feeling'[133]). These attributes pertain to man's unique capacity to receive and respond in freedom to God.[134] While the non-human natural world 'resembles' God, it is not capable of replying to 'the Word, through which it arose'.[135] This distinction between creation and conservation is that which leads Dorner to absorb the evolutionary model of human origins without detriment either to the freedom of God (to be the 'creative power'[136] behind the creation of the first man) or the freedom of man (to be an organism who is not determined by its natural

---

[132] *SCD*, II, p. 50.

[133] Ibid. p. 72.

[134] In an otherwise flawed definition of Dorner's doctrine of *imago dei*, J. Bobertag cor-rectly recognizes 'receptivity…for God' as an integral part, J. Bobertag, *Isaak August Dorner: Sein Leben und seine Lehre* (Gütersloh: Gütersloh, 1906), p. 105.

[135] *SCD*, II, p. 65.

[136] Ibid. p. 41.

constitution but is an ethical being whose destiny is to live in free obedience with God).

However, while this distinction pertains to the *origin* of the spiritual con-stitution of humanity, as we have already noted, Dorner's conception of the creation is as that which progresses towards perfection and is not originally perfect. That is to say, the creature is posited and conserved as that which is 'able to determine the character of his existence i.e. to determine whether he will be a good or evil causal power'.[137] The question of how this creaturely freedom remains free in the fulfilment of the divine intentions for the world is addressed in the final section on divine providence, to which we now turn.

IV. Divine Providence

As Dorner has repeatedly affirmed, the world is *destined* to be 'an image of the triune God'.[138] However, this teleological conception of creation and conservation is one which is brought to fulfilment by God with the free co-operation of the creature, and thus he must delineate an account of prov-idence which holds together as compatible and non-competitive divine con-trol of the world and creaturely freedom. It is an account which must not only demonstrate the congruity of divine providence and human freedom in the abstract. It must also provide the resources and background for Dorner's later explication of the incarnation. There he will seek to establish that the union of divine and human natures was perfected by a process of Jesus' free creaturely response to His divine identity, without implying that the perfec-tion of this process was at any stage uncertain. We will see in Chapter 5 on the doctrine of Jesus Christ how this is worked out. For now, we will lay out the details of his understanding of the scope and nature of providence itself, and how the key to his approach lies in an essentially molinist view of divine foreknowledge and divine-creaturely co-operation.

a. The Nature and Scope of Providence

For Dorner, providence is the means of describing the teleological con-tent of God's creative and conserving faculties. As such it pertains to the maintenance of God's intentions for individual creatures to be part of the Kingdom of Love towards which the world is destined. Providence is that which maintains the conjunction between the divine purpose and the free activities of the creatures; as such it is *preservative*: God 'permits nothing to take place that would interfere with His world-plan'.[139] Yet it is also

---

[137] Ibid. p. 51.
[138] Ibid. p. 54.
[139] Ibid. p. 55.

reactive, by co-ordinating the free activities of the world in such a way that they correspond to the divinely determined destination: 'Providence, in its governing capacity is that divine activity which keeps both the spontaneous activity of the established system, and the new combinations entering into it, in harmony with the aim of the divine world-idea.'[140] It is an account of providence which on the one hand is profoundly delimiting and on the other hand responsive. In the conjunction of divine vigour and reflexivity we see the trace of Dorner's doctrine of divine immutability, in which God remains consistent – immutable – even in the very moment of being affected by the world. It is *in* the state of responsiveness that He reveals His ethical constancy. This description of providence, as the conjunction of divine preservation and reaction, results from this decisive aspect of his doctrine of God. It ought not surprise us that Dorner should have what appears to be both a very strong view of divine providence as well as a strong view of the capacity of creatures to affect God. Yet we need to set out in more detail the way in which he feels able to have both a risk-free view of providence and an expansive view of creaturely freedom. We suggest that there are in fact two aspects to his account. The first amounts to a kind of divine fore-*planning*, in which there is a limiting of creaturely possibilities. The second pertains to the divine fore-*knowledge*, and gives an explanation of the way in which the remaining creaturely freedom (which is of a substantial nature) does not present an obstacle to the divine certainty concerning the attainment of the world's end (without obfuscating the distinction between divine and creaturely causality or advocating a predestinarian account of the world). To that end, we will look in turn at each of these aspects of his account, before bringing this present chapter to a close.

b. Human Freedom and Divine Fore-planning

In his account of the constitution of the world, Dorner sets clear boundaries to the realm of what is possible in and for the world. The world is posited in such a way that already it is limited by the divine determination as that which is 'destined to be an image of the triune God'. As such the world is ordered as that which from its beginning bears the imprint of its triune creator: 'accordingly, the triune form of life is *already incorporated therein*' (my italics).[141] Since it bears this impression, indeed, lives in the form of its creator,[142] there are limits set to its possibilities. The world does not possess what might be called *absolute* freedom. Rather, it is a freedom which

---

[140] *SCD*, II, p. 53.

[141] Ibid. p. 54.

[142] The original German is 'Daher ist [the world] die trinitarische Lebensform *einverleibt schon*' (my italics), *SCG*, I, p. 492. 'Einverleiben' carries also the sense of annexation. It does not merely bear the form but is in the *possession* of its former. Dorner later

is limited by its circumstances. Dorner speaks of providence in terms of God's *permissive will*: 'He permits nothing to take place that would interfere with His world plan.'[143] This means that the possibility of evil, which is maintained by God Himself and is not outside of His providence, is that which is permitted only insofar as it serves the divinely appointed ends: 'Arbitrariness is only permitted a place in the world of the instrumental means by which the absolute final aim is accomplished.'[144] It is not merely that God foreknows what will happen in His creation (which He certainly does) but that *the manner of His knowing is consistent with His determination of the world's end.*

This, then, is the first key move which Dorner makes in his account. The second, related to the first, concerns the freedom which is afforded to the creature. The crucial step that Dorner takes is to suggest that this freedom is 'conditioned by God'.[145] That is to say, the freedom in the possession of the creature is that which is sustained by God alone. This freedom is the 'possibility of arbitrariness'[146] (by which he means the possibility for which there is no reason and as such is a *chance* occurrence). Yet such enacting of arbitrariness is not a threat to the divine purposes precisely *because* this very possibility is itself *included* in the world-idea. It does not fall outside the purview of the divine intentions. On this basis, then, arbitrariness may not be said to possess a quality of absoluteness. As Dorner himself puts it, with freedom comes the possibility of arbitrariness, and with it 'the principle of chance'.[147] This is not, however, *absolute* chance since God's vision of the world includes all possible configurations of its creaturely actors. It has the character of 'comparative chance',[148] according to which the free agent acts in an arbitrary way, but this is not absolutely arbitrary because the freedom of the agent is itself maintained by God, and as such is not 'accidental'.[149] The arbitrary act by the free agent is not absolutely arbitrary because the agent is himself not absolutely arbitrary.

Dorner navigates his way through this issue with a carefully defined account of the nature and scope of creaturely freedom, in which it is said to be delimited both by the form of the world and the fact of the creaturely dependence on God (without involving a confusion of causalities).

speaks of the incorporation of individuals into the attainment of the divine world-plan, *SCD*, II, p. 61.

[143] *SCD*, II, p. 55.
[144] Ibid. p. 57.
[145] Ibid. p. 55.
[146] Ibid.
[147] Ibid.
[148] Ibid.
[149] Ibid. p. 56.

The overall picture given by Dorner is of a God who has configured the world in such a way as to preclude the possibility of the world attaining an absolute and uncontrollable status. Yet even though an absolute freedom is excluded, this does not mean that there is absolutely *no* freedom. On the contrary, while there is a *delimiting* of creaturely possibilities and freedom, this is coterminus with the affirmation of creaturely freedom as that which, while dependent *on*, remains in perpetuity independent *from* the divine causality. The final grounds for Dorner's no-risk understanding of providence does not reside merely in the divine conditioning of the world (since this would of course not properly account for his insistence on the role of creaturely co-operation). Rather it is the first part of an account in which he suggests that God may be confident of the world's end because He is continually governing the world's contents without causing (apart from indirectly) the creaturely co-operation of the attainment of the world's ends. The final piece of Dorner's account of providence resides in his account of divine foreknowledge to which we now turn.

c. Divine Foreknowledge, Human Freedom and the Attainment of the End

Thus far in our presentation of Dorner's account of providence, we have focused on the way in which he has sought to lay out the divine control of the world's elements. Yet it is inaccurate to conclude that Dorner's is a deterministic account. Rather, it is an account which sees freedom operating within ordered spheres. It is within the divinely ordered sphere of the world that creatures may be said to be free and even to be arbitrary, while not being free to be absolutely arbitrary in the sense of having the capacity to devastate the divine intentions for the world. Yet, within this tightly defined account of the divine constitution of the world remains the notion that the creature is free to decide or act without the direct causality of God. This means of course that while there are limits to absolute creaturely freedom, creaturely freedom is not absolutely limited. For Dorner there remains a question, therefore, of how God may be certain that these free creatures will freely *co-operate* in the attainment of the world's end, since the delimiting of freedom does not mean the eradication of freedom, and it therefore remains possible to envisage a world in which *only* arbitrary choices are made.

At this stage of Dorner's dogmatics, he is setting out merely the *basis* of the divine relationship to the world and its end, and is not yet speaking of the way in which creaturely freedom will be manifest in the redemptive scheme (i.e. in terms of those who are saved and not saved by God). He will come to this later on in his discussion of the doctrine of salvation. However, it is worth noting that Dorner insists at this stage that God's providential relation to the world extends not only to a general object, of race or nations, but is related to the care[150] of individuals. On this point Dorner differs from his contemporaries, Martensen[151] and Rothe[152] who maintain that God's providence extends only to the general world aim and does not – cannot – extend to individuals who will be a part of that future world. God's providential relationship to the world, then, includes a certainty about *who* will make up the future Kingdom of Love. As such His is an expansive and detailed confidence in the future, and one which is not itself limited by the freedom of His creatures to be arbitrary, being able to know their future free actions without negating creaturely freedom.

We suggest that the key lies in Dorner's reference to what he calls God's 'intuitive knowledge',[153] by which He knows which definite individuals are incorporated into the destiny of the world. As such He is confident that their free co-operation with the divine intentions the world's fulfilment will be brought about (presumably together with the existence of some who have remained uncooperative). While God foreknows He has not predestined (apart from having been responsible for the conditions in which free creatures respond in freedom). As already intimated, Dorner rejects those predestinarian accounts of divine providence which place, finally, the

---

[150] *SCD*, II, p. 61. The English translation on this point speaks of an inclusion in this 'highest grace' – which would be the first time that Dorner has spoken of providence in terms of grace – yet the original German is of an inclusion in the 'höchsten *Gute*' (my italics), which is probably more accurately translated 'highest good', *SCG*, I, p. 499.

[151] On this point, in fact, Martensen seeks to differentiate the way in which the individual is the 'proper subject of divine providence', but only insofar as he is a member of the 'Kingdom of God'. Thus, the individual is the object of providential care via the community, Hans Martensen, *Christian Dogmatics*, (Edinburgh: T & T Clark, 1886), p. 215. Martensen argues that God's foreknowledge is conditional on the actual choices of free creatures and while God may have a fixed view of the 'final goal of the world's development' (Ibid. p. 219) He does not foreknow the details of how this end will be attained. This would be to impugn creaturely freedom and the divine relation to the world, since He would be merely a 'spectator of events decided and predestined from eternity' (Ibid. p. 218).

[152] *SCD*, II, p. 60. Rothe contends that while the goal of the world is held firm in God's grasp, He is limited in His foreknowledge of who, among the individual members of the world, will be participators of this future Kingdom. Creaturely freedom is unpredictable, even for God: 'Das Ziel also der Entwicklung der Welt steht in Gottes Rathschluß fest und die organische Reihe der an sich notwendigen Stufen und Knoten der Entwicklung, über welche hinweg sie zu diesem Ziele hingeführt werden soll, weil mit innerer Nothwendigkeit muß. Mehr ist aber auch nicht vorherbestimmt; der Weltplan befaßt nur die abstracte Formel (in unbenannten Grösen) für den Verlauf der Weltentwicklung. Ihre Realisierung in dem Stoff der concreten Wirklichkeit ist ja von Gott selbst ausdrücklich als durch die eigene freie Wirksamkeit der persönlichen Kreatur vermittelt gedacht und geordnet, und folglich ist sie dem freien Spiel des Handelns der persönlichen Weltwesen anheim gegeben', Richard Rothe, *Dogmatik*, Bd. I (Heidelberg: J. C. B. Mohr, 1870), pp. 198–199.

[153] *SCD*, II, p. 61.

responsibility for the attainment of the world's ends only on the divine side. Whether or not this is a fair evaluation of such theologies (he does not spend any time in detailed analysis of such approaches), he maintains that this model fatally undermines the real freedom of individuals to respond to God's 'revelation of love':

> [T]o wish to exclude human freedom in the interests of God's all-comprehending Providence would mean that God was able to effect His purposes only by means of unfree, impersonal forces.[154]

This reluctance to reduce the place of creaturely freedom in the attaining of the divine end is consonant with his concern, which will later be explored in the doctrine of atonement, to ensure that the salvation of the world is rooted firmly in the historical, creaturely sphere and is not merely an exchange which takes place within the Godhead. Here, however, his concern is to display the way in which there is no risk involved in God's positing human creatures who are really free to choose the Good or not. He does this, as we have already noted, with an appeal to what he calls God's *intuitive knowledge*; and since he specifically distinguishes his way of conceiving how God may be confident of the presence of individuals in His world-plan from that of divine predestination, we must deduce that the way in which he resolves the question of how God is provident and man is free, is by an appeal to something which looks very similar[155] to the concept of middle-knowledge formulated by Luís de Molina.[156] According to this view, creaturely freedom and divine confidence in the future are maintained by positing the notion

---

[154] *SCD*, II, p. 55.

[155] Dorner refers much later to the *Scientia Dei media*, and rejects it because he suggests it is merely another form of determinism. However, this reference comes in a discussion of the generic nature of sin, and not the attainment of the end to which God purposes the world, and as such Dorner rejects it because he suggests it implies God treating humanity 'according to what they have not done' (since it argues that God knows that all humanity would have fallen if put in the same position as Adam), *SCD*, III, p. 53. We propose that middle-knowledge has a place in reference to the ends, because it pertains to the divine recognition of actual human action. Stanley Russell describes Dorner's account as an 'attenuated Molinism', 'I. A. Dorner: A Centenary Appreciation', in *The Expository Times*, Vol. 96, No. 3 (December 1984), p. 79.

[156] This is of course a model with a chequered history. He makes no reference to Molina or any other historical advocates of the view he espouses. William Lane Craig has suggested that the debate between Thomists and Molinists following the decisive papal endorsement of the latter's consistency with Catholic doctrine in 1607, took place 'pretty much in a corner', William Lane Craig, *The Problems of Divine Foreknowledge and Future Contingents from Aristotle to Suarez* (Leiden: E. J. Brill, 1988), p. 170. In more recent times it has enjoyed a renaissance among philosophers of religion following its use by Alvin Plantinga in *The Nature of Necessity* (Oxford: Clarendon Press, 1974), ch. 9.

that God's omniscience allows Him to know how even free creatures will behave in any given situation, and on this basis creates a world in which He may ordain its ends without detriment to the creaturely freedom.

Conclusion

We have sought to demonstrate the way in which Dorner's doctrine of God provides the platform for an account of the divine economic activity in which the distinctiveness of God and world is maintained without detriment either to the divine immanence or worldly dependence on God. What is of most significance is the way in which he uses the doctrine of God's aseity to maintain both the distinction and relation between God and world, and this is a theme which will emerge as integral to his account of the doctrine of the incarnation. Furthermore, the way in which he seeks to distinguish between divine and creaturely activity without disrupting the latter's continual dependence on God is a theme which will be operative throughout the account. It is the resources which he has collected from his account of God's self-sufficiency – trinitarianly configured – which provide the grounds for this distinction to be maintained. The details of his account of God's triunity prove decisive, and as we turn now to an analysis of his doctrines of the Creature and the Unity of the God-man, we will argue that he avoids the criticism levelled at him of proposing a theological vision which divinizes humanity because of the keenness of his interest in the unique singularity of God's being and the corresponding distinctiveness of the creation.

3

THE DOCTRINES OF THE CREATURE AND THE UNITY[1] OF GOD AND HUMANITY

Introduction

In our discussion of Dorner's account of the relation between God and world in the previous chapter, we saw how he understands the Creator–created *distinction*. Pointing to the doctrines of conservation and concursus he argues it is consonant with the divine intention for the world to become 'an image of Himself'.[2] This brings into focus the role that divinely maintained[3] *creaturely* co-operation has in the attainment of the divine intentions for the world's perfection. This arrangement completes his doctrine of the economic Trinity (and the First Main Division of Fundamental Christian Doctrine), and anticipates the Second and Third Main Divisions. It clears a space for human activity which is not in competition with the divine intentions for

---

[1] The German is 'Einheit', and Dorner's translator gives the English word 'Unity' rather than 'oneness' which he 'shrinks from using in this connection', *SCD*, II, p. 105. The problem of rendering this German term into English is not, of course, unique to Dorner's text. The translators of F. C. Baur's use of the same term contend that it is intended to suggest neither a 'sheer identity on the one hand' nor 'an outward combination of factors on the other', but rather a unity in which the distinctive factors are preserved. We do not wish to suggest Baur's and Dorner's use of the terms are identical, but suggest that this translator's note is a helpful gloss on the use of a term which might even allow us to use 'oneness' if these considerations are observed, *Ferdinand Christian Baur on the Writing of Church History*, ed. and trans. Peter C. Hodgson (New York: Oxford University Press, 1968), p. 244.

[2] *SCD*, II, p. 27.

[3] God 'wills the divine concursus, consisting in this, that every moment God wills the world to be self-reproductive, and confers upon its several structures a power of self-conservation', Ibid. p. 49.

the world since it is *God Himself* who continuously confers on humanity the capacity to be the 'cause of his own causal action, i.e. as a good or evil causal power'.[4] This configuration of concursus is Dorner's attempt to circumvent the extremes of accounts which posit *either* God *or* humanity as the singular determinants of the world's end; and reflects his concern to avoid what he sees as the two major enemies of orthodoxy: pantheism and deism.[5]

It is an arrangement, however, which would still be expected to invest in the doctrine of humanity[6] a high level of significance (perhaps reflecting what has been described as the 'anthropocentrism' of 19th c. theology[7]). It would need to be an account which displayed the capacity of humanity to conform freely to the divine purposes for the world while not denuding the

---

[4] *SCD*, II, p. 51.

[5] Ibid. p. 22. Thomas Koppehl correctly observes that these are the only types of heresy identified by Dorner in his historical survey of church doctrine, in contrast to Schleiermacher (*The Christian Faith*, p. 97 ff.) who identified four (docetism, nazorism, manichean and pelagianism), Koppehl, *Standpunkt*, p. 74. Dorner argues that it was the doctrine of a Trinity of the divine essence which prevented the early Church from assimilating the 'pantheistic or heathenish' and 'deistic' idea of God, *History of Development*, Div. I, Vol. II, p. 291 ff., a point which he rejoins in his considerable critique of Hegel and his notion that God comes to self-realization in the world: 'the immanent Trinity' alone 'now as formerly, will be in a position to secure the living, personal, ethical conception of God against Pantheism and Deism', *History of Development*, Div. II, Vol. III, p. 150.

[6] We shall use 'humanity' except when Dorner is himself quoted. The term God-man will, however, be preserved.

[7] This is how Pannenberg, commenting on Barth's analysis of nineteenth-century theology in *Protestant Theology in the Nineteenth Century*, New Edition (London: SCM, 2001), describes Barth's critique of that era, Wolfhart Pannenberg, *Anthropology in Theological Perspective* (Edinburgh: T & T Clark, 1985), p. 18. Barth partially excuses Dorner from the charge of excessive anthropomorphism, since he sees his project as that which seeks to affirm faith *and* revelation without 'allowing now the one and now the other to issue in a human possibility' (p. 563). However, he considers that this commendable principle is obscured by what he calls Dorner's pursuit of a '*speculation* about God' which arranges Christian doctrine according to human philosophical principles (as we have seen Axt-Piscalar argue), and may be said finally to be an anthropocentric project. However, as Barth himself acknowledges, Dorner's firm commitment to the *priority* of the objective above the subjective. ('faith can never...dispense [with] objectivity', *Protestant Theology*, p. 569), distinguishes him considerably from the contemporary theological trends. What may certainly be said of Dorner is that *his repeated concern* is to provide a theological account which seeks to avoid the kind of turn to human subjectivity which obviates the need for a privileged objective foundation. Yet, as we shall see in our evaluation of his doctrines of humanity and God-man (and particularly in the manner with which he treats the doctrine of Atonement), his approach is one which threatens to break out into an account of the Christian Gospel which elevates the capacity of humanity to achieve its perfecting end rather than the triumph of God in salvation. We will address this question in Chapter 6.

divine capacity to achieve the world's perfection mediately. Of considerable significance here is the fact that the culmination of the Second and Third Main Divisions lies *not* in the doctrine of humanity (which occupies a brief section[8]), but instead in the doctrine of the God-man. It is the demonstration of the necessity of the Incarnation for the world's perfection rather than the doctrine of the creature, which represents the dénouement of Fundamental Doctrine.

Dorner's dogmatic arrangement of these points differs considerably from those of his contemporaries, not least in the careful way in which he organizes the doctrines of Humanity and God-man so as to present the latter as the proper conclusion of the theological enquiry which began with the doctrine of the immanent and economic Trinity. That is to say, Dorner's theological commitment to what is, as we shall see, basically a supralapsarian position is not merely the choice of one from among the different options available from the history of doctrine (e.g. supralapsarianism, infralapsarianism or sublapsarianism), but rather is the considered result of first principles and *carefully interweaved into the dogmatic structure*. This point may be best observed in a comparison of Dorner's dogmatic arrangement with that of his close associate Hans Martensen who also commends the supralapsarian approach to the incarnation: 'If the divine Logos did not Himself become man, the Ideal of humanity would not be realized.'[9] Martensen includes this comment within a general discussion of the doctrine of *imago dei*, but it does not *inform* the dogmatic structure of his system and so, unlike Dorner's, remains *structurally* peripheral to the theological project (which is ordered according to what Karl Nitzsch describes as the 'Trichotomy' of Father, Son and Spirit.[10] Dorner, arguably, demonstrates a greater capacity to order his doctrinal treatment according to its dogmatic principles.

Concluding with the doctrine of the God-man accords with Dorner's earlier announcement that the primary aim of the first section of his project is the 'demonstration of the necessity of Jesus'.[11] The arguments in this first section are marshalled to display the *fittedness* of the actual Jesus of Nazareth with the *idea* of the God-man[12] which he will now develop on the basis of his doctrine of God *in* and *ad* extra. His concern is to display

[8] The relative brevity of this section is correctly observed by Hans Walter Frei, *I. A. Dorners Christologie und Trinitätslehre* (Leipzig: Sturm & Koppe, 1930), p. 61.

[9] Hans Martensen, *Christian Dogmatics*, p. 147.

[10] Karl Immanuel Nitzsch *System of Christian Doctrine*, trans. Robert Montgomery (Edinburgh: T & T Clark, 1849), p. 126).

[11] *SCD*, I, p. 177.

[12] A point on which Emanuel Hirsch, rather cynically we suggest, says Dorner offers Jesus as the fulfilment of the classical, German ideal of humanity, the 'allseitigen goethischen Menschlichkeit', *Geschichte der neuern evangelischen Theologie*, Bd. 5 (Gütersloh: Bertelsman, 1951), p. 384.

indubitably that the incarnation has occurred in Jesus not merely by appealing to its *occurrence* but by grounding it in the *idea* of God – immanent and economic – which he has set out in the first part of the System ('To the explanation of the appearance of Christ, there belongs...a very definite idea of God'[13]). For Dorner, there is a demonstrable progression from the doctrine of God contained in the First Main Division, whose 'result' was to 'show that God's will is to communicate Himself',[14] to the exhibition of the divine incarnation as the 'ethically necessary'[15] consummation of the divine purpose of perfect self-communication. This move signals Dorner's concern to demonstrate the certainty of the divine economic operation by displaying its conformity with the immanent divine essence. While it is an account which seeks to provide verification for the object of faith, and as such has an epistemological import, it also points towards the ultimate end of that faith in its identification of the idea of the God-man as that whose actualization will represent the centrepoint of the divine purposes for creation. It means that there is a clear distinction between the representation of the God-man as the fulfilment of the world-idea, and his representation as the saviour of the world (which will be treated only in the second part of the System). Dorner's Christology may best be described as *bifurcated*.[16] This has led Karl Barth to complain that this means the divine purpose is focused on the 'ideal man and the process of his spiritualization or deification', rather than the 'divine work of reconciliation'.[17]

This evaluation, in our estimation, is only partially correct. Dorner's approach does mean that the divine focus is not primarily salvific,[18] since the particular way in which the Incarnation takes place is not, by itself,

---

[13] *SCD*, I, p. 51. This concern to seek a connection between the Ideal and the Real is a key feature of Dorner's and the wider mediating school of theology. Ragnar Holte, during his exposition of C. Ullmann, identifies as the foundational principle of the 'vermittlungstheologischen Programmes: Der Zusammenhang zwischen dem Idealen und Realen', *Die Vermittlungstheologie: Ihre theologischen Grundbegriffe kritisch untersucht* (Upsalla: Almquist & Wiksells, 1965), p. 96.

[14] *SCD*, II, p. 106.

[15] Ibid. p. 206.

[16] Michael Hüttenhoff has correctly identified this distinction as the consequence of Dorner's concern to discern 'scientific verification of Christianity' according to 'epistemologischen Gesichtspunkten', Hüttenhoff, *Erkenntnistheorie*, p. 61.

[17] Karl Barth, *Church Dogmatics, Vol. III, The Doctrine of Creation, Part I* (Edinburgh: T & T Clark, 1958), p. 47.

[18] Gunther Wenz draws attention to the suggestion that Dorner's influence on the young Martin Kähler concerning the idea of the incarnation as a growing personal union with God gave way to an interest in soteriology alone, Gunther Wenz, *Geschichte der Versöhnungslehre in der evangelischen Theologie der Neuzeit*, Band II (München, Kaiser Verlag, 1986), p. 134. For Dorner, such an opposition between Person and Work is inappropriate because it endangers the necessity of the God-man by hanging his appearance on the contingent occurrence of sin.

the fundamental basis for its occurrence.[19] In this we perceive problems which impact the capacity of Dorner's account to delineate the full weight of sin and salvation. Yet Barth overstates the case when he suggests that this is displaced by a focus on *deification*. We suggest that while Dorner's account leans towards this tendency, a final analysis offers *communion* between God and humanity as the more appropriate description of Dorner's understanding of the realization in history of the idea of the God-man. Central to this defence lie the resources of his doctrine of God which preserve distinction while proposing union or communion. We shall see also that the details of his account of God's triunity provide the basis for his exposition of how humanity attains perfection as living, ethical being in relation to God.

To this end we will consider Dorner's treatment of the major sites in the Second and Third Main Divisions of Fundamental doctrine which work towards a demonstration of the necessity of incarnation and prepare for the exhibition of Jesus as the realized God-man.

I. The Doctrine of the Creature

The Second Main Division of Fundamental theology is divided into two parts. The first part treats the doctrine of the world as nature; the second treats the doctrine of humanity. The length of Dorner's treatment of these *loci* is considerably shorter than the subsequent section. Yet while the comparative brevity reflects the importance Dorner attaches to a fuller account of the idea of Incarnation as the primary focus of concern, he furnishes his concise account with features which:

i. Express continuity with the theological model which he has thus far constructed;
ii. Lead into the doctrine of the God-man;
iii. Anticipate the structure of his accounts of the Person and Work of Christ, and the status of the Christian believer which he will develop in the Second Part of the System (most notably in his use of the concept of ethical development).

We will excavate the last of these connections in Chapters 5 and 6. For now, we will seek to lay out the first two elements by exploring the major features

---

[19] Central to this arrangement is, of course, Dorner's concern not to admit the necessity of the God-man as *Erlöser*, because he holds that this would mean presupposing the necessity of sin, which he rejects as inconsistent with the ideas of God and world. Hüttenhoff has correctly observed this point, Hüttenhoff, *Erkenntnistheorie*, p. 61. Furthermore, J. Bobertag insists there should be no surprise about this feature in Dorner's project, J. Bobertag, *Isaak August Dorner*, pp. 108–109.

of Dorner's treatment, before proceeding to an investigation of the Third Main Division and the doctrine of the God-man.

a. The World as Nature

The first section sees Dorner attend to the status and function of the natural world, and its relation to God and humanity. He sees the created order as *distinct* from, yet *dependent* on God, and as such it is maintained in a state of *relative* independence.[20] He employs this principle by speaking of the natural world having in it a 'pulse of life'.[21] The natural world itself is the *relative* origin of life ('Kraftcentren oder Lebensherde'[22]) and sustainer of its being; a capacity which does not come at the expense of divine involvement in the ongoing sustenance or direction of the world, but rather is established *by* this original and continual interest. It is only in these terms that Dorner contends it possible to posit the natural world as the sphere which 'bears [God's] seal, even the life that is in it already reflecting the triune life-law'.[23] Only as it is capable of *establishing* and *producing* can the *established* and *produced* natural world resemble God.[24] This is the triune life law to which he refers: a created analogy of the uncreated divine relations which he laid out in the First Main Division in terms of Absolute Personality. As he does this, Dorner lays out how it is not the world *tout simple*, but *humanity* which is destined to bear the divine image in its fullness. He thus sets out the relation of nature to humanity; and part of this includes a descriptive shift he makes from speaking of the 'world's' destiny as *divine image* bearer[25] in the First Main Division to the narrower definition of the *natural* world bearing a *resemblance* to God, anticipating the representation of humanity as the proper owner of this title. Central to this is humanity's capacity, unique

---

[20] This notion of a relative independence stands as an important revision of the idea of creation existing in a state of absolute dependence, which C. Gunton has noted of Schleiermacher's treatment, Colin Gunton, *The Triune Creator* (Edinburgh: Edinburgh University Press, 1998), p. 156. Cf. Schleiermacher, *The Christian Faith*, p. 143 ff.

[21] *SCD*, II, p. 65.

[22] *SCG*, I, p. 502.

[23] *SCD*, II, p. 65.

[24] 'It has not in it merely the essence of the established, commanded; but whatever proceeds from God's creating mouth must carry in itself establishing, productive force.' Ibid.

[25] Ibid. pp. 9, 15, 27, 47. That Dorner does use this term to describe the world is not insignificant, and displays a concern to depict the organic relationship between the various strata of the created order. He does this in such a way as to avoid the pantheistic tendencies which such descriptions might lean towards. We suggest that in this, Dorner provides an account which filled a gap noted by the natural theologian Otto Zöckler for a theological account which describes the creation as the divine image, Otto Zöckler, *Theologia naturalis. Erster Band: Die Prolegomena und die specielle Theologie enthaltend* (Frankfurt: Herder & Zimmer, 1860), pp. 170–171.

in the natural world to *respond* to the world's creator:

> Nature makes no reply to the Word, through which it arose. It is not
> dead, but speechless and blind. Only in man does awakened nature
> open its eyes to recognise its Maker, to reply to His voice.[26]

Dorner had earlier framed this unique capacity in terms of humanity's
power of 'reciprocal love',[27] which itself was indicative of his likeness to
God. However, before he goes on to delineate the full extent of this likeness,
he first seeks to lay out the ways in which nature prepares for and itself is
affected by the realization of the *imago dei* in humanity. While the natural
world is incapable of responding to its creator, it retains an interest in the
consequences of humanity's relation to God. It is an interest which Dorner
conceives as teleological in nature ('Nature is good by reason of its teleological relation to man'[28]). The natural world is a sphere of creation which has
a mediating role in the attainment of the divine purposes for what has been
made. As and when this end is reached the natural world will find its own
completion, for while in its origins it does not lack goodness, it *does* exist in
a state of provisionality:

> The world is created good and perfect, not in the same sense as God,
> but in the sense that as Nature it is fitted and destined, and continues
> to be a means in reference to the world-aim, which finds its realization
> through spirit.[29]

The natural world, then, has a functional role in the attainment of the purpose of creation; and Dorner's account of how it works brings out a key
feature of his project's concern not to allow the entrance of sin and its consequences to distract from what he sees as the more primary issue of establishing the non-contingent grounds for the attainment of the world-aim (a move
which, of course, recalls Barth's analysis concerning the place of his doctrine
of reconciliation). Dorner presents the natural world as having a positive
role in the ethical ordering of humanity which, crucially, is not a scenario
which begins with the Fall: Nature 'restrains or punishes (man) now, acts as
a spur to his indolence, rewards his industry, *but need not, in order to do
this, ever have been different*' (my italics).[30] These are the beginnings of an
account which frames the strivings of the ethical life *not primarily* in terms
of their relation to the recovery of original righteousness (within the wider

---

[26] *SCD*, II, p. 65.
[27] Ibid. p 25.
[28] Ibid. p. 67.
[29] Ibid. p. 64.
[30] Ibid. p. 67.

matrix of sin and salvation) but in terms of how they pertain to the original intentions for the attainment of the world-aim.

The goodness of the natural world hangs not on the absence of death[31] but on its original and ongoing capacity to be an instrument in the attainment of the divine world-plan. Yet, just as Dorner's account of 'Right' marks the point of transition from nature to spirit in his arrangement of the divine proof[32], so too the natural world's limitedness does not represent the final condition of its existence but, through its relationship with rational humanity, looks forward to participating in an 'incorruptibleness'[33] which is the destiny of the 'children of God'.[34] It is preserved not because of what it is, but of what it will be. In detailing the future hope of the natural order together with its present function in the attainment of that end Dorner displays a key feature of his dogmatic vision: the created realm is that which *moves* or develops towards its fulfilment.[35]

Finally, before we leave the doctrine of the natural world, we must take note of a feature which displays a crucial component of Dorner's project and which has particular importance for the subsequent doctrines of sin and atonement: *the extent to which the natural world remains unchanged by the Fall*:

Nature is good, because it was prepared for man before the Fall, *but also prepared for him as he is after the Fall.* (my italics)[36]

This pertains to Dorner's plan to posit the idea of incarnation as that which is a necessity even *without* the entrance of sin. The natural world remains essentially impervious to the Fall[37], and continues, albeit in a somewhat *modified* way, to restrain and punish humanity as it would have done *without* sin's arrival. As such it retains its original teleological relation to humanity, as that which will find its fulfilment in the God-man. It is the weight of this essentially unchanged teleological relation which is significant, rather than his suggestions about the prior existence of death in the natural world

[31] Ibid. p. 66.
[32] Cf. §25, *SCD*, I, pp. 303–305.
[33] *SCD*, II, p. 66.
[34] Ibid.
[35] D. O. Zöckler observes that Dorner is indebted to the ideas of development prevalent in the natural sciences, D. O. Zöckler, *Geschichte der Beziehungen zwischen Theologie und Naturwissenschaft, mit besondrer Rücksicht auf Schöpfungsgeschichte* (Gütersloh: Bertelsmann, 1879), p. 714.
[36] *SCD*, II, p. 67.
[37] Dorner speaks of Nature being 'detained by sin' and existing in an 'unnecessary' long-enduring state of corruptibleness (Ibid. p. 66), but the problem is not the corruption as such (which is normal to the natural world), but the length of time it has to wait for its fulfilment.

which is seemingly shared by a number of his near contemporaries, e.g. Julius Müller, who argues that the natural world, considered solely in terms of its organic processes, leads inevitably and not improperly to death because individual examples of any biological genus do not deserve preservation but contribute to the general life of nature.[38] Martensen also takes this view suggesting that 'death is natural for existence generally' (man's relation to death is considered separately).[39]

Dorner's position means that the natural world did not *begin* with one relation to humanity (of complete perfection which is now lost) and with the arrival of sin *acquire a new one* (that of needing to be restored to an original paradisical state). Rather, it began and retained the same relation to humanity which will be fulfilled in the incarnation.

While his account of the world as nature forms only a short section of the Doctrine of the Creature, it sets the scene for the rest of the Second Main Division which, in turn, is always anticipating the decisive site of the Third Main Division and the delineation of the idea of the God-man. We will ourselves turn now to a brief assessment of Dorner's doctrine of humanity.

b. The Doctrine of Humanity[40]

Dorner's doctrine of God is intended to clear a space for free human activity as that not in competition but consonant with the divine intentions for the world. Following his account of the natural world, he continues to set out how this free conformity occurs in humanity. The natural world manifests *temporally* (in its processes of production and reproduction) the *movement* which is characteristic of the uncreated triune relations conceived in terms

---

[38] Julius Müller, *The Christian Doctrine of Sin*, Vol. II, trans. W. Pulsford (Edinburgh: T & T Clark, 1853), pp. 315–316.

[39] Hans Martensen, *Christian Dogmatics*, p. 210.

[40] One interesting feature of Dorner's doctrine of man is its similarity to the account he gives in *History of Development, Div. II, Vol. I*, of Theodore of Mopsuestia. Common themes are: conceptualizing man as that part of creation in which spirit and matter are united (though, unlike Mopsuestia, Dorner does not see this as the reconciling of antagonistic forces) (p. 31); holding to the freedom of souls to learn the nature of the good, rather than being originally posited as the possessors of the good (p. 33); the notion that the moral law cannot be perfect at the beginning but is connected to a moral process (p. 33); the original disunity, apart from the Fall, of Adam (p. 34). This connection is, on one level, unsurprising since Dorner produced a separate study of Theodore (in Latin) on his doctrine of the *imago dei* (I. A. Dorner, *Inest Theodori Mopsuesteni doctrina de Imagine Dei exposita* (Regiomonti, Hartungianis, 1844)). However, it displays a tendency in Dorner to situate his dogmatic project within a theological trajectory which sees the concept of ethical development as a normative feature of proper Christian accounts of man and, as we will see in the subsequent section and next chapter, God-man.

of the concept of Personality. We will see that in the content of his doctrine of humanity a similar set of moves takes place.

Central to his treatment is the presentation of humanity as *destined* for 'community of life with God'.[41] Like his doctrine of the natural world, Dorner's anthropology is teleological, and characterized by a concern to depict relationality with God as its end. While humanity is offered as the 'goal and crown'[42] of the natural world, it is so in two distinct ways, standing in a liminal space in relation to the world's natural constitution.

Although humanity is the 'highest *natural* being' (my italics),[43] it is also subject to the exigencies of nature's processes and finitude (including its susceptibility to death), and thereby it is simply but importantly the *microcosm* of the natural world: 'the various systems of life…which in nature appear apart in different classes of beings, are united in man' and 'each one of these systems thus attains its proper perfection'.[44] Yet, humanity is the 'king of creation' in its *distinction* from nature, being able to comprehend nature as a *spiritual* being, by virtue of its unique possession of knowledge, will and feeling.[45] These attributes pertain to its capacity to distinguish between the good and its opposite, the freedom to choose the good undeterminately, and the faculty to receive infinite (as well as finite) truth.[46] We shall say more of these attributes in the discussion of the divine image. For the moment, we want only to observe that prior to a consideration of its attributes, humanity stands apart from the natural world on account of its origins as a 'new distinct divine conception'.[47] As the product of divine inspiration, it is set apart as the appointed means by which 'knowledge of and desire for the divine may be possible'.[48] In its status as both natural and spiritual being humanity is the end and apex[49] of nature (and accordingly Dorner divides his account into a treatment first of humanity as natural being and second as spiritual being); an end which is defined by a capacity for communion with God. Yet as already noted, Dorner's anthropology is primarily teleological in tone. This means that it is not as it is *originally* posited, but in what it will *become* that the ultimate end and fullness of creation will be attained. It is as humanity is *capable* of relating with God that it is *provisionally* the apex of the

---

[41] *SCD*, II, p. 77.
[42] Ibid. p. 68.
[43] Ibid.
[44] Ibid. p. 69.
[45] Ibid. p. 72.
[46] Ibid. p. 73.
[47] Ibid.
[48] Ibid. p. 69.
[49] 'End' and 'apex' are our renderings of Dorner's original term, 'Spitze' (*SCG*, I, p. 505), to describe man's relation to nature.

natural world. While humanity is both natural and spiritual being, its original state does not involve a settled unity of these aspects. This means that such disjunction as originally obtained in humanity ('an original incongruity between soul and body'[50]) expressed itself in a natural pre-disposition to death ('man *potuit mori*, nay *non potuit non mori*'[51]). This would be overcome only by the attainment of a unity with spirit, coming as the product of an *ethical process*.

This scenario instantiates Dorner's concern to provide an account which sees humanity's completion *neither* as the product of a single, immediate divine act (which would bypass creaturely involvement and impinge upon its liberty[52]), *or* as the consequence of humanity's own self-actualization (as a kind of *homo faber*). A middle ground is sought so that 'man is not precluded from a course of ethical development by a too-much or too-little'.[53] It means, for Dorner, that humanity is not a completely realized moral being since a requisite of the good is that it be 'willed freely, constrained neither by determination from without, nor yet from within by a constitution not due to freedom'.[54] It is a future state, and Dorner is defining free human activity and its consonance with divine intentions for the world. There must be an undetermined response to the ethically necessary in order for that freedom to have explicable content. Yet this is not an arbitrary choice of the good, since God 'implants the moral, existing in Him and conceived and willed by Him as the good, in man's knowledge'.[55] Humanity is originally ordered to the good (and as such is capable of sinless development), but it is in its free choice of the good that this origination is actualized. We see in this is a doctrine of humanity arranged according to the structure of the divine life (as the free obedience to the necessary). It is also a scheme which mirrors Dorner's teleological account of the divine image.

c. The Divine Image

Man's collective organization has its unity in the fact of his being destined for community of life with God or for religion. With religion the portrayal of God in the personal creature is realized, in order that man

---

[50] *SCD*, II, p. 71.

[51] Ibid.

[52] Such an account would make it a 'physical' act because it would remove entirely from the creature any part in his realization, and be an instance merely of the revelation of God's power rather than His love. It recalls, of course, Dorner's handling of the relation between the physical and ethical attributes in the doctrine of God, according to which the triune God exists as free obedience to the necessary, *SCD*, I, p. 431 ff.

[53] *SCD*, II, p. 83.

[54] Ibid. p. 73. Dorner does not take this ethical incompletion as a sign of evil. Rather, it is the 'necessary condition' of a properly ethical life (Ibid. p. 74).

[55] Ibid. p. 75.

may be God's image. *This is to be viewed partly as original endowment, partly as destination.*[56]

With this opening proposition, Dorner continues his teleological account, and introduces to the discussion the concept of religion, to which he gives a twofold significance: religion as the *portrayal* of a certain 'reciprocal, living relation'[57] between humanity and God; and religion as the *actual* community of life with God. The last of these is fulfilled in the idea of the God-man and realized in the historical Jesus of Nazareth.[58] Prior to this actualization, religion is the means of describing the general grounds on which this particular combination of God's will to communicate Himself and humanity's capacity to receive His self-communication is prepared. Dorner's configuration of the divine image is, therefore, conceived in terms of religion rather than, say, an original positum residing *somewhere* in humanity's constitution.

This means that the key issues are, first, the *relation* between the divine and the human (since it has to do with the way in which both humanity and God are correlated and not, say, the kind of attributes, such as righteousness, which humanity possesses), and, second, in whom this future union is realized (with the schema of the connection between the *idea* of union and its *realization* functioning as a presiding principle). It reduces immediately the significance of the first human[59] (as well as branching away from what has been described as the 'orthodox emphasis on the original state as a *completed* state'[60]), and continues to set up the dogmatic arrangement for its decisive site, which is the God-man considered in its ideal and historical forms. He makes these moves with what he takes as the consent both of the biblical sources and an important thread in ecclesiastical doctrine[61], proposing the endowment – destination schema as the most appropriate rendering of the often noted[62] (and often

---

[56] Ibid. p. 77.

[57] Ibid. p. 114.

[58] Ibid. p. 280.

[59] Indeed, in the whole of the Second Main Division, Dorner makes only *one* explicit reference to Adam (and this in a remark about the NT's teaching that Christ and not Adam is the *imago dei* (Ibid. p. 78)).

[60] Holte, *Vermittlunsgtheologie*, p. 124 (my translation). Schlink demonstrates that the Lutheran confessions presupposed an original possession which, after the Fall, is lost and with it the image of God, E. Schlink, *Theology of the Lutheran Confessions*, trans. P. Koehneke & H. Bouman (St. Louis: Concordia, 1961), p. 47.

[61] Dorner appeals to the distinction made in the early church between εἰκών and ὁμοωίσις.

[62] Pannenberg suggests that the nineteenth-century rendering of this distinction (due in large part, he argues, to J. G. Herder) owes much to the discovery of the 'saga character of the Yahwist story in the creation and fall of Adam' which prompted that century's theology no longer to regard 'the image of God as a perfection of the original state that

disputed[63]) distinction in Gen. 1.26 between *d'mut* (likeness) and *tselem* (image) to point towards the future orientation of the image concept:

> [Man's] spiritual powers and capacities bear the imprint of the divine *likeness*. Still, capacities are not God's actual *image*, but merely its possibility. The higher import of the word 'image' points to the future. In reference to what he possesses already, he is created 'in' the divine image as his model; but in reference to the chief matter – his destination – he has in God a norm and ideal.[64]

In ascribing to humanity original divine *likeness* but not *imaging*, Dorner appeals to humanity's relational *capacities* and ethical *potentialities* as the point of contact with the idea of the divine image. It pushes the dogmatic agenda forwards out of the domain of humanity's origins and towards the question of when and in whom this image will be actualized. Its ultimate realization in Jesus means that, for Dorner, the concept of *imago dei* is one which, properly speaking, is not an anthropological appellation and description *tout simple*, to be treated merely within the confines of a doctrine of humanity, but a doctrine to be determined by the idea and act of incarnation. Its initial setting within this discussion of humanity does have preparatory import in that it lays out the terms by which the God-man will demonstrate his true humanity by displaying these capacities, revealing his union with God by the realization of these capacities; and the final form of this will be Jesus' free obedience to the Father. This will be the actualization of humanity as that creature destined to exist in a relationship of loving reciprocity with God, within which humanity's free acts will be marked out as '*receptive*'.[65] The reciprocity will not be a meeting of equally self-determining agents, but the coincidence of humanity's *free obedience* to God's demands. This is the trope which will inform Dorner's later explication of the Christian Life. It

---

was lost at the fall', but as 'the destiny that human beings have still to attain', Wolfhart Pannenberg, *Anthropology*, p. 54 ff. Robert F. Brown, in his essay 'On the Necessary Imperfection of Creation: Iranaeus' *Adversus Haereses*, iv. 38', *Scottish Journal of Theology*, No. 1, February 1975 (Edinburgh: Scottish Academic Press, 1975), suggests 'it was not until eighteenth-century scholars began to break the monopoly which biblical literalism held over the church...that the presupposition of an original imperfection of human nature could be taken with real seriousness', p. 25.

[63] Dorner's own confidence in the distinction does not reflect a wholesale consensus in biblical scholarship at the time of the publication of his System. Delitzsch, for example, argues that the differentiation of the words comes from the level of presupposition rather than linguistic necessity, Franz Delitzsch, *Commentar über die Genesis* (Leipzig: Dörffling und Franke, 1872), p. 102.

[64] *SCD*, II, p. 77.

[65] Ibid. p. 80.

will be the temporal manifestation of the uncreated triune unity of freedom and necessity which characterizes the *divine* life as Love in Dorner's account of the doctrine of God: 'love is the unity of ethical necessity and freedom because it wills the ethically necessary as such, that is, with consciousness and absolute desire.'[66] The *life* which characterizes God will characterize humanity. At the heart of the brief discussion of the doctrine of the divine image we see the extent to which Dorner's concern is always to lead up to and from the doctrine of the God-man.

We suggest, however, that this arrangement suffers from its account of the original endowment and indicates a systemic failure to accommodate the significance of the entrance of sin and its eventual removal. While the matrix of endowment and destination means that Dorner pushes the doctrine of the divine image away from being considered *merely* in terms of origins (and the often attendant vagaries of situating the image *somewhere* in humanity[67]) and orders it according to the import of his doctrines of God and incarnation, its *futurity* eventuates in an incapacity to account properly for the full impact of the Fall and weight of the *reconciling* activity of God. It disengages it from the doctrine of salvation, by removing from *homo creatus* an original determination as a creature in *actual* communion with God. While the '*idea* of man' *includes* an 'actual, life relation to God',[68] the 'idea and the actuality of the idea exist *apart*, the latter being the fruit of free acts and coming gradually into existence' (my italics).[69] The entrance of sin occurs *before* humanity is in actual relation to God, making it difficult to grasp how the activity of a creature who has not yet acquired ethical vitality would result in a divine *curse*.[70] An orienta-

---

[66] *SCD*, I, p. 437.

[67] G. C. Berkouwer refers to Von Rad's dismissal of all such efforts to identify the divine image according to 'one or another set of anthropological concepts alien to the O. T. writers' so that it is seen in man's 'personality', 'free ego', human 'worth', or 'free use of moral tendencies', G. C. Berkouwer, *Man: The Image of God* (Michigan: Eerdmans, 1962), p. 75.

[68] *SCD*, II, p. 79.

[69] Ibid. p. 80.

[70] This point is observed by John Macquarrie who quotes approvingly William Adam Brown in saying that 'the doctrine of a kinship between God and man gives the standard for measuring the significance of sin', and himself suggests that if 'one minimizes the kinship, then what we call the "fall" of man must be correspondingly minimized, for he has less to fall', John Macquarrie, *Principles of Christian Theology* (London: SCM, 1977), p. 230. While Macquarrie is clearly intending to criticize those theological projects which seek to foreground divine sovereignty at the expense of creaturely freedom, and himself wants to propose the *imago dei* more in terms of a 'potentiality' than a fixed 'endowment' or 'nature' (p. 231), there is some bearing on Dorner's account in the extent to which his account of potentiality does not provide a depiction of *kinship* which will suffice for a fully rigorous explication of the doctrine of the Fall.

tion *towards* the good, or the presence of the *possibility* of an actual life relation to God, is in danger of evacuating from humanity's original state a sufficient connection with the consequent sites of sin and salvation. A marked feature of Dorner's treatment is that he will not treat the relationship between Christ and Adam in terms of a *'typological reverse'*[71] of the Fall, but instead the incomplete Adam will be *contrasted* with the complete Christ.

This supports Barth's analysis that Dorner's account of the divine purpose is focused not on the 'divine work of reconciliation' but on 'ideal man and the process of his spiritualisation or deification'.[72] Indeed, it accords with Dorner's own insistence that since one cannot lose what one does not possess the divine image is not lost or removed by sin. Rather, the image remains humanity's destination and is merely 'deflected into a by-path by the Fall'.[73] For Dorner the Fall is more of a *stumble*. His teleological account serves the wider theological vision by allowing the doctrine of the God-man to take centre ground. Yet while we will see that in Dorner's concern to *distinguish* between God and humanity he avoids Barth's charge of *deifying* humanity, we see adumbrated in his doctrine of the divine image the motifs (ethical development, receptivity, Fall as deviation) which will find full expression in an account of the *actual* instantiation of the God-man which will expose him to the charge of ultimately proffering the Christian Gospel as the triumph of the capacity of *humanity* to achieve its perfecting end rather than the triumph of God in salvation.

We continue here, however, by delineating his account in the Third Main Division of the doctrine of the God-man which he offers as the conclusion to the propositions given in the first two: that God wills to communicate Himself; and that in humanity God made a creature destined to receive His self-communication.[74]

II. The Doctrine of the God-man

The form and contents of Revelation only attain their consummation in the divine Incarnation, and in such a way that the consummation of divine revelation in itself becomes also the consummation of religion, and therewith of humanity. This perfective process is carried into effect

---

[71] This distinction has been noted of Theodore's arrangement of the Two Ages which are divided by Christ, and we suggest that again the pattern has purchase in Dorner's own treatment, Rowan Greer, *The Captain of our Salvation* (Tübingen: Mohr-Siebeck, 1973), p. 190.

[72] Karl Barth, *Church Dogmatics*, Vol. III, Part I, p. 47.

[73] *SCD*, II, p. 83.

[74] Ibid. pp. 106–107.

first of all in One who, as absolute God-man, is both the Revealer in the absolute sense and the Man embodying God's perfect image, while at the same time bringing about the consummation of the world.[75]

Dorner offers this statement midway through the Third Main Division. The section it introduces follows a detailed discussion of Religion (§46–49) and Revelation (§50–61), and precedes a threefold consideration of how the consummated incarnation is preserved (§63), what the relation of the incarnation is to the historic religions (§64–69), and what the keys are to demonstrating that the idea of incarnation has been realized (§70). That Dorner incorporates such material into his account of the unity of God and humanity displays his concern to depict the full scope of the Christian idea of incarnation. Consonant with the apologetic concerns of the first part of the system, he is laying out an account which seeks to demonstrate how the idea of the God-man is both the key to explicating the concepts of religion and revelation and the *telos* of creaturely and divine activity to which those concepts pertain. His intention is to exhibit the idea of the incarnation as that which is *demanded* by the ideas of God and humanity previously mapped out, and to explicate the grounds on which its actual instantiation in Jesus Christ may be said to be verifiable. He speaks, therefore, in the Third Main Division of the need to present the 'concrete combination'[76] of God's 'will to communicate Himself'[77] (which was the result of the First Main Division) and of humanity as the creature 'destined to receive His perfect self-communication'[78] (which was the subject of the Second Main Division). The terms of this combination (attained in the divine incarnation) are not delineated, however, until he has set out the principle of 'reciprocal, living'[79] relations between God and humanity *and* the divine institution and preservation of these relations (considered in terms of the concepts of miracle and inspiration). Dorner depicts the incarnation as that which may be *inferred* from the general conditions which obtain in creaturely existence and divine relations with the world: 'The idea of the God-man is cognizable as one destined to realization.'[80] Yet, it is important that we do not think of Dorner's account of these *general* conditions as the result of empirical observation (of the sort which might consider first the *religiousness* of humanity in history).[81] Rather, religion is conceptualized primarily as the 'reciprocal,

---

[75] Ibid. p. 205.
[76] Ibid. p. 107.
[77] Ibid. p. 106.
[78] Ibid. p. 107.
[79] Ibid. p. 114.
[80] Ibid. p. 206.
[81] With this observation we recall his ambivalent assessment of the efficaciousness of the Teleological proof in determining the existence or nature of God: 'nature shows us

living relation'[82] between God and humanity, and not a practice defined by cultic norms and traditions.[83]

There is high significance in Dorner's placement of the concepts of religion and revelation under the general rubric of the union of God and humanity. This means they are considered in the immediate vicinity of the proposition concerning the idea of the God-man, and not, say, at the level of prolegomena (as do Martensen and Nitzsch[84]). It displays a concern to locate the discussion within the *realm* of the Christian idea of the God-man, and even though he states his intention to examine religion first as a 'general concept' (i.e. not in its actual instantiation) it is so on the basis of the 'results already gained'.[85] The concepts of religion and revelation are treated in order to *prepare* for the proposition concerning the God-man. They are not considered *remoto Christi*. We shall see that the concepts acquire a *teleological* character since they too, like the doctrine of the creature, are organized in order to point towards their completion in the idea of the God-man.

a. Religion

Religion is the living, reciprocal relationship of God to man and man to God. Thus, on God's part it is His self-manifestation, first of His

no all-embracing purpose upon which we could rely: it is rather a cycle of rising and setting' (*SCD*, I, p. 266). That is to say, his observations concerning religion are not, like his observations about the world, based on empirical data upon which theological propositions are built; but rather, the empirical is assessed on the basis of the theological proposition concerning the ideas of God and the God-man.

[82] *SCD*, II, p. 114.
[83] That is not to say, of course, that for Dorner religion does not include what has been called the 'bestimmte Funktionselemente in der Kultur und im Prozeß der Gesellschaft' (D. Rössler, *Die Vernunft der Religion*, [München: Piper, 1976], p. 8) as his subsequent account of the historic religions demonstrates (in *SCD*, II, §64–69). Rather, religion is a concept which pertains primarily to the 'complete idea of human nature' (Ibid. p. 107), and as such it is not to be reduced to a set of practices but defined by this idea which, as we have seen in the doctrine of the creature, is a teleologically constituted reality.
[84] Martensen gives a brief account of the concepts of Religion and Revelation in the Introduction to his *Christian Dogmatics* (pp. 5–15); Nitzsch uses the concepts of Religion and Revelation as the first two of three divisions of his introduction to the exposition of Christian doctrines, and does so according to the understanding that the *scientific* apprehension of Christianity can be achieved only when its 'specific resemblances' and 'differences' from 'other forms of man's spiritual life' are acknowledged (Nitzsch, *System*, pp. 3–4). This, of course, makes the depiction of the spiritual life *apart* from its specifically Christian orientation more pressing. Accordingly, Nitzsch provides lengthy accounts at the introductory stage of his system.
[85] *SCD*, II, p. 107.

> *majesty and power, secondly of His will; on man's part, primarily the consciousness of absolute dependence on God and surrender to Him.... [M]an is in religion filled with divine life in knowledge, freedom, and blessedness.*[86]

Dorner's conceptualization of religion hangs on the notion of *reciprocal relationality*. With this definition he offers the grounds on which he will seek to demonstrate that the idea of the God-man is both explicable and necessary.

Yet it is not merely preparatory since he is, in fact, establishing how the spiritual receptivity of the human creature helps constitute religion, as well as setting out the form of this receptivity (conceptualized in the act of faith). In advance of his account of the *nature* of religion he seeks to delineate the 'seat of religion'.[87]

He thus interprets the nature of religion as *reciprocal relationship*. What is central to the whole treatment is that in his dogmatic arrangement he seeks to offer a *balance* to the issue. As we will see in our following section on his doctrine of Revelation, we 'only come to know God through God'.[88] Though religion is a creaturely activity it is not by itself *creative* but freely (and obediently) co-operative with the *prior* divine operation. The fundamental activity of religion is, therefore, faith.

1. Faith

In his Prolegomena Dorner has given a thorough assessment of faith as the 'postulate of the apprehension of Christianity as truth'.[89] There he conceives of faith as an *epistemological* category. His primary concern was to determine the relationship between the act of faith and its objects, and the extent to which faith as a property tied to its objective content may be said to provide certainty to the believer (as opposed to the mere principle of faith itself). As we have seen in his doctrine of God, it is as the 'evangelical principle of faith' is connected to the 'Trinity' that the Christian personality 'finds its objective and absolute foundation'.[90] Here however, in the brief definition of faith as the fundamental activity

---

[86] Ibid. pp. 114–115.
[87] Ibid. p. 107.
[88] Ibid. p. 133.
[89] *SCD*, I, p. 31.
[90] Ibid. p. 417. A point on which K. Barth praises Dorner as one of the few modern theologians to see this as the only alternative to the 'Übel' of seeing the doctrine of Trinity not merely as the *work* – 'die Werke' of faith but also its object – 'der Gegenstand', Karl Barth, *Die Christliche Dogmatik im Entwurf*, Erster band, Die Lehre vom Worte Gottes, 1927 (Zürich: Theologischer Verlag, 1982), p. 267.

of religion we find that he is not concerned with that aspect (although he does refer to the 'firm certainty' which attends 'religious faith'[91]). Neither does he attend to the *soteriological* function of faith. (This will come in his treatment of the origin of the Church through 'Faith and Regeneration' in §130–133 of the Second main Division of the Second Part of his *System*.) The focus here is how faith is that creaturely activity by which the reciprocal relationship is instantiated and maintained, since it unites in itself 'activity and receptivity' (manifest in the 'essential function of faith – prayer'[92]). It pertains to the *whole* human person (and not a mere aspect of him),[93] since it implies the 'personal participation of the heart':[94]

> [O]n the subjective side, through knowledge, through exercise of will and trust, and through personal participation, faith is the link of connection binding the entire man in heart to God.[95]

It is part of the normative constitution of the creature in his relation to God, and the concept with which he describes how the *ideal* relations between the spiritual creature and God are instantiated. Crucially, in its depiction as the union of activity and receptivity, Dorner conceives faith as that which *both* displays the human creature as one who lives in a state of ethical development, *and* which instantiates the mutual relationship of humanity to God and God to humanity. The development is *ethical* because it is to be marked by an ever deeper free obedience to God, and a process not initiated or defined by the loss of an original state (consistent with his teleological doctrine of humanity), but the normal characteristic of humanity in its relation to God and His purposes:

> *By no means* can *sin* be primarily regarded as the reason why the life of religion or faith has to pass through a series of stages. Rather, man's ethical destination requires ethical self-determination on his part, and to this a law of succession, entrance upon a course of progressive development, is requisite.[96]

---

[91] *SCD*, I, p. 122. This comment comes as part of a cursory effort to distinguish faith as what we may call *a species of knowledge* rather than a type of opinion.

[92] *SCD*, II, p. 121.

[93] 'Es ist wichtig, diese Gründung des Glaubens im ganzen Menschen zu beachten', Heinrich Benckert, 'Isaak August Dorners "Pisteologie"', in *Zeitschrift für Theologie und Kirche*, 14 Jahrgang, 1933 (Tübingen: J. C. B. Mohr/Siebeck, 1933), p. 265.

[94] *SCD*, II, p. 122.

[95] Ibid.

[96] Ibid.

Consequent to this interchange of activity and receptivity, faith also instantiates the reciprocal relationship of God and humanity, so that Dorner speaks of a 'twofold surrender of God to man, and of man to God'.[97] This demonstrates how faith, as the fundamental activity of religion, pertains to and institutes a relation between humanity and God which is holistic, preparing the ground for God in His fullness being embodied by the God-man. We will turn to that account after we have provided a brief survey of the parallel section to Religion, that of Revelation, which precedes his section on the divine incarnation.

b. Revelation

Dorner offers an account of the doctrine of revelation in which he purposes, first, to demonstrate that God *Himself* is its contents without detriment *either* to the creaturely constitution of the recipients and mediators *or* God's own self-possession; and, second, that the culmination of revelation consists in the freely willed perfect reception of God by the human creature. This conforms to his strategy of preparing for the demonstration of Jesus as the culmination of divine revelation. That Dorner provides an extended survey of the doctrine *here* in his preparation for the demonstration of the idea of the incarnation (and not at the level of prolegomena) displays the extent to which this account of revelation is not merely a *general* concept either to be used as the *basis* of our knowledge of God or as an overarching theological principle. Rather, its placement displays Dorner's concern to depict the incarnation as itself the central or 'fundamental idea of Christianity'.[98] The doctrine of revelation is intended to aid the cognition of the idea of the God-man as that which is 'destined to realization'.[99] Situating the doctrine of revelation within the division of the unity of God and humanity means that it becomes the place in which the nature and forms of the divine 'Self-communication'[100] are expressed as pertaining to this discrete end, that is, the idea of the God-man. This means that Dorner treats the doctrines of Miracles (§53–56) and Inspiration (§57–59) in terms of their *inadequacy* to describe the divine Self-communication in its fullness, but also of their *relationship* to and *fulfilment* in the God-man. In both aspects, it is the extent to which they pertain to that end which interests and occupies Dorner. We will see how this manifests itself in the details of his account as we continue by analysing two of the three subdivisions in this section: (1) The nature of revelation (§50–51); and, (2) The form of revelation (§52–59).

[97] Ibid.
[98] *SCD*, I, p. 28.
[99] *SCD*, II, p. 206.
[100] Ibid. p. 205.

1. The Nature of Revelation

[R]eligious Revelation is subjective and central in nature, and is related to man's entire nature or the heart, while pointing to the objective, absolute centre – God – and revealing the latter. Often, indeed, Revelation is applied to the mere communication of higher truths, as in the old Supranaturalism. But revelation, being related to man's entire nature, is meant to impart to him a share in the divine life in general, not merely in the divine knowledge.[101]

Dorner propounds the concept of revelation as that which is oriented towards bringing together humanity and God. It is *subjective* in nature (by which he means, it pertains to the *whole* of the human creature[102]) and involves the creature not as the originator of revelation but, in its role as the recipient, as an essential factor in the divine activity of revelation. Yet Dorner points also to the objective centre of revelation, namely God. *Religious* revelation is not, therefore, the mere 'exhibition of subjective energy',[103] but the divine impartation of something new to the creature. What is at stake is a need to remain consistent with the effort to clear a space for creaturely freedom in relation to God's self-communication, and provide an account of revelation which does not 'violate human autonomy'.[104] He attempts this by proposing a Subjective–Objective schema, offering revelation as that in which the receiving human creature has an interest and, therefore, *contributes* to its end. While he goes on to speak of revelation as that divine activity in which 'something new has been instituted',[105] it becomes the object of 'conservation'.[106] With this Dorner interweaves his theological gradualism or theory of development: 'Revelation assumes the form of gradual progress.'[107] While revelation is first of all an innovative divine activity, in its reception is instantiated the creaturely component to the activity. According to this view, mere

---

[101] *SCD*, II, p. 134.

[102] The German word, translated as 'heart', is *Gemüth*, (*SCG*, I, p. 570) which carries with it the meaning of 'nature', or 'disposition', and certainly that which is characteristic of the complete person rather than, say, pertaining merely to one aspect, such as the mind. It is a word, however, which can also have an *affective* significance i.e. it can mean, 'emotion', or 'feeling'. However, it is, of course, not *Gefühl*, and as we have already noted, Dorner locates the heart of man not in any one of his attributes and certainly not in his feelings or emotions.

[103] Ibid.

[104] Colin Gunton, *A Brief Theology of Revelation* (Edinburgh: T & T Clark, 1995), p. 31. Gunton speaks of this as the 'modern offence with revelation'.

[105] *SCD*, II, p. 135.

[106] Ibid.

[107] Ibid. p. 136.

human 'passivity'[108] is excluded, and instead 'vital receptiveness' means that the human creature *co-operates* in the purpose of the divine revealing activity.

2. The Form of Revelation

Dorner assesses the form of revelation according to the categories indicative of its external and internal aspects: Miracle and Inspiration. They are the aspects which pertain to the depiction of humanity as natural and spiritual being. The miraculous belongs to the *'receptiveness of Nature'*, by which it acknowledges itself not as its 'own end, but designed to have spirit as its master'.[109] Inspiration 'refers to the spiritual side of man':[110]

> Revelation as regards its form is of necessity partly external, partly internal, one co-operating with the other. External Revelation or Manifestation, intervening in the system of nature, is called Miracle in the strict sense; internal Revelation, related to the spirit, is Inspiration.[111]

His intention is not to offer an account of these two doctrines as isolated sites (of the kind that sees, for example, the doctrine of inspiration merely in terms of a doctrine of Scripture). Rather, he seeks to demonstrate how these forms of revelation relate to the consummation of Revelation. He treats both forms as *preparatory* but also *contributory* to that consummation. The account is, therefore, ordered to serve the depiction of the idea of the God-man as the most appropriate, indeed necessary, location of the 'perfecting' of the divine 'self-communication'.[112] It alone allows the distinction between God and humanity to give way to a unity without abolishing the distinction. We will address in more detail later the way in which Dorner conceives this as capable of occurring only in the incarnation. For the moment, we want to observe the *singular* focus in his treatment:

> *God's collective activity in revelation, directed to the end of completely satisfying man's receptivity and need*, is exhausted or precluded neither by the original creation nor by the conservation of the world, but joins on to the world of conservation, both physical and human (my italics).[113]

---

108 Ibid.
109 Ibid. p. 175.
110 Ibid. p. 190.
111 Ibid. pp. 140–141.
112 Ibid. p. 146.
113 Ibid. p. 141.

This statement demonstrates the extent to which divine revelation, while having more than one form, has a singular purpose which is neither *alien* to the original constitution of creation (because of its teleological configuration) nor *interchangeable* with the divine work of conservation (since it becomes reality *only* on 'the ground of the divine agency'[114]). It is connected to the satisfaction of humanity's receptivity and need.

However, the *benefits* which come to the creature from this revelation are themselves not to be identified *as* the final cause of the divine activity (Dorner is not a eudaimonian). Rather, it is the 'actual communion between God and man', coming as a result of 'reciprocal acts of spontaneous mutual surrender',[115] which has this status. With this we want to take note of a focus on communion which functions both as the norm for his subsequent accounts of miracle and inspiration and also holds the key to determining whether Barth's analysis of Dorner's project – as the deification of humanity – is accurate.

i. The idea of communion

Dorner speaks of communion ('Gemeinschaft') as that which represents a decisive form of relation between humanity and God. It is the state marked by, and is the consequence of, a process of reciprocity. The human creature demonstrates the *ethical* vitality of this relation by his *free* obedience to God not merely as the One on whom he is absolutely dependent[116] but as He who, in His self-communication, is *holy* Love (recalling Dorner's account of the triune God as Personality) and the willing object of free creaturely conformity to the good. Since God is holy Love, communion between God and humanity is to be characterized as holy love, according to which the creature will respond to God's self-communication by actively receiving Him and 'personally appropriating'[117] that which God has designed for him (including 'moral duties'[118] which have a function of displaying the divine will). This arrangement recalls the definition of love which Dorner offered in his account of the doctrine of God: 'love is the unity of ethical necessity and freedom because it wills the ethically necessary as such, that is, with consciousness and absolute desire.'[119] The unity of necessity and freedom should characterize the God-man relation, without the abolition of their distinction.

It is this concept of communion which functions as the guiding principle for his accounts of miracle and inspiration. It is the means by which

---

[114] *SCD*, II, p. 116.
[115] Ibid. p. 141.
[116] Ibid.
[117] Ibid. p. 201.
[118] Ibid.
[119] *SCD*, I, p. 437.

he speaks of a relation between God and humanity which pertains to the perfecting of revelation and the transition from the distinction between God and humanity to their unity without the abolition of the distinction. At the heart of his account of these two forms of revelation is, therefore, a concern to display their connection to this particular end. Dorner begins his discussion of miracles by noting that they have their 'centre in the revelation of God in Christ',[120] and concludes his account of inspiration by suggesting that the proper view is to 'conceive the divine and human personality as co-operative in Inspiration'.[121] As these forms of revelation are related to the '*ends* of revelation'[122] they are defined and receive their significance. Dorner classifies two types of miracle: those which are related to the natural world as revelation,[123] and those which are 'not produced by God Himself directly' but 'those performed through the instrumentality of men'.[124] In both it is the end to which the revelation pertains which receives primary attention. For the first class of miracles, as they point to a 'higher power holding sway over Nature' and, in this, signify both the non-finality of Nature and the 'secret bond'[125] which exists between Nature and spirit, they are intended to display how Nature may be 'made serviceable for the ends of revelation'.[126] They pertain to and disclose the teleological condition of Nature. For the second class also, the focus is on how they relate to the end of the divine purposes for the world. This class of miracles attest not *merely* to divine authority or activity in the world (which Dorner describes as 'insufficient'[127] and a characteristic of Biblical Supernaturalism), but to the *co-operation* of humanity with this form of divine revelation. Dorner depicts carefully the part played by the creature in their instantiation to demonstrate that this form of revelation conforms to the *ethical* nature of the divine purposes for, and end of, the world: the instantiation of a relation between God and humanity characterized by free obedience. He

[120] *SCD*, II, p. 147.
[121] Ibid. p. 198.
[122] Ibid. p. 171.
[123] Ibid. p. 168.
[124] Ibid. p. 171.
[125] Ibid. p. 169. With this first class of miracles, in which God alone is the active agent of change, Dorner seeks to demonstrate that since God is the continual upholder of the created order and its laws, His miraculous activity does not represent an aberration but the continuous, though unusual, divine upholding of the world for the ends to which He has purposed creation. It is not, as Dorner's contemporary and friend I. Lotzte maintained, the temporary positing of external power but rather 'durch eine unmittelbare Einwirkung, welche die innere Natur der Dinge verändert', quoted in Eduard von Hartmann, *Lotze's Philosophie*, (Leipzig: Wilhelm Friedrich, 1888), p. 39.
[126] *SCD*, II, p. 69.
[127] Ibid. p. 171.

argues of such miracles:

> Man is not a mere channel for divine actions or a mere spectator, but his power of will receives this enhancement or freedom[128]

and

> [T]he application of miraculous power in a particular case, stands perpetually under ethical laws, because it is the human will that has to perform the miracles.[129]

With the identification of the essential place of the human will in this second class of miracles, Dorner demonstrates how his treatment is ordered according to the idea of communion between God and humanity. It comes in the middle of a highly significant discussion of the status of miracles for Christ, which will give an opportunity to respond to Barth concerning Dorner's treatment of humanity, and provide a bridge to the final section of the doctrine of the God-man:

ii. Miracles and the will of the creature

> [I]n the case of Christ, according to the N. T., it is not God or the divine nature that does the miracles, but this ἐξουσία is given Him as man, given as a power of His own, with which as with the other powers He has to exercise authority. Man is not a mere channel for divine actions or a mere spectator, but his power of will receives this enhancement or freedom...the miraculous works, as expressions of such really existing works, form part of the world of conservation...We may then endeavour to regard this divine act, by which the ability to work miracles is implanted, as a divine quickening of existent but slumbering capacities, or as a 'liberation of previously imprisoned forces' by God, or again (a view which the representations of the N. T. favour) as a communication of the divine living Spirit to men.[130]

In this exposition of the nature of Christ's miracles Dorner sees the acts as the result of divinely given and awakened creaturely capacities. This means linking these acts with the world of conservation, even though the *origins* of the force reside in a creative divine act and therefore pertain to creation. This arrangement seeks a non-competitive account of divine-creaturely action. Yet in its representation of the *capacity* for the miraculous as intrinsic, albeit slumbering, to the creature, it is perhaps unsurprising that Dorner

[128] *SCD*, II, p. 174.
[129] Ibid. p. 180.
[130] Ibid. p. 174.

may be thought to be proposing an account which *spiritualizes* the creature rather than demonstrates the primacy of God in salvation (by, for example, depicting the miracles of Christ in terms of their relation to the Kingdom of God[131]). It attributes to the creature capacities whose manifestation displays what has been called the 'highest development of the spiritual activity of man',[132] rather than the primacy of the divine operation and 'presence'.[133] For Dorner, the miraculous performances are to be attributed to the creaturely will empowered by the Spirit. The bringing to fruition or consummation of creaturely potentiality instantiates humanity's co-operation in the conservation of the world.

Dorner's account appears to justify Barth's remarks concerning Dorner's lack of focus on the divine activity of reconciliation.[134] However, in his representation of the relation between the divine origins and the creaturely enactment of the miraculous powers Dorner does enough to demarcate the activity as that which displays the *dependence* of the creature on the divine action (again we hear the echoes of Dorner's investment in the divine aseity). The miracles are to be seen as the 'outbursts or self-manifestations of a higher, divine Spirit in human organs employed by God'.[135] Even if the authority is given to humanity, it is authority which hangs on his necessary dependence on God. Insofar as these class of miracles have an 'inner teleological connection' with 'religion and revelation', they pertain to the divine purpose to see instantiated a relationship between God and humanity which is characterized by humanity's willed obedience and reception of God Himself. God's priority is neither neglected nor proffered at the expense of creaturely freedom. We have already seen how this is expressed in the preparations for his account of the God-man in terms of fellowship and communion. We will now turn to the final stage in Dorner's apologetic section, and seek to delineate the way in which he renders the idea of *theanthropos* or the God-man as the culmination and fulfilment of the first two divisions.

---

[131] Hendrikus Berkhof, *Christian Faith* (Michigan: Eerdmans, 1986), p. 169.

[132] Felix Flückiger, *Die protestantische Theologie des 19 Jahrhunderts* (Göttingen: Vandenhoek & Ruprecht, 1975), p. 67.

[133] Gerald O'Collins, for example, speaks of the connection between Jesus' miracles and the presence of 'God's rule' in his person and presence, *Christology* (Oxford: Oxford University Press, 1995), p. 56.

[134] This is, of course, an inevitable consequence of his supralapsarianism, a position which has been correctly said to 'influence one's whole outlook on the incarnation itself', by which it is intended that the soteriological import is at the very least informed at least as much by the idea that the incarnation was always necessary for the completion of creation as it is by the sites of sin and salvation, Lewis B. Smedes, *The Incarnation: Trends in Modern Anglican Thought* (Amsterdam: Kampen, 1953), p. 135.

[135] *SCD*, II, p. 174.

c. The Divine Incarnation, or the God-manhood

*Since it is God's will in His eternal love to make an absolute communication of Himself as regards His entire communicable being, in the
world-idea or world-counsel He willed not merely the spiritual existence of relative receptiveness for Him, but as Revealer or λόγος He wills
absolutely such cosmical existence as is endowed with perfect receptiveness for Him and His presence, i.e. He wills the perfect divine image
in the form of realization in the world, which again is the Son of His
love.*[136]

Dorner offers an account of the idea of the incarnation as that which brings
together *all* the elements thus far delineated: God's will to self-communicate;
receptivity in the world; the form and content of revelation. It is explicated
according to the dogmatic decisions already made concerning, for example,
the reason for God's creation of the world (§33–34), the status of the world
as that relatively independent sphere intended for a relation with Himself (a
relation to be characterized by free obedience). It is also excavated as the final
destination of the *form* ('The most perfect organ of revelation can only be
the man...never separated from God'[137]) and *content* ('God Himself wills to
live and dwell in the absolute organ of divine revelation'[138]) of revelation. It
refers back to the divine determination to create and sustain a created object
which, 'loved and loving', will become a 'relatively self-dependent image of
His perfect triune nature and attributes'.[139] What is of concern here is the
inference that only in the divine incarnation may the divine purpose for
Self-communication reach its satisfying conclusion, and bring the attendant
perfection of religion as the perfect relation of God and humanity.

However, Dorner's account is not here merely a kind of advanced theological geometry (i.e. God + humanity = God-man) of the sort which offers the
idea of incarnation as the result of 'pure thought'.[140] His intention is to map

---

[136] *SCD*, II, p. 207.

[137] Ibid. p. 206.

[138] Ibid. p. 207.

[139] Ibid. p. 9.

[140] Ibid. p. 205. On this point, it is probably fair to say that Dorner is seeking to distinguish his project from those with a more explicitly Hegelian intention to depict the
idea of Incarnation as capable of being *re-enacted* in the form of thought, so that the
major dogmatic sites of Christian theology (Trinity and Incarnation) are represented
as merely the 'same truth' as the philosophical system of pure thought (James Yerkes,
The Christology of Hegel [Albany: State University of New York, 1983], p. 112),
rather than the truths appropriated by faith *by which* their verifiableness is to be
based. There may also be an implicit criticism, in particular, of Richard Rothe's speculative theological method (on which, see Robert S. Franks, *A History of the Doctrine
of the Work of Christ, Vol. II* (London: Hodder & Stoughton, 1918) pp. 281–282; &
Axt-Piscalar, *Grund*, p. 136).

out the *coherence* of the idea of Incarnation with the 'divine thoughts' (concerning the world and His purposes for the world) and the 'nature of God in His character of love'.[141] This first stage in his doctrine of incarnation is to demonstrate, by preparing for the depiction of its occurrence, the *appropriateness* of the idea of incarnation to the ideas of God (ethically conceived as Love and inclined to the establishment of fellowship with the world) and humanity (as constituted capable of actively receiving God for the sake of his own and God's satisfaction). In this, of course, is Dorner's apologetic concern to provide certainty to faith by demonstrating that the object of faith hangs not on 'caprice'[142] or the accidents of creaturely history (e.g. sin), even if the actual historical form of the divine activity pertains to these (in the economy of salvation), but rather on the eternal determinations of God to establish a union with humanity in the God-man. It is the outworking of the theological method which aspired to connect to the contents of faith an objective verification. In submitting this at the concluding stage of the *Apologetic* phase of his dogmatic project, Dorner is suggesting that this verification has arrived, since the contents of faith (in Christ) provide the resources to demonstrate its certainty: that the 'idea of the God-man is cognizable as one destined to realization, not merely possible but ethically necessary'.[143] *Arrived*, however, only *together* with the depiction of its actual instantiation:

> [I]f God willed a world, and that in order to consummation, which no one can question, by logically necessary inference he willed the God-man, because in Him this consummation is attained. That it *is* found in Him is corroborated...beyond reach of doubt by Christianity.[144]

The first part of Dorner's two stage doctrine of the incarnation is, then, not the end of the beginning but the beginning of the end. In his exposition of the *reasons* for the verifiableness of the incarnation he sets out the features which will inform his characterization of the actual incarnation:

1. The intensity of the divine self-communication
2. The capacity of humanity to receive God: *finitum capax infiniti*
3. The God-man as Central Individual
4. The relationship of the God-man to the relation between God and humanity.

Since the first and second pair are connected, we shall briefly survey them together, before bringing the present chapter to a close.

[141] *SCD*, II, p. 205.
[142] Ibid.
[143] Ibid. p. 206.
[144] Ibid. p. 217.

1. The Intensity of Divine Self-communication and
Finitum Capax Infiniti

The major inference Dorner draws from the ideas of God and world is that *only* in the divine incarnation may the perfect relation between God and world be instantiated. This is occasioned by two key moves he makes with regard to the constitutions of both God and humanity (to which we have already made reference). The first is that the revelation of God is a *Self-*revelation; the second is that the vital capacity of humanity is *receptivity* to God. Dorner returns to these features and depicts the idea of divine incarnation as the only place in which they have proper purchase:

> God Himself wills to live and dwell in the absolute organ of divine revelation. In harmony with His own form of being, belonging to Him as λόγος or the Principle of revelation, he wills to possess existence and self-consciousness in man, forming with him one unity of life, willing even in the world to live His triune life. Since it is God's will in His eternal love to make an absolute communication of Himself as regards His entire communicable being, in the world-idea or world-counsel He willed not merely the spiritual existence of relative receptiveness for Him, but as Revealer or λόγος He wills absolutely such cosmical existence as is endowed with perfect receptiveness for Him and His presence.[145]

This *maximal* account of the divine involvement in the creaturely sphere as *an absolute communication of Himself* is predicated on the divine mode of being (Seinsweise[146]); and it is perhaps surprising that Dorner does not make explicit the significance of this connection. He leaves unexplained exactly *how* the fullness of the divine self-communication is related to the divine being. Later he affirms that what is not communicated is the divine 'self-existence',[147] but he gives only the trace of a reference to the doctrinal site which we suggest *ought* to be invoked in order to account properly for the insistence on the absolute *fullness* of the divine revelation. The site in question is the complex of ideas with which he has previously formed the concept of God as the 'Organism of the Absolute divine Personality'.[148] In his 'presentation of the being of God as the unity of God's acts of self-preservation [*Selbstbehauptung*] and self-communication [*Selbstmittheilung*]',[149] Dorner has already set out how he is able to posit this maximal account of revelation

[145] *SCD*, II, p. 207.
[146] *SCG*, I, p. 644.
[147] *SCD*, II, p. 208.
[148] *SCD*, I, p. 412.
[149] John Webster, 'The Divine Perfections' (unpublished).

as consistent with God's mode of being. This is so that it does not come at the expense either of His own abiding distinctiveness (since His Self-preservation and Self-communication are functions of His Self-existence), or to the detriment of the creaturely integrity of the object of the revelation (who will be preserved by God from receiving what is proper only to God Himself but not precluded from receiving God, because He remains Himself even as He gives Himself). If we make explicit the connection between these accounts (and we suggest it is a weakness of Dorner's account that he does not), then we see an understanding of incarnation being unfurled which is *enabled* by the form and structure of the Christian idea of God. With this Dorner avoids a divinizing Christology and, contra Barth, anthropology. Since God's Self-preservation and Self-communication are not opposed He *remains Himself* in His Self-communication as He unites Himself with a human who receives His 'entire communicable being' and as such is the 'embodied expression of God's eternal image in time'[150] without the creatureliness of his humanity (his *non-aseity*) being divinized.

We conclude this analysis of the incarnation as it relates to the divine *fullness* with a brief consideration of Dorner's insistence on the *finitum capax infiniti*, which he accounts for with reference to his previously expressed understanding of divine infinity:

> God must not be contemplated as a Quantum, an infinitely extended, extensively infinite quantity. Otherwise, there would be no room, so to speak, for God in the narrow limits of humanity. On the contrary, we have recognised as the innermost Essence or heart of God His intensive infinity ($\S\S 27$–32), His love, upon which everything physical in God must be regarded as dependent. But that intensive infinity, God's love and wisdom, finds room even in a human heart destined to partake in the divine likeness.[151]

The perfect being of God makes possible His full Self-revelation, and God's infinity makes possible His instantiation in a human. His infinity is not extensive but *intensive*; it is not a mere physical attribute but ethically determined. Rather than being a *limit* to divine activity, it is the very basis of its possibility. God as Love is in control of His own attributes and free to establish Himself in the particular. This flows from Dorner's ethical account of God not as Absolute Substance (subject to His physical attributes) but Absolute Personality (the eternal result and cause of His own being). God is free to establish a creaturely location capable of being this particular mode of receptivity, without detriment either to His unique Self-existence or the

---

[150] *SCD*, II, p. 207.
[151] Ibid. p. 208.

creature's *creatureliness*. It is part of its creatureliness to be receptive for God. The key to this lies, for Dorner, in the depiction of the divine essence as holy Love. Only then can the relation between God and humanity be determined in terms of holy (ethical) relations rather than the (only ever near) meeting of distinct spheres defined substantively according to their physical constitutions e.g. *extensive* infinity/finity. Dorner argues that the potential for this problem to be resolved came with the Lutheran church's development of the doctrine of Christ with the 'decisive new fundamental christological idea, that "finitum capax infiniti"'.[152]

Dorner eschews the language of 'dwelling'[153] to describe the incarnation since it does not properly express the extent to which *this* human has *received* the fullness of the divine revelation. Not merely as a passive instrument of divine activity but as the *active* receiver of God's Self-communication which, as Love, is desirous of loving response. By appealing to the Lutheran formula he observes the notion of creaturely receptivity for God, identified in his doctrine of humanity, which both defines humanity's distinctiveness but is a future-oriented capacity.

Yet with the identification of this capacity as conducive to the establishment of intensive relations between God and humanity, Dorner seeks to identify the reasons for this occurring in only one place, in one human. He suggests first that what marks out the God-man from the rest of humanity is the unique *condition* of his creatureliness willed as the 'perfect organ of revelation' who 'from the first moment of his existence in his entire person lives in a sphere of being pertaining to revelation and never separated from God'.[154] The incarnation is not a development from *within* humanity (even though it is humanity's telos); it is not an immanent self-actualization of humanity, but the act which is occasioned by God, but not 'against (human) nature'.[155] The creature may be said to *co-operate* in its completion by the manner of its reception of God. As we shall see in Chapter 5 this finds full expression in Dorner's rejection of the doctrine of the non-personality of Christ's human nature. Here we want to observe that the notion of the necessary *singularity* of the God-man finds its first point of reference in the divine action of assuming a creaturely 'shape' that 'embodies and manifests the divine life in human form'.[156] The first move is God's, and not the immanent development of the creature. In laying out the way in which this unique God-man, set apart by God, remains in essential connection with humanity (and not the *tertium quid*) Dorner presents his case using the notion of the *Central Individual*.

---

[152] *History of Development*, Div. II, Vol. I, p. 263.
[153] *SCD*, II, p. 207.
[154] Ibid. p. 206.
[155] Stephen Edmondson, *Calvin's Christology* (Cambridge: Cambridge University Press, 2004), p. 214.
[156] *SCD*, II, p. 206.

2. The God-man as Central Individual and the Relationship of the God-man to the Relation between God and Humanity

Dorner's representation of the necessary uniqueness of the God-man has several aspects. What is not present in the discussion is the identification of the incarnate one's necessarily unique role as the mediator of salvation (although he does argue that the basis of his account is no different from Anselm's 'doctrine of the necessity of the God-man in order to atonement' since it too 'flows from the perfection of God's love to us'[157]). The key features of his programme pertain to the instantiation of a *created* location as itself the scene of a perfect union with God. This will bring to perfection the *whole* creaturely realm by having at its centre a figure through whom God will be perfectly revealed to the world and in whom the world will make its perfect loving response to God. It is as the mediator of *perfection* that Dorner presents this one site: the God-man. What concerns Dorner is the depiction of the God-man as unique insofar as he alone brings to completion the entire purposes of God for creation. It is in this very singularity that his connection with the whole of humanity (and creation) is realized (and with this we notice Dorner's insistence that it is not in spite of but because of God's distinctness that He is related to the world). Dorner commends the necessity of the *one* God-man for multiple reasons, chief among which are the following:

1. It is in this one that 'absolute or perfect God-manhood'[158] alone will be realized, since (contra Baur[159] and Strauß) an incarnation in the whole of humanity would not ever come to a completion: 'a contradiction to the divine idea of the God-manhood for God never to attain what He wills, but only ever to be seeking Himself in the world.'[160] Key to the account

---

[157] Ibid. p. 217. We will suggest in Chapter 6 that Dorner does enough to demonstrate that the atonement coheres with the *general* divine disposition to the world, even if his supralapsarianism problematizes the precise place of the atonement in the eternal purposes of God.

[158] Ibid. p. 208.

[159] Thomas Koppehl has provided an exhaustive account of the debate between Dorner and Baur in the 1840s concerning the question of whether the God-man is a generic or an individual concept, cf. Koppehl, *Standpunkt*, pp. 21–35. He argues that it is in Dorner's controversy with Baur that we find the 'starting point of Dorner's christology' (p. 21), and notes the crucial move made by Dorner in opposition to Baur's 'Gattungschristologie' is the appeal to subjectivity (p. 25) rather than substance in order to see how human genus may be realized in one individual (p. 26), since the relation between God and world is not conceived in terms of the 'competition of universals' (p. 25), but the relation of subjects, since the human genus may be realized in one individual who sees himself in relation to the whole.

[160] *SCD*, II, p. 209.

(and the rejection of Schelling[161] and the left-Hegelian Strauß) is the identification of the God-man in terms of *Personality*, which requires a 'living
unity'[162] of God and humanity rather than a constant immanent search
for unity in the whole of humanity. The parallel here with Dorner's configuration of the doctrine of God as also a living unity or *Life* is obvious
and highly significant, pointing as it does to the triune *structure* of his
idea of the God-man as that which is a *complete* but *not static* unity of
the divine and human. We shall see in Chapter 5 that this completion,
since it is the divine union with a temporal creature, is not perfected
immediately in the actual incarnation but is held by Dorner to be the
result of a gradual development.;

2. It will secure for humanity its 'distinctive worth'[163] since through him it
will be united with God rather than seeking its end in itself;

3. It is the basis for the realization in the world of a 'higher religious' community, since a unified humanity needs an 'objective central personage
cognizable by all' as 'pledge to all of union with each other'.[164] Through
the individual God-man humanity (by faith in him) identifies itself as that
whose end is holy love – fellowship – with God, by becoming cognizant[165]
of the God-man's 'true humanity': perfect loving obedience to God. Human
creatures become participators in a 'perfected revelation' which is not mere
'salvation of believers' (by which we take him to mean an atomistic volun-
tarism) but the 'fellowship of believing men with each other in giving and
receiving'.[166] The connection Dorner wishes to make is clear: the individu-
ality of the God-man (with its attendant perfection) is the basis of fellowship between men and the bond of creaturely holy living.

4. The Logos has united Himself only to one human and in so doing this
one human is related to the whole of creation because the Logos is that
mode of God's being by and through whom the world has its being and
form: 'He is the Son of Man by the fact that He is the Son of God';[167]

---

[161] 'For Schelling, humanity as such is God's eternal Son' (my translation), Holte,
Vermittlungstheologie, p. 115.

[162] Holte identifies the significance of the concept of Personality advanced by Schelling
as that which for Dorner helps conceive as a 'living unity of subject and object, particular and general' the Gottmenscheit, Ibid. p. 117. The point here is that the unity
is alive (vitally whole), but not restless (endlessly seeking completion in the whole of
humanity).

[163] *SCD*, II, p. 209.

[164] Ibid. p. 210.

[165] The German text refers to the true man as 'erkennbaren', which we have used as the
basis of cognition, but take Dorner's original term to imply not merely an intellectual
appropriation but a becoming aware of this central personage, *SGC*, I, p. 648.

[166] Ibid. p. 222.

[167] Ibid. Rothermundt helpfully observes that Dorner understands 'Son of Man' to mean
merely 'man', Rothermundt, *Synthese*, p. 165, n. 92.

What these aspects coalesce to demonstrate is an idea of the God-man as one who brings the creaturely order to a unified conclusion. All created beings pertain to Him as the perfect creature and as such find their end in Him, since humanity's 'craving for God and receptiveness for God'[168] has been perfectly satisfied. As humanity is brought to completion in the God-man, so too are the divine purposes for the world, in the instantiation of an individual through whom the created order has responded in loving obedience to God: in the God-man the world answers 'Yes' to God.

Conclusion

In this account of the God-man as the fulfilment of the ideas of God and humanity set out in the first part of his system, Dorner has prepared the ground for his representation of the actual instantiation of these doctrines in the person of Jesus Christ in the second part as demonstrably true. His conclusion is centred on the question, 'Does the history of Jesus of Nazareth satisfy the demands?'[169] which he has made in the first part of his *System*. To this he answers, 'Not merely is there nothing of a historical nature that would justify the denial of this dignity (God-manhood) as belonging to Christ, but whatever *a priori* be expected to belong to the figure of the absolute God-man is given abundantly in the history of Christ.'[170] With this final flourish to the Apologetic section, in preparation of his account of *Specific* Christian doctrine, there is a recollection of the pre-eminent intentions for the project: the demonstration of the certainty of the contents of the Christian faith, the solving of the problem 'presented by Christian faith itself – the exhibition of Christianity *as truth*'.[171]

We have sought to argue that his account of the creature and the God-man, while on occasion tending towards the charge of divinization, is indebted to the details of his doctrine of God in such a way as to conceptualize the relation between God and humanity as one of communion. In this way, the Creator–creature distinction is preserved. We have, however, observed a systemic problem concerning the extent to which the soteriological import of the incarnation is reduced because of the supralapsarian structure of the project. We will see that it is a feature which becomes more obviously problematic in the details of his *Specific* doctrine, to which we turn now in Chapter 4 on the doctrine of Sin. However, while there is this ongoing concern (which we will address in the following chapters), we suggest that with Dorner's arguments concerning the Self-possession of God *in* His activity of

---

168 Ibid. p. 209.
169 Ibid. p. 284.
170 Ibid. p. 285.
171 *SCD*, I, p. 17.

Self-communication are significant moves in advancing an account of the relation between God and world – culminating in the incarnation – in which their distinction is not inimical to union. This non-competitive dimension of his proposal stands as a valuable theological contribution, even if it is accompanied by a less satisfying acknowledgement of God's reconciling activities. We will see, however, how this final question may be resolved during the course of the remaining chapters.

4

THE DOCTRINE OF SIN

Introduction

The doctrine of sin opens the second part of Dorner's *System of Christian Faith*. It functions as the *dogmatic* point of contact between his account of the idea of the God-man as the 'fixed objective principle of the Christian religion'[1] and the 'exposition'[2] of 'the way in which the consummation' of this principle 'is carried out by means of redemption'.[3] The doctrine of sin marks, therefore, the entrance to the discussion of the *actual* incarnation of God. Yet while it stands at the *structural* centre of the dogmatic arrangement, in accordance with Dorner's insistence that sin should not form the *grounds* for the depiction of the certainty of the Christian faith, it is not offered as the *explanatory* centre of the dogmatic project. Rather, it takes its place as the first port of call in the *Specific* doctrines because the 'manifestation of Christ's person and work', while not 'exclusively motivated' (that is, wholly contingent on[4]), is 'essentially *modified* by sin'.[5] Thus, as has earlier been noted, Dorner's placing of the doctrine of sin *after* the account of the idea of the God-man is intended to demonstrate that the entrance of sin does not represent the *motivation* or purpose of the divine incarnation. However, the extent to which it *is* modified means that Dorner presents his account of sin as an 'introduction' to the 'exposition of Christology'[6] without, of course, this implying *the* exhaustive justification for the incarnation. The doctrine of sin stands in the middle. It is the point of connection between the *idea* of the God-man and His *historic* manifestation; between the motivation for the incarnation and the cause of its modification.

---

[1] *SCD*, II, p. 293.
[2] Ibid. p. 294.
[3] Ibid. p. 297.
[4] Elsewhere Dorner describes such contingency as that which 'comes from without', *SCD*, III, p. 285.
[5] *SCD*, II, p. 298.
[6] Ibid. p. 299.

This is not the first time that Dorner has assessed the place of sin in the course of his dogmatic project. It was previously considered under the aspect of its 'possibility' in the doctrine of 'man's original capacity',[7] and as such was treated in relation to the conditions necessary for humanity to be posited as ethically vital.[8] The *possibility* (though, of course, not the necessity[9]) of sin in the ethical development of humankind was proposed in order to exclude the idea that original human 'goodness would be an innate quality'[10] incapable of being distracted by its opposite. Here it is treated under the aspect of its non-necessary 'realization'.[11]

A consequence of this twofold treatment of sin is the extent to which it displays Dorner's interest in locating the doctrine within the wider dogmatic project and not, as has been said of one of his contemporaries,[12] as a locus which may be expounded in isolation from his overall theological enterprise. Later he suggests of evil that its 'correct definition...depends in the last resort on the true idea of God'.[13] This demonstrates once again the decisive significance to the content and ordering of all dogmatic material of the Christian idea of God. Accordingly, Dorner explains at the outset of his exposition that the doctrine of God 'must preserve its fundamental position because of the regulative influence it exerts in reference to all principal doctrines, securing in this way systematic coherence'.[14] This means that it is *as* the doctrine of sin and evil coheres with and is informed by the specific contours of the identity of God that it is assessed. As such, it is granted dogmatic space as that which is neither outside the purview of the divine purposes for the world nor a *problem* to be delineated apart from the details of God's prior being as 'the absolutely perfect, blessed, and glorious Personality who is to be conceived in Trinitarian form'.[15] It is a clear

---

[7] *SCD*, II, p. 298.

[8] Ibid. p. 73.

[9] Humanity did not become ethically engaged *by* sinning. This is, according to Dorner, merely the resolution of Manichaeism, Ibid. p. 74.

[10] Ibid.

[11] Ibid. p. 298.

[12] Rothermundt accuses Rothe of providing a doctrine of sin which has no connection with the rest of his theological system, but instead seeking a merely rational explanation of this problem. He compares this with Dorner's strategy which works out the doctrine of sin from the corresponding concepts of God and man (even if those concepts are in themselves problematic or 'zu kritisieren war' [p. 171]), Rothermundt, *Synthese*, pp. 171–173. Furthermore, as we will see later on in the chapter, Dorner himself criticizes Julius Müller for separating the consciousness of sin from any Christological considerations. This point is ably noted by Christine Axt-Piscalar in *Ohnmächtige Freiheit* (Tübingen: Mohr-Siebeck, 1996), p. 34.

[13] *SCD*, II, p. 359.

[14] Ibid.

[15] Ibid. p. 360.

example of Dorner's trinitarian agenda. Yet, as we observed in Chapter 1, this commitment is allied to the apprehension of Jesus Christ as the 'fundamental idea of Christianity'.[16] As such the doctrine of sin – *regulated* by the idea of God as Absolute Personality – is situated as an *introduction* to Christology since it is as realized sin pertains to the actualization of the necessary God-man that it has its proper place.

This is indicative of a singular, systemic eagerness to see Jesus of Nazareth, whom Dorner has identified at the close of the Fundamental section as the one who putatively fulfils the criteria of the ideal God-man, depicted *with certainty* as the *God-man* who brings to *completion* the divine intentions for the creation. When we join Dorner in his account of realized sin, his initial apologetic interest in seeking scientific verification for the truthfulness of the Christian faith (by its reconciliation 'with thought'[17]) is brought back into direct connection with the actual form in which the 'fundamental Christian idea [of] God-manhood' *occurred*. This is so that its truthfulness can be articulated in terms of (but not reduced to) the fittedness of Jesus of Nazareth for the task of bringing *perfection* '[a point which Apologetics has to place in the foreground]…solely by means of *redemption*'.[18] Since the idea of the God-man has been accounted as the only appropriate end and explanation of the ideas of God and world, what remains is the need to demonstrate how this Jesus meets these demands in actuality. Accordingly, Dorner defines the *purpose* of the doctrine of sin as seeking the depiction and definition of evil and sin in order to contribute to the demonstration of how perfection is brought by the God-man, via the occasions of sin and salvation, to the world. Thus, in his introduction to the doctrine of sin, he states:

> Our present business is to exhibit the relation in which Christ, who came into existence despite sin by a volition of God's transcendent, almighty love, stands to sin, in order to make it clear how he came on account of sin, and for the purpose of destroying the existing state of sin. Only such an exposition can give us the more concrete image of his historic manifestation and work.[19]

Sin, in its realized form is therefore a doctrine whose role it is to serve the purpose of the proper depiction of Jesus Christ as the God-man; contributing to the explanation of how the necessary idea actually occurred by providing the resources for the stable representation of his actual manifestation. This conceptualization is part of a strategy intended to display the connection of

[16] *SCD*, I, p. 28.
[17] *SCD*, II, p. 293.
[18] Ibid. p. 298.
[19] Ibid.

idea and history. While it *relativizes*, by reducing, the *dogmatic* significance of the doctrine of sin (by refusing to make sin the basis of the incarnation[20]), it does not seek its removal, since it is the immediate cause of the incarnation. As a result, it also provides the foundational insight of the Christian personality since sin (and its removal) is the backdrop to the new moral agency of the Christian who is enabled to live in free obedience to the good in contrast to the old life of wilful orientation to the bad:

> The Christian Church knows itself to be a Church *redeemed* by Christ from sin. It knows Christ not merely as a Perfector...but as One who came to perfect it solely by means of redemption.[21]

Yet while the reduction of its dogmatic significance does not *intend* to evacuate from sin its important place in the construction of an account of the actual person and work of Christ we suggest, because of Dorner's supralapsarianism, his account of sin is exposed to the charge that it fails to provide sufficient justification for the God-man to come as *Saviour*. We will suggest that Dorner's treatment displays a consistent concern to cohere with the terms and contents of his key dogmatic principles (originating in his doctrine of God), and yet the question asked by Anselm concerning the *weight* of sin[22] is one on which he appears exposed. It has been suggested that the appreciation of the gravity of sin functions as a useful aid to evaluating theories of reconciliation,[23] and we suggest that Dorner's theory of sin at times seems to suffer from an *under*weighing, and as we shall see in Chapter 6, this continues to be a question in his treatment of the *weight* of the sacrifice of atonement. It is a problem which Søren Kierkegaard identified (somewhat elliptically) as not properly answering the question of *why* Christ 'came into the world'.[24] We will set out the details of Dorner's account, following the broad contours of his plan, and seek to lay out the grounds for these concerns.[25] We begin with a discussion of Dorner's analysis of the nature or essence of evil.

[20] Dorner had earlier identified this as necessary to the recognition of the non-contingency and 'absolute significance' of the 'historical in Christ', *History of Development*, Div II, Vol. III, p. 236.

[21] *SCD*, II, p. 298.

[22] St Anselm, *Cur deus homo?*, Book 1, Chapter 21, (Edinburgh: John Grant, 1909), pp. 49–52.

[23] H. R. Mackintosh argues that there is a direct link between the accounts of the seriousness attributed to sin and accounts of forgiveness and therefore atonement, *The Christian Experience of Forgiveness* (London: Nisbet and Co., 1934), p. 51,

[24] *Søren Kierkegaard's Journals and Papers*, F–K, Volume 2, ed. and trans. Howard V. Hong and Edna H. Hong (Bloomington and London: Indiana University Press), 1970, p. 196.

[25] Dorner's theory and our criticism of it recalls the observations made of Zwingli's doctrine of sin as 'Erbprest' – original weakness – rather than 'Erbsünd' – original

THE DOCTRINE OF SIN

I. The Nature of Evil

Dorner begins his formal account of sin by seeking the 'principle or the essence of evil', maintaining that 'it is possible to understand this without affirming or knowing anything definite beforehand respecting its ultimate origin'.[26] This confident[27] (though somewhat unconventional[28]) ordering of the material is not incidental, but recalls the decisive principle with which he constructed his doctrine of God (leading to the interlinking of attributes and proofs): 'There is no idea of a thing apart from its essential characteristics.'[29] The privileging of the question of essence, while not excluding the question of origins (which would lead to the problem of assuming evil a normal part of the created order),[30] typifies Dorner's belief in the superiority of doctrinal excavation which hangs not merely on the *description* of occurrences (in this case, the historical *circumstances* in which sin and evil entered the world through Adam), but rather relies on the explanatory power which comes from the *definition* of the principles according to which an 'actual fact'[31] may have (and does have) existence, through connection and deduction from the 'true idea of God'.[32]

In the present case, of course, it is the quest for the proper definition of the *essence* of *evil* which takes precedence over the account of its *origins* since, according to this understanding, an affirmation of the latter would not provide sufficient resources to account for how evil and sin pertain to the *idea of man as he is intended to relate to God*.[33] To make decisive the question of derivation would be to make the doctrine of man in his *primal state* – as he *is* and not as he is *intended* – the 'regulative influence'

---

sin – which led him to be accused of giving 'insufficient grounds for condemnation'. For more on this controversy see Henri Blocher, *Original Sin* (Leicester: Apollos, 1997), p. 15, n. 2.

[26] *SCD*, II, p. 299.

[27] '[D]efinition is not derivation, – a point certainly often overlooked', Ibid. p. 300.

[28] Ernst Luthardt provides his summary of the Lutheran tradition's approach to sin by considering the essence of sin (§42, pp. 169–171) *after* the doctrines of Fall (§40, pp. 160–162), and Original Sin (§41, pp. 162–168), *Kompendium der Dogmatik,* (Leipzig, Dörffling und Franke, 1893).

[29] *SCD*, I, p. 190.

[30] *SCD*, II, p. 300.

[31] Ibid. p. 299.

[32] *SCD*, II, p. 359.

[33] Interestingly, Dorner commends Julius Müller for increasing the amount of space devoted to the question of the essence of sin in the 1844 revision (*Die christliche Lehre von der Sünde*, 2 Bde [Breslau: Josef Mar, 1844]) of the 1839 work *Vom Wesen und Grund der Sünde* (Breslau: Josef Mar, 1839) (although Dorner confusingly refers to an *1838* edition), in his review of the updated work in *H. Reuters Repertorium für theologische Literatur und kirchliche Statistik*, Berlin, 1845, Bd. I, p. 162.

121

on all the 'principal doctrines',[34] a position which Dorner contends the Christian idea of God alone must have. An appeal to humanity's pre-fallen origins might, he suggests, appear more 'natural...since the normal must decide what the abnormal is'. Yet of this primal state he contends 'we have no immediate knowledge as of God' and furthermore, as seen in the previous chapter, since the first human pair did not represent the 'absolute realization of the idea of man'[35] they may not be referred to as the pristine template from which to assess the extent or nature of the problem of evil.

Thus, consistent with his determination of the human creature as one whose final and not original status is the most consequential and graspable[36] subject of theological focus, Dorner begins with the question of essence before origins because the most pressing question is not how the state of affairs can be explained by recourse to historical analysis.[37] Indeed, this is not, for Dorner even the most *difficult* question, since what is required to account for sin's entrance into the world is, apparently, merely a recognition of the human creature's 'imperfect spiritual beginnings, where there is still a possibility of deception'.[38] Rather, most pressing is the definition of the *essence* of evil because what must be accounted for is the way in which this human creature, who is destined for fellowship, can be defined as such even *as he is accounted sinful*. Therefore, he must offer a definition of evil which will cohere with the teleological structure of God's purposes for the world. He makes two key moves in order to attain this end. First, he makes a link between the creature's sinfulness – and its punitive consequences, the terms of which, we will go on to suggest, are problematical – and his *capacity for redemption*. Second, he defines evil as an *abnormal* development in the divinely appointed relational structures for which the world is intended. We will attend first to the second of these features, since his teleological exposition of sin provides the background to the subsequent and, we suggest, more pressing question of *how* such abnormality attracts the status of liability to condemnation and invokes the attendant question of how the inheritance or transmission of sin relates to the instancing of guilt. We suggest that it is in this discussion that Dorner's approach appears most problematical. But we begin with the notion of abnormality in order to prepare the ground for this discussion.

---

[34] *SCD*, II, p. 359.

[35] Ibid. p. 360.

[36] Ibid. p. 360.

[37] This is not to say that he has no place for the notion of an actual, historical Fall. Indeed, as Axt-Piscalar points out, he criticizes J. Müller for reducing the significance of Adam's Fall for the rest of humanity, *SGC*, II.i., p. 158, *Ohnmächtige Freiheit*, p. 118.

[38] *SCD*, II, p. 381.

a. Sin as Abnormal Development

Central to Dorner's depiction of the essence of evil is its deviation from the purposes for which God intended the world. This leads him to provide an account which sees evil as both the 'opposite or contradiction' of God as the 'absolute Good',[39] and as that which pertains to the frustration of the plans for the *unity* of God and man for which the world was created. Accordingly, we see displayed the connectedness (or as Dorner himself says 'mutual relation'[40]) of the two aspects of this theory in the two-handed definition of evil (in terms of its *form* and *contents*) which he furnishes at the midpoint of his thetic exposition of the nature of evil (§77). We will survey first the proposition concerning the form of evil, before turning to its contents.

1. The Form of Evil

> The general...nature of...evil generally, is as to form a God-opposing *abnormity, disturbing the right relation of the spirit as well to the corporeal, natural life in a downward aspect and to the world, as to the divine life in an upward aspect. But what the abnormal is appears from the normal, i.e. the true ethical idea of God, whose image the rational creature is meant to be in unity with Him who is the principle of all good.*[41]

According to this definition, as to its form, evil is the disturbance of right relations to the world and to God. Yet crucially, for Dorner, this disturbance is abnormal not merely because it is in discord with the goodness instituted and instantiated by God, but much more because it is the deviation *from* the God who has designated the rational creature as destined to be his image (a point we observed in the previous chapter[42]) through being united with Him. As such, it marks also the disruption of the creature's own proper teleological constitution. Since this is the case, Dorner is loathe to attribute to evil an essential being (notwithstanding his own use of the term *essence* of evil) except as a merely *derivative* stage in the divinely constituted and maintained progress of the world. As he concludes of those theories of evil which appeal to some kind of dualist metaphysics, while good 'can be conceived without contradiction even apart from evil' this is not so with evil, since it is 'contradiction to something good'[43] and as such is not *absolute*.[44] Yet to

---

[39] Ibid. p. 360.
[40] Ibid. p. 382.
[41] Ibid. p. 382.
[42] Ibid. p. 83.
[43] Ibid. p. 361.
[44] On this point, Dorner finds himself in agreement with Müller who was also, as has been correctly noted by Stanley Russell, sure that evil could not be accounted for in terms of a 'higher necessity', 'Two Nineteenth Century Theologies of Sin – Julius

speak of evil as a derivative *stage* does not imply that it is a *necessary* phase in the 'way of moral development'.[45]

This view of evil, which he locates in Schiller[46] and Hegel, is found wanting by Dorner because it is predicated on an erroneous view of freedom, according to which only the opposition – and not the obedience – to the 'absolute universal law'[47] marks the stride of humanity from 'mere moral indifference, immaturity'[48] and pre-morality to free action: 'Hegel calls Paradise a garden of animals and exit from it the beginning of human development.'[49] This view defines evil as the necessary precondition for the coming to fruition of proper creaturely consciousness. As such evil is characterized as a necessary corollary to the progress from pre-moral innocence to proper ethical engagement. Dorner's inevitable rejection of this view displays a consistency with his dogmatic convictions concerning the relationship between ethical necessity and freedom (exemplified in his doctrine of God). It manifests a desire to refute the idea of the inevitability of evil for the normal ethical progress of the human creature to fulness.

However, while Dorner seeks to close off the dualist tendencies which attribute to evil a substantial essence, he affords the traditional Reformation definition of sin as *privatio* only modified significance. It is not that it has no place in his account. He refers, without disparagement, to the Reformation doctrine of evil as that which is different from good not in a 'mere quantitative sense, a minus of good' since 'in the spirit itself there is not a mere *defectus*, but an *affectus* which ought not to be'.[50] There is thus an acknowledgement of the insight that privation is an 'active, dynamic and

Müller and Søren Kierkegaard', in *Scottish Journal of Theology*, Vol. 40, No. 2 (1987), p. 235.

[45] *SCD*, II, p. 367.
[46] Friedrich Schiller, *Etwas über die erste Menschengesellschaft*, Bd. IX (Haag: Hartmann, 1838), p. 387 ff.
[47] *SCD*, II, p. 367.
[48] Ibid. pp. 367–368.
[49] Ibid. p. 367, n. 1. The trace of such a notion may be found in Marheineke's treatment of evil, which he deals with within the confines of his doctrine of creation, Philipp Marheineke, *Die Grundlehren der christlichen Dogmatik als Wissenschaft* (Berlin: Duncker und Humbolt, 1827), §260–268, pp. 153–159. It is highly significant that Dorner distinguishes clearly between those doctrines which pertain only to divine agency (e.g. creation) and those which pertain to the secondary causality within the created order. He is determined to find the source of evil in the creature and not the creator, and his ordering of material is a formal indicator of this. Marheineke's reading of the Fall sees it as a consequence of the necessary discernment of the difference between good and evil required for the 'kindlichen Unschuld' to become proper self-consciousness, Ibid. p. 151. In this detail alone, we see a variance with Dorner, for whom it is not in the distinction of good and evil, but in the free obedience to the good that completion comes to the human creature.
[50] *SCD*, II, p. 347.

destructive force',[51] and as such, Dorner is in agreement with this aspect of the Reformation tradition.[52] Yet the teleological structure of his anthropology (with its christological orientation) leads him to account for the variance between what *is* and what *ought* to be in a way which differs significantly from that tradition. While he posits evil as a 'defect of that which ought to exist, a defect forming a contradiction to the idea of man – that finite being',[53] the standard by which the discrepancy is assessed is not the human creature's *justitia originalis* – which is the basis of his original 'likeness to God'[54] – but what he *will* be or, more precisely, *ought* to be, according to the divine intentions. This is the dogmatic move which ultimately leads the concept of evil as *privation* or – as Dorner more often speaks – *defect* to be considered in conjunction with the divine image *as it finds its fulfilment in the God-man*. This reconstitution of the concept of privation brings to it the idea, crucial for Dorner, that the entrance of evil to the creaturely realm pertains primarily to the divine *intentions* for the world – the union of God and man in the theanthropos – and not primarily to creaturely origins.

Furthermore, since this union is one which is conceived in ethical-developmental terms, with its completion arriving with the conjunction of free obedience to the ethical necessary, it is the disjunction of this arrangement which holds Dorner's attention most appreciably. In his critique of the argument that the Law *'springs from sin'*,[55] which he finds untenable on the grounds that it means that evil is 'traceable to the Creator'[56] (since unless there is an 'obligatory good' which precedes evil, there would be no 'violation of what ought to be'[57]) – in partial agreement with this otherwise discarded theory – he concludes:

> Holy Scripture does not call every imperfection evil, least of all the inevitable imperfection of the beginning. Man is not made evil by the fact of his will still having duties to fulfil in order to self-improvement, but simply by his will not overtaking the duty of the moment, but instead obstinately lagging behind. Thus, according to the apostle [Paul], it is certain that so little does the law spring from sin, that it is rather the objective ground of sin's possibility.[58]

---

[51] G. C. Berkouwer, *Sin* (Grand Rapids: Eerdmans, 1971), p. 259.
[52] Bavinck defines sin as 'a privation of the moral perfection a human ought to possess', Herman Bavinck, *Reformed Dogmatics, Sin and Salvation in Christ*, Vol. 3, ed. John Bolt, trans. John Vriend, (Grand Rapids: Baker, 2006), p. 137.
[53] *SCD*, II, p. 363.
[54] Ibid. p. 347.
[55] Ibid. p. 307.
[56] Ibid. p. 308.
[57] Ibid.
[58] Ibid. p. 308.

It is as evil is actualized as a consequence of the human creature's ethical *development* that Dorner concedes privation as the disconnection between what the creature *ought* to do, in order to move ever closer to the completion of his intended identity as the divine image bearer, and what he *does* do. Accordingly, the decisive metaphors which he uses to describe this state of affairs are those associated with false progress:

> [I]nstead of forward, there is backward movement, which ever originates abnormal forms of development; or, to change the figure, instead of advance in a straight line, there is divergence into a bypath, return from which alone can give salvation.[59]

Sin is, then, a teleological disorder; but since the human creature's proper telos is 'to *be in unity with Him* who is the principle of all good',[60] it issues forth, not merely as *objectless* disorder, but as a disunity with the *purposing God*. In this the creature refuses both its designation as that created sphere which has a particular and unique identity – as destined for union with God – and as a dependent creature with responsibilities to the Creator – to be obedient to God as good: '[E]vil, in forming a false centre of the powers, withdraws them from their destination, and sets them in contradiction to their nature.'[61] In this way, evil is properly conceived as the opposite of *love* for God, ethically conceived as the 'unity of self-affirmation and surrender', and issues forth in the redirection of those constituent features of holy love (allowing Dorner to configure his account so as to incorporate *both* selfishness and sensuousness as the decisive components of sin) to 'God-opposing surrender' and 'God-opposing self-affirmation'.[62] Thus, the form of evil is marked out by theological hostility. The way in which this hostility is manifest is surveyed in the second proposition.

2. The Contents of Evil

> *Regarded as to contents, a God-opposing,* perverted love of the creature *is included in sensuousness as in spiritual selfishness, in false surrender as in self-affirmation of the personality....To exclude love to God, is to exclude the primal image and principle of true love, and to give to the finite that place in the love of the heart which is due only*

---

[59] *SCD*, II, p. 364. Dorner's use of such metaphors is, of course, not incidental, but consonant with the shift, which we observed of his doctrine of God away from Absolute Substance to that of Personality, in order to accommodate the idea that God is Life: it is a shift towards *mobility* as a divine characteristic, and the references to sin as the leaving of a path is, we suggest, a consequence of this in Dorner's dogmatic construction.

[60] Ibid. p. 382.

[61] Ibid. p. 400.

[62] Ibid.

> to God. *All false creature-love has therefore a coeval alienation from*
> *God for its coefficient....But therewith a separation from the abso-*
> *lute source of life is implied, although not at once an absolute one.*
> *This* alienation from God is in contradiction to the nature of man,
> because loving connection with God is the constituent of that nature.
> (my italics)[63]

The contents of evil, thus, represent a decisive turn towards the creature. In
this determination of perverted love as that which includes *both* sensuousness
and selfishness, Dorner demonstrates his independence from his contemporaries Julius Müller and Richard Rothe,[64] as well as that part of the dogmatic
tradition which has tended to see the essence of evil in *either* sensuousness *or*
selfishness.[65] Rather, he suggests that sensuousness and selfishness are 'merely
different stages of one and the same moral evil'.[66] This dogmatic move is significant since it displays the extent to which Dorner seeks to depict both sensuousness and selfishness together, when correctly oriented, as vital aspects of
the progress towards the creature's proper end. That is to say, sensuousness
is defined by Dorner as '*false surrender*'[67] only when it is *not* accompanied
by 'self-affirmation'[68] of the kind which sees 'self-improvement'[69] coming by
way of freely conforming to the designated means of attaining perfection
(Dorner does not, as Pannenberg correctly notes, say that 'self-centeredness
of life is itself sinful',[70] since the 'self-affirmation of the sensuous-spiritual
nature of man is an essential side of goodness' because it is the basis and not
contradiction of the human creature's capacity to serve others 'in accordance with its complete idea'.[71]). Furthermore, '*false self-affirmation*' occurs
when it does not surrender to God in 'self-sufficiency' and may even despise
'corporeity'.[72] Thus, false self-affirmation and sensuousness are conceived as
indicators of 'one and the same moral evil'[73] (even though they may occur at

---

[63] Ibid. p. 383.

[64] Dorner rejects Rothe's view that selfishness is the product of sensuousness, and
Müller's view that sensuousness is the product of selfishness, Ibid. p. 382. It seems
that Bavinck too agrees with Dorner's assessment, *Sin and Salvation in Christ*,
p. 152.

[65] For a clear account of this fluctuating doctrinal history, see Hendrikus Berkhof,
Christian Faith, pp. 195.

[66] *SCD*, II, p. 385.

[67] Ibid. p. 382.

[68] Ibid. p. 383.

[69] Ibid. p. 308.

[70] Wolfhart Pannenberg, *Systematic Theology*, Vol. II, trans. Geoffrey W. Bromiley
(Edinburgh: T & T Clark, 1994), p. 260.

[71] *SCD*, II, p. 379.

[72] Ibid. p. 389.

[73] Ibid. p. 386.

different stages in the human creature[74]): the *'perverted love of the creature'* and its 'coeval *alienation from God'*.[75]

These conclusions about the nature of evil display obvious continuity with the teleological account of the human creature which he lays out in the first section. However, it remains unclear to what extent the form and contents of evil are to be considered as 'chargeable with guilt'.[76] Since evil has been accounted as an abnormal development and the return to the proper road as the basic definition of salvation, we must now assess his notions of its status as the object of divine censure. We will first address this question by way of his account of the transmission or universality of sin. The way in which sin is said to acquire the status of guilt will prepare us for the final section on the decisive nature of the actual incarnation. In it we will see how Dorner's concern to configure the advancement of sin to guilt according to the concept of *ethical personality* impacts and informs his account of its relation to the crucial topos of the *actual* incarnation.

II. Evil and Guilt

Dorner treats the question of the culpability of evil in two parts. He begins his account in the latter stages of his section on the nature of evil,[77] before laying out the theory in relation to the *problematic*[78] of sin's universality in the section on the origin of evil. He treats first the concept of guilt in relation to actualized evil and the free-will of the human creature, since evil 'cannot be regarded as the work of Nature or physical necessity' but the 'will has an essential part therein'.[79] Afterwards, he addresses the question in terms of the relationship between the individual and the genus. As we have already suggested, it is the first question which holds the most importance for Dorner

---

[74] Dorner suggests that self-affirmation represents a higher stage of evil since it is marked by a 'greater energy of will' than the rather more passive 'deification of the world', *SCD*, II, p. 385.

[75] Ibid. p. 383.

[76] Ibid. p. 397.

[77] Ibid. §78, pp. 397–405.

[78] F. R. Tennant states that the problem for modern theology was the 'necessity of always correlating the sinful and the guilty and making them exactly coextensive terms. *It retains original sin; it repudiates original guilt*' (my italics), *The Origin and Propagation of Sin* (Cambridge: Cambridge University Press, 1902), p. 20. Gunther Wenz summarizes the self-conscious modern Subject as wanting 'selbst schuld', and quotes the eighteenth-century theologian J. G. Töllner's assertion: 'Wir haben in Adam nichts verloren', to exemplify the prevailing dogmatic trend to speak of guilt only in terms of 'Selbstverfehlung', 'Vom Unwesen der Sünde', in *Kerygma und Dogma*, Vol. 30 (1984), p. 298.

[79] *SCD*, II, p. 397.

since the 'recognition of (sin's universality) does not depend upon a definite theory of the origin of evil and its universal spread, but is already certain empirically'.[80] However, the question of origins still has a place in the dogmatic depiction of evil since it provides, subsequently, the grounds for seeing how evil is, according to its 'nature',[81] that which is *necessarily* universal. We will follow Dorner's ordering and set out the details of the essence of evil as it relates both to acts and inherency; and map out the way in which this configuration relates to the question of origins.

a. The Essence of Evil and Its Relation to Freedom and the Will

Dorner comes to speak positively of the relationship between evil and guilt first in a critique of the great nineteenth-century ponerologist Julius Müller. His comments come as he lays out the grounds for distinguishing between the different stages of evil – following their two chief forms of sensuousness and selfishness – according to which the decisive factor is the extent to which they 'participate in energy of will and consciousness, or in the principle of freedom'.[82] Yet, even though he has himself noted a connection between the different *stages* of evil and the operation of the will, he finds himself at variance with Müller who seeks to make the connection between evil and freedom absolute:

> Will and freedom come into view in all evil at least as consenting, if not as already existing, still as future. We cannot go so far as to say, that what is not due to free personal volition and conscious free act is morally indifferent, and cannot wear the character of abnormity and absolute wrong. No doubt guilt and punishment are so closely connected with freedom when already existing, that they are conditioned by it. But we cannot with Müller resolve the idea of evil into that of personal guilt. We cannot acknowledge evil merely where guilt is found. Insensibility to God, unlovingness or hate, wherever they are found in a rational being, are contrary to the idea of man, abnormal, nay absolutely wrong, and just so ungodly love of the world. We must therefore regard as wrong not merely purely spiritual conscious selfishness, and sensuousness as wrong for its own sake, but every abuse, every perversion of powers and spheres, contrary to man's moral duty. Since the law maintains his moral destination, it condemns even involuntary sin and appeals from the present absence of freedom to a freedom at least possible hereafter, which it is man's duty to acquire.[83]

---

[80] *SCD*, III, p. 11.
[81] Ibid.
[82] *SCD*, II, p. 385.
[83] Ibid. p. 386.

With this *Anmerkung,* Dorner lays out the principle insights by which he orders his account of the scope and reach of the guiltiness of evil. The will is acknowledged, in agreement with his earlier doctrine of man, as having an 'essential part'[84] in the (future) possibility and actual instantiation of evil (since, as we have seen, it cannot be regarded as the work of 'Nature or physical necessity'[85]). However, as he is at pains to point out, this does not exhaust the matter, since evil is to be acknowledged even *without* its being directly caused by the free motions of the will (viz. Müller). For Dorner, this would provide too narrow a view of evil and its repercussions (both vertical and horizontal) and overlook the wholly negative view of evil not merely as the *manifestation* of the wrong but of the *absence* of the good. As such, the status of evil as culpable may be extended even to those forms or occurrences of evil which are not caused directly by the will. Thus, 'even involuntary sin'[86] is subject to condemnation. Highly instructive in this regard is his representation of the twofold or, as he (rather inelegantly) puts it, the 'amphibiological'[87] character of guilt. Evil may be attributed as guilty first because it is *caused* by the will:

> [T]he will emerges in particular conscious acts. Thus it becomes a causality, to which the action must be assigned by logical necessity. The first, in itself still amphibiological, signification of *guilt* is just this, to affirm that the will has become the cause of an action.[88]

This, we suggest, posits the idea of guilt in terms of *responsible* action, since the will does not appear in a vacuum but is that aspect of the human creature which manifests its ethical constitution according to the constitution of the human creature as having a highly specified telos. However, this is only the first signification of sin as guilt, since it is finally established as such by its *contrariness*:

> If this action was evil, and was therefore contrariety to the law and its just claim upon the man, the right of the law is not annihilated by his disregarding it. Based on God's own will, that right stands in its inviolable sanctity, it renounces not its claim on man. On the contrary, that

[84] *SCD,* II, p. 397.
[85] Ibid.
[86] Ibid. p. 386.
[87] The 1860 edition of *Wörterbuch der Deutschen Sprache,* von Daniel Sanders, (Leipzig: Otto Wigand, 1860), gives as a definition of *amphibolisch* 'zweideutig' (two-sided), p. 29. Presumably Dorner's use of this term is intended to convey the two-sided aspect of guilt.
[88] *SCD,* II, p. 397.

claim remains binding upon him, and...the idea of guilt thus receiving a more *intensive* signification. (my italics)[89]

This affords to the culpability of evil, as that which is caused by the will, the idea that it is so because of its conclusive connection with God's *own* will. While the will is indubitably involved in the attribution to evil of guilt, it is because it comes into conflict with *God's* will (and the inescapable *right*) that the guiltiness of the evil caused by the will does not *end* with that act. It is so because it is the human creature – who has the will to cause either good or evil acts – who is made guilty by this sequence of causality and connection (to God) and not merely the will or its acts themselves:

> First, the law does not describe his act as culpable, but himself, so far as his personal will combined with the act, depreciates the worth of his life;

and

> Secondly, since by the evil act both a good is neglected, which man was under obligation to do, and the validity and honour of the law are called in question, the evil carries guilt with it in the sense that something neglected has to be made good.[90]

The human creature is bound up with the acts of his will and in his evil action is also the passing over of his duties. This means, for Dorner, that the guiltiness of evil extends further than its immediate causal relation to the will. It is the will of the *creature* and not merely the *will* of the creature which is in an accountable relationship to God and His ethical demands. Accordingly, it is not merely with individual acts that the locus of evil resides. Even 'law refers not merely to acts, but also to states,' because its concern is not merely to 'have legal acts, but also to regulate Being, the latter being the consequence of the conjunction of the act and the disposition'.[91] It is the creature's *life* – as the instantiation, but not aggregation of its acts – which represents the decisive source of ethical assessment. The crucial template for this assessment (which Dorner invokes again in connection with the question of whether evil is avoidable even if the will is *not* free) is the human creature's ordained telos: 'the divine idea of man'.[92] This, Dorner argues, is the basis for any determination of the culpability of evil: if the creature, whether on account of actual or inherent evil, is at ethical developmental variance with

---

[89] Ibid.
[90] Ibid. p. 398.
[91] Ibid. p. 402.
[92] Ibid. p. 405.

his teleological destination. This is the key feature of the account, and it is this insight which forms the centre of his definition of the relation between the universality of sin and the guilt of the individual which he details in the second section on origins. According to this framework, the assessment of the idea of guilt must be made within the context of the ethical 'development or history'[93] of the human creature. We will turn to the specifics of his treatment now and seek to lay out the way in which he configures his account according to this principle.

b. The Origin of Evil and Its Universal Spread and Culpability

As the individual evil deed does not vanish without traces, but produces an evil state (eine böse Zuständlichkeit), so inherent evil (das zuständliche Böse) cannot remain isolated in such a species as man; the community is seized thereby, and that not simply by the agency of teaching, example, and a common evil spirit; a still more original mode of its continuous passage from one individual to another is established in the nature of man as a secondary causality, by which the origination of other human beings is brought about, as well as, on the other hand, in the nature of evil which perverts the various powers and functions of human nature, and having become inherent draws the coherence of the race into the sphere of its power.[94]

As we have sought to display, Dorner's account of the culpability of evil as residing not merely in acts of the will finds further, detailed, expression in his understanding of the way in which individual evil deeds produce evil states at a universal level. From the extract given above we see that his initial attention is drawn to the *connectedness* of humanity as the general basis for sin's universality, together with the very nature of evil itself as that which tends towards proliferation and escalation on account of its perverting character. Yet this account of the reason for evil's universality is distinctly different from the question of universal guilt. The way in which he lays out the relation between this universal or generic sin and the guilt of the individual reflects his concern to see these two factors affirmed without detriment to 'personal moral freedom, nor the truth of the idea of guilt, nor the ethical idea of God'.[95] We will set out now the major features of his suggestion.

c. The Problem of Original Sin

Dorner arrives at his positive thesis after assessing what he depicts as the two contrary streams within ecclesial tradition which he sees as emphasizing

[93] *SCD*, III, p. 59.
[94] Ibid. p. 42.
[95] Ibid. p. 43.

too much either the individual or generic character of sin's universality. According to his review, those theories which seek to locate evil merely in the continual misappropriation of freedom (he cites, of course, Pelagius,[96] and places Müller's theory of the pre-temporal fall in the same category[97]) fail because they are unable to account properly for sin's universal persistence: 'Whence then the universality of evil if every individual begins his life pure and fully free?'[98] Yet the problem is more than merely about the demonstration of evil's unbroken pervasiveness, but pertains to the question of how humanity *en masse* exists in a state of unity, crucially, in relation to the universal significance and scope of redemption (on this point we recall of course the christological focus of Dorner's treatment). An underplaying of the generic character of sin threatens the universal applicability of the redemption as well as the more particular, though integral, point of the relation of the God-man to all human creatures:

> The slackening of the significance of the coherence of the race in reference to sin must also have important consequences for the homousia of Christ with us, for the doctrine of the atonement and that of the church.[99]

Yet while it is the problem of the genus which besets those theories which foreground the freedom of the individual, the reverse is true of those accounts which he sees as *focusing* only on the genus (he identifies this component in the Formula of Concord[100]):

> Redemption must also be transformed into a merely physical process. If all sins arise from the nature of Adam, then do his sins also arise from his nature? If not, but if they arise from his freedom still his act is not

---

[96] Ibid. p. 44.

[97] Ibid. p. 48 ff.

[98] Ibid. p. 45.

[99] Ibid. p. 48.

[100] He suggests that there is in fact a double-sided character to the Formula since it also seeks to maintain the freedom of the individual with regard to guilt. Dorner's critique of the federal view is, of course, a critique of the Augustinian tradition. He offers, elsewhere, a more detailed analysis of Augustine's account of original sin and the law of inheritance. While he sees great 'merit' (*SCD*, II, p. 341) in his system – mostly because it at least sought to uphold the place of individuals in the responsibility for sin by positing them as having participated in Adam's act (Ibid. p. 341) – he sees this conclusion as undervaluing post-Fall free will, as well as making inexplicable the Fall by investing the 'original state with a perfection which anticipates the work of freedom' (Ibid. p. 342). In all of this, of course, Dorner is resisting what he sees as the exclusivity of Augustine's notion of salvation as entirely 'God's work in virtue of absolute and particular predestination', Ibid.

ours. His personality cannot pertain to all his posterity. A physical constitution may be common to many, but not a personality. From Adam's
nature, which we possess, his first sin cannot be derived without falling
into some mode of deterministic thought...all these theories of representation, they may regard Adam as the principium et caput seminale
or federale, fail to present an equalisation of Adam and his posterity,
and just as little present an actual explanation of the enigma.[101]

What this part of the doctrinal tradition fails in is a proper regard for the
ethical constitution of the human creature as *personality*. The federal vision
(as exemplar of the generic model) does not adequately account for the
way in which ethical responsibility comes with the development of *personal*
responsibility. While Adam may be the one through whom sin entered the
world of irresistibly interconnected humanity, he alone is neither responsible for evil's persistence or the source of our guilt. Rather, unique though
Adam is as the first sinner and bequeather of sin to the genus, to set him
apart as exceptional and decisive is to remove ourselves as his heirs from
the responsibility for sin. Furthermore, since guilt is the product of 'personal
(not generic) responsibility',[102] all appeals to *culpa hereditaria* rest merely on
'physical' and not, as he sees it, ethical definitions of how the good is instantiated (bringing Dorner, of course, back to his guiding principle of the idea of
God as ethical Personality). While Adam hands to his descendents a *corruptio
humanae naturae hereditaria*, it is not passed over as 'personal punishment'
and inherited guilt but instead as 'inherent abnormity and irregularity'.[103]
The *connection* of the race (Gattungszusammenhangs[104]) means that the sin
of the parents passes to the children because the individual is constituted
as such not in opposition to but on the *basis* of his relationship to the race.
Thus, the 'individual is nothing isolated; being thought and willed in and
with the thought of the race, the individual is consummated by means of the
race as original causality likewise at hand and endowed and conserved by
God with power to act'.[105]

   In this arrangement we see an important reference to that axiomatic theological principle underlying the distinction between God and world: God's
aseity. It is the nature of the creature to lack the capacity for self-existence
and self-maintenance and in God's capacity and inclination to maintain
creaturely existence in such a way as to enable it to reach its end. Dorner
affirms later, 'The creation of man having designed a free moral personality,
the divine order must be directed towards bringing all the forces of good and

---

[101] *SCD*, III, p. 51.
[102] *SCD*, II, p. 326.
[103] *SCD*, III, p. 55.
[104] *SCG*, II.i., p. 159.
[105] *SCD*, III, p. 55.

evil in decision.'[106] The relation in which the individual stands to the genus is both a reflection of the relation between God and creature (since the individual does not – could not – exist without the genus), but also it is in the divine upholding of the human creature's existence as an *original cause with power to act* which secures the status of the individual as not 'mere manifestation of the race'.[107] What is highly significant in this suggestion is the extent to which the idea of divine preservation, while it includes the notion of a greater evil being caused by annihilation,[108] is posited in terms of its consistency with the divine determination of the human creature as that destined to come to perfection through development. This means that the doctrine of inherent sin – as opposed to original sin – is arranged in order to foreground the place of free obedience to the good which, with the entrance of sin into the world, comes in the form of a remedial God-man in whom it is decisive to believe:

> [G]eneric sin has the character of the morally exceptional or evil, although it is not decisive of the definitive worth of the fate of man. The members of the human race, on the other hand, are destined to personal responsibility and there is also a personal guilt, which is not the effect of generic sin, and has not a universality equally referable to all, constituting them from a new side needy of redemption, and causing common guilt. The definitive worth and the ultimate fate of the individual are annexed to personal decision.[109]

While the sinfulness which defines the genus is evil, it does not have the kind of indefatigable purchase on the human creature which characterizes, as Dorner sees it, doctrines of original sin. The creature's teleological constitution – his *fate* – is not altered by the entrance of this abnormity. Rather, it is actually instantiated in the process of being found as one of a sinful genus and having to respond to the attendant demands of gaining 'control over (itself) gradually'.[110] This means that the human being 'must become an actual personality, whether good or evil', by a process in which the creature's capacity to be condemned or saved increases with the increased measure of clarity of the ethical demand to which he is responsible. Thus, Dorner speaks of a three-staged process which leads up to the basis of judgement:

1. The First Stage is the infantile in which the creature, while participating in the 'evil constitution' of the genus is not yet an active ethical

---

[106] Ibid. p. 69.
[107] Ibid.
[108] Ibid. p. 58.
[109] Ibid. p. 54.
[110] Ibid.

being – an actual person but 'only a potential punctual existence for future personalities';[111]

2. The Second Stage is that of moral subjectivity, when the 'intellectual ego' emerges with the 'faculty of choice between finite things'[112] and a cognizance of good and evil which brings with it a 'share in moral freedom of choice',[113] and capacity to perform 'legal acts' or 'individual good acts', but which are not yet 'decisive of the total worth of man' because it is the, as yet undetermined, 'fundamental disposition' which furnishes acts with ultimate value. At this *legal stage* there is not yet revealed good as that which is not merely the opposite of evil, but the absolutely necessary, and so a 'pure decision for good is not yet present'.[114] This stage both raises the creature to a level of partial awareness of the good and yet since the law is not 'yet the highest revelation (of the) good'[115] it may not be said that good has been rejected. As such, as 'far as punishment is concerned, the subject, although punishable, is not yet ripe for absolute judgement, because he is in himself in process'.[116]

3. The Third stage is that of 'personal free decision'[117] or crisis, which arrives with the 'manifestation of Christ'.[118] This represents the 'perfectly revealed good' and as such 'makes free decision possible' because its manifestation is an indication not of ineluctable incapacity for the good but rather of the *possibility* of redemption. The appearance of Christ (and Christianity in the history of religions) is the occasion of a crisis since it 'necessitates every one to decide for or against good itself'.[119] In the act of decision, whether for Christ or against him, the 'man crosses in a moral and religious respect to the stage of personality as distinguished from the generic character'.[120]

It is with this three stage process that Dorner holds it possible to reconcile the entrance to the world of sin with the properly ethical completion of creaturely development. Rather than sin making it impossible for the human creature to be fulfilled in free obedience to God, the divinely maintained developmental constitution – proceeding through these three stages – is posited both as subject to the influences of sin (since it is as *Saviour* and not

[111] *SCD*, III, p. 62.
[112] Ibid. p. 65.
[113] Ibid. p. 66.
[114] Ibid. p. 68.
[115] Ibid.
[116] Ibid. p. 69.
[117] Ibid.
[118] Ibid. p. 70.
[119] Ibid. p. 71.
[120] Ibid.

merely perfector that Christ as the perfect revelation must be apprehended) but not absolutely determined by this status. Indeed, sin only becomes *ineluctably* guilty after the redemption from sin has been rejected. In this way, Dorner holds as solved the problem of reconciling inherited sin with the ethical category of guilt without denying either component, and in such a way as making the actual manifestation of the God-man as the decisive event in the fulfilment of the divine intentions for the world.

However, we suggest that these doctrinal decisions, while seeking to retain the concepts of universal sin and guilt in a way consistent with the ethical idea of God at the heart of the dogmatic project, are exposed to the question of whether he adequately represents sin as that which would occasion the manifestation of the God-man as Saviour. We will look at this point in detail in the concluding section on the relationship between sin and the capacity for redemption.

III. Sin and the Capacity for Redemption

The universality of liability to condemnation or guilt is the presupposition underlying the all embracing significance of redemption, which addresses itself to universal receptiveness for it and for that restoration of the unity of mankind, which Christianity will effect.[121]

In the course of his survey of the biblical material at the opening of his section on the essence of evil, Dorner offers this summary of the *reach* of sin – universal – and its *consequences* – condemnation; but he does so by observing that it is on the *basis* of the universality of redemption that the universality of those aspects are ultimately disclosed.

While the Old Testament had provided an account of how 'evil actually exists in all men',[122] and that 'O. T. piety and righteousness are marked by that form of humility which rests upon the sense of sin',[123] the New Testament produced a 'still profounder knowledge of sin' because 'only

---

[121] Ibid. p. 305. The translators have given the phrase *'liability* to condemnation' for the original 'Verdammlichkeit', (*SCG*, II.i. p. 8), and with this, we suggest, they have sought to represent the sense in which the state in which the sinner stands is as one *heading towards* judgement or condemnation rather than standing *already* condemned. This is a translation consistent with Dorner's own emphasis which, as we shall see, is ordered more towards representing sin as that which occasions future condemnation in the death of the God-man or as absolute condemnation after the rejection of this God-man. We suggest, however, that the concept of condemnation suffers from this almost exclusive futurity and provides little explanation of condemnation which exists either before the historic death of Christ or the post-resurrection encounter with him.

[122] *SCD*, II, p. 302.

[123] Ibid. p. 303.

after (the apostles) have entered the kingdom of light and life do they thoroughly understand the danger and depth of the night, from which they have been rescued'.[124] There is, thus, a *noetic* intensification of the significance of sin. Yet, it is not merely noetic. Much more, Dorner notes in the N. T. a shift in the *status* of sin in its connection with the *soteriological* status of the sinful human creature: 'Such is the close relation between sin and Christ's appearance.'[125] He argues that with the advent of Christ come the conditions in which sin is to be defined either as punishable and therefore redeemable or unpunishable and therefore unredeemable. He interprets the 'time of forebearance' (Rom. 3.25 f.) as evidence of both the culpability of pre-Christian sin but also its corresponding capacity to be forgiven. For Dorner, condemnation and forgiveness are intimately connected realities: 'what is not punishable needs no forgiveness'[126] (*ergo* what *is* punishable *needs* forgiveness). The crucial component in this is the notion that all sin committed before Christ is capable of being forgiven, and therefore condemnable, because it does not include, *could* not include, the rejection of the 'perfect revelation'[127] of God. Thus, what holds his attention is not the culpability of sin *tout simple*, but rather the *capacity of sin to be forgiven*.

As such, it is as there *is* or *is not* the capacity for redemption from sin which represents the major focus for his investigation of the biblical material so that he observes in both O. T.[128] and N. T.[129] the connection between the definition and condemnation of sin and the call to repentance (although his use of this material is not detailed exposition, but amounts only to a general survey and the posting of multiple verses as evidence for his position[130]). Furthermore, this schema informs his construction of a theory of the essence of sin which seeks to account for the nature of its universality, its culpability in the individual, and the proper accounting of its relationship to the actual appearance of the God-man who is to bring to perfection the divine purposes for the world, including the human creature.

He writes:

[O]n the basis of the essentially equal, i.e. absolute, need of redemption by all a distinction arises, accordingly as one possesses more or less living receptiveness for redemption. To this more or less of receptiveness

[124] *SCD*, II, p. 304.
[125] Ibid.
[126] Ibid. p. 305.
[127] Ibid. p. 306.
[128] Ibid. p. 303.
[129] Repent 'is also the first word of the N. T....Such is the close relation between sin and Christ's appearance, that the coming of God's kingdom is above all the most powerful call to repentance', Ibid. p. 304.
[130] C.f. Ibid. fn. 1–4, Ibid. p. 305, fn. 1–8.

corresponds a distinction in the degree of sin and guilt....But the sin against the Holy Spirit is described as the most grievous although avoidable sin, i.e. the rejection of Christ as Saviour in definitive unbelief, after He has begun to reveal Himself in man's spirit. Nowhere is it said that man must needs commit this sin on account of his natural sinful constitution. On the contrary, Christianity which so perfectly restores personal responsibility, that no one can be finally lost or forced to reject Christ on account of his connection with the race.

From this it follows that sin is more perilous and deadly in the degree that it urges to unbelief in Christ.[131]

As indicated by these concluding remarks on the biblical material, Dorner does not identify the essence of sin, and therefore the *really* culpable sin (as that which can be condemned only in the death of the God-man), as coming to its complete reality *before* the appearance of Christ. It is this appearance that brings the ultimate and final grounds for sin's definition: the rejection of Christ as Saviour. Thus, the essence of sin, according to this reading of the Scriptures, finds its most complete definition with reference to the *response to Christ*, bringing it into a direct connection with what we might call his understanding of the *essence of redemption* (and way to perfection): the *acceptance* of Christ as Saviour.[132] In laying out the biblical evidence in this way, Dorner provides a means of defining sin as that which has *purchase* in the history of the human creature such that its essence is determined ultimately by the actual incarnation and not as that which has a final form *before* the God-man has appeared.[133] The consequences of this configuration

---

[131] Ibid. p. 333. In his historical survey of Christology, Dorner identified this notion as forming an important part of the doctrinal development of post-apostolic theology in Polycarp's singling out the 'worst sin' as 'unbelief in Him', *History of Development*, Div. I, Vol. I, p. 117.

[132] The high significance which Dorner attributes to the sin against the Holy Spirit (Mt. 12.28; Mk 3.28f; Lk 12.10) is not accompanied by a detailed exegetical account of how this sin *is* to be described as the sin against Jesus Christ, a point of obvious concern given the long and complicated history of debate surrounding this logion. For a brief account of this history see C. Clemen, *Die Christliche Lehre der Sünde* (Göttingen: Vandenhoeck und Ruprecht, 1897), p. 89 f. Clemen himself suggests that there are dangers attached to making generalizations on the basis of this one utterance in isolation from other passages which seem to indicate the forgivableness of all sins, a point on which he finds August Tholuck in agreement, '*Über die Natur der Sünde wider den heiligen Geist*', in *Theologische Studien und kritiken*, Vol. 9 (1836), p. 407 f.

[133] This doctrinal emphasis found many advocates in the nineteenth century cf. F. Schleiermacher, *The Christian Faith*, §112, p. 5; A. Ritschl, *The Christian Doctrine of Justification and Reconciliation* (Clifton, NJ: Reference Book Publishers, 1966), p. 407 ff; J. Kaftan, *The Truth of the Christian Religion* (Edinburgh: T & T Clark, 1894), p. 250. However, as Carl Clemen observes, there is significant disagreement between those who occupy this point. Most notably, Ritschl argues that this entails no

are clear. It means that the essence of sin cannot be properly identified as a condition or state in isolation from the divine offer of forgiveness. It cannot be correctly explicated apart from the idea that the human creature – both with or without sin – has his defining moment in relation to the God-man. In this way, Dorner's representation of the biblical material coalesces to provide a way of harmonizing his views of the teleological structure of the human creature with the appearance of sin in the world. The terms of this ponerology, furthermore, inform the way in which he imagines how the appearance of Christ informs the human creature's relationship to himself as an individual and as a part of the human race. If Christ is central to the intensification of sin and its culpability or guilt he is also central, for Dorner, to the manageable representation of the way in which the individual human creature is both distinctly accountable for his own sin and yet not in isolation from the genus. This formulation functions, of course, as the decisive means by which Dorner addresses the question of the doctrine of original sin and the relationship between the individual and the genus.

Conclusion

In positing the doctrine of sin in this way, however, Dorner is exposed to the accusation that he provides insufficient grounds for the depiction of the *death* of the God-man as the necessary divine response to human sinfulness. Søren Kierkegaard has commented:

> If it is true that all sins prior [to Christ] are merely something provisional in the sense of being insignificant, something which cannot as such be an object of God's wrath...[that the individual] is not properly [guilty] anyway since the individual is not really guilty...if this is so, why in the world did Christ come into the world? If guilt was no greater than that, he was not necessary. In such a case Christ comes to the world as proclaimer of the law and as demand.[134]

While we resist Kierkegaard's suggestion that the provisionality of sins prior to Christ are 'insignificant' (since they occasion a change in the divine disposition towards the world), we acknowledge a problem Dorner has in preparing for an account of the divine response to generic sin in the sacrificial *death* of Christ.

judgement, a point from which Dorner distances himself (Vol. II, p. 305), and which Clemen himself suggests is at variance with the biblical sources, C. Clemen, *Die christliche Lehre*, p. 87. Clemen is in more agreement with Dorner's suggestion (although he questions his handling of the proof texts) that sins committed before Christ are seen by God as not fully realized or as 'Sünden teilweiser Unmündigkeit', Ibid.

[134] Kierkegaard, *Journals and Papers*, p. 196.

While the twofold definition of sin as forgivable and unforgivable is intended to centralize Christ and His appearance as that which defines the essence and telos of sin ('Christ as the one who brings the crisis, and the one against whom alone the highest guilt can be committed'[135]), what his particular usage of and investment in the (much disputed) idea of the unforgivable sin does is suggest a doctrine of sin and condemnation in which the absolute weight – and *reach* – of Christ's death is reduced. By it is condemned not *absolute* guilt and sinfulness, but that which has yet to reach such a degree or measure. This is, of course, Kierkegaard's complaint and the reason why he questions the rationale for Christ to come as anything other than law giver. Why the need for an absolute theanthropic guilt offering when the guilt has not yet attained its fullest or most potent form?

We will address in more detail the full implications of this position and the import of Kierkegaard's question as they emerge in the details of his doctrine of the atonement in Chapter 6. Here we wish to acknowledge the systemic consistency in his account. Dorner does undoubtedly threaten to reduce the weight of that sin condemned in the death of Christ by describing it as non-personal and merely generic. However, this stems from his concern to see Christ as the fulcrum of his exposition. For this reason he interprets the sin against the Holy Spirit as that which pertains specifically to the rejection of Christ. This approach brings attention to Christ as the central figure not only in sin's removal but also in the development of the absolute currency of sin (as definite unbelief or rejection of Christ). This means that he is able to define sin and evil – as he intended – as that which is regulated by the 'Christian idea of God'.[136] This is because it is Christ's godhumanity – as it finds fulfilment and perfection in the death and resurrection – which provides the definitive interpretative scheme for the definition of sin in its two-sided aspect; as that which is condemned in the death of Christ and thereby forgivable, and as that which is condemned in the unbelieving human creature and thereby unforgivable. In this we recall Dorner's early discussion of the place of the doctrine of God in the search for the 'objective idea of evil' which is, he argues, 'only possible by recurring to the idea of the absolute Good, i.e. God, whose opposite or contradiction it is'.[137] With regard to sin and its condemnation, therefore, Dorner recurs to Christ's *the*anthropic identity as the basis for his definition of the essence and scope of sin and in this he has maintained a crucial dogmatic connection.

[135] *SCD*, III, p. 72.
[136] *SCD*, II, p. 359.
[137] Ibid. p. 360.

5

THE DOCTRINE OF CHRIST

Introduction

As we have already noted, Dorner's exposition of the doctrine of Christ begins *before* its formal treatment as the Second Part of the *Specific* section of his *System*. His account of the doctrines of sin and evil is offered as the 'introduction' to the 'exposition of Christology'.[1] For this reason, the Christology *division* in his dogmatic investigation is best understood as the place in which the principles of his overall dogmatic project come to full expression.

Dorner is not inappropriately described as the Christologian *par excellence* of the nineteenth century.[2] Not merely for the sheer magnitude[3] of his output in the area, but more particularly for the manner in which he handles the *totality* of the content of the Christian faith so as to bring all doctrinal spheres into relationship with the realized idea of the

[1] *SCD*, III, p. 299.
[2] E. Günther, *Die Entwicklung der Lehre von der Person Christi im XIX Jahrhundert*, p. 235. Claude Welch also notes the particularly important role of Dorner in a post-Hegel 'renewal of incarnation theology', *Protestant Theology in the Nineteenth Century, 1799–1870*, Vol. 1, (New Haven: Yale, 1972), p. 104. It is, however, wise to acknowledge, as Richard A. Muller does, that theologians diverse and multitudinous have been described as 'Christocentric', yet much more important is the precise way in which the doctrine of Christ occupies central ground in systems of Christian thought, 'A Note on "Christocentrism" and the Impudent Use of Such Terminology', in *The Westminster Theological Journal*, Vol. 68. No. 2 (Fall 2006), p. 254. For our part, we suggest that Muller's threefold classification of Christocentricism provides a helpful matrix for explaining different dogmatic agendas, though, as with all such determinations, can too easily lead to unnecessary simplifications. Thus, Dorner's trinitarian agenda is invariably missed as and when he is described as Christocentric.
[3] Dorner is, of course, the author of the magisterial multi-volume *History of the Development of the Doctrine of the Person of Christ*, in which he 'masterfully clarified...the history of christological problems in a work of approximately *2500 pages*', Ragnar Holte, p. 114.

incarnation of the Son of God in Jesus Christ. As we shall demonstrate, what occurs in his doctrinal treatment is an unfurling of details which have their foundations in the preceding material; and this interconnectedness is manifest most specifically in the careful linking of the doctrines of Trinity and Christology.[4] For this reason, it is important that accounts which emphasize – not without reason – the pivotal role of his doctrine of Jesus Christ as 'Zentralindividuum' (which we will come to later) need always to be supplemented by a clear acknowledgement of the trinitarian construction of his Christology, and specifically his *reconstruction* of the doctrine with the explication of the divine hypostases as *Modes of Being* rather than *Persons*.[5] A proper reading of Dorner ought to admit the attempt – even if not successful – to connect, rather than treat in isolation, the twin doctrines of God and Christ.[6] Dorner *may* be described as a Christologian, but only if this does not obscure his wider vision for a thorough linking of doctrines.

Indeed, it is certain aspects of Dorner's configuration of the doctrine of God that we hold to be of durable value in the development of Christology. As we shall go on to see, the significance of his doctrine of Modes of Being for the solution of a pervasive doctrinal problem (the double Personality of Christ) has already been well noted by Christine Axt-Piscalar. However, we suggest that in addition to this (and lacking in her study) should be acknowledged the productive scope of Dorner's account of God's *aseity* – trinitarianly arranged – for a depiction of Jesus Christ as God-man without detriment either to the *union* or distinction of natures. This obtains, we argue, even though the attendant details of his account fall more easily

---

[4] In his survey of the Christocentricism of much nineteenth-century theology, Reinhard Slenczka takes particular note of Dorner's ambition to fuse the question of the historical Jesus within the context of a wider consideration of the relationship between the trinitarian and Christological dogmas, *Geschichtlichkeit und Personsein Jesu Christi* (Göttingen: Vandenhoek & Ruprecht, 1967), p. 227. Dorner's *tightly* bound treatment of trinitarian and Christological questions is also noted by H. Walter Frei, *I. A. Dorners Christologie und Trinitätslehre*, p. 51.

[5] Axt-Piscalar notes the recognition of this feature in O. Kirn, E. Günther and E. Hirsch, Axt-Piscalar, *Grund*, p. 248.

[6] We acknowledge that this connection has been made in the major monographs on Dorner (e.g. Rothermundt & Axt-Piscalar); but it is the less rigorous descriptions of Dorner which abound in many accounts of mediating theology or nineteenth-century theology, offering a picture of Dorner as something of a one-trick-pony whose only major contribution to the history of doctrine is the rather eccentric and now obsolete developmental or progressive doctrine of Incarnation. We suggest that this presents a seriously skewed picture of his theological project. An example of this kind of representation may be found in E. Y. Mullins' description of Dorner's account of incarnation which focuses *exclusively* on the doctrine of progression without any reference to the wider venture, *The Christian Religion in its Doctrinal Expression* (Philadelphia: The Judson Press, 1917, repr. 1945), p. 190.

into disrepute (most notably his rendering of the development of Jesus' Godhumanity).[7]

In the course of this chapter, we will seek to lay out the key features of Dorner's account, and along the way set out the major objections which have arisen in response. As we shall see, a consequence of the eclecticism of his doctrine (displaying features from both Lutheran and Reformed traditions), as well as his doctrine of God's triunity, is that he has faced criticism from all sides, not least in the extent to which he remains faithful to (or limited by) the *intentions* of the two-natures doctrine of Chalcedon.[8] We will suggest that Dorner's project, though problematic, contains resources which, if properly marshalled, may be retained in the service of a positive statement concerning the Person and work of Jesus Christ. We begin by laying out the grounds on which he begins the formal account of his Christology.

I. The Transition from Ponerology to Christology

Following his treatment of the doctrine of sin and evil, which we assessed in the previous chapter, Dorner delineates the specific grounds on which the ideal God-man may be said to have become actual in such a way as to meet the demands of the contingent occurrence of sin. His intention is to demonstrate that the arrival of the Christ meets the specific needs of the world and in doing so brings the divine purposes for the world to their destined conclusion. This impugns *neither* the holiness of God nor what we might call His eternal *agapaic* purposes for the world. He does this by positing the idea that the definitive divine response to the world is properly displayed only in the manifestation of both the divine justice and love, an occurrence which he links exclusively to the appearance of Jesus Christ:

> The punitive reaction against evil is indeed necessarily based in the justice of God; but this necessity also leaves room for a revelation, which, arising from the depths of the eternal free-will of love, and acknowledging the right of justice, is reckoned to humanity, lost as

---

[7] It is also the case that Dorner's Christological formulations have also suffered from some considerable misinterpretation. For example, B. B. Warfield gives a wholly inadequate representation of Dorner in *The Person and Work of Christ*, B. B. Warfield, ed. Samuel G. Craig (Philadelphia: The Presbyterian and Reformed Publishing Company, 1950), p. 200.

[8] We say 'intentions' in order to signal the acceptance of Chalcedon's enduring provisionality for critics of Dorner like H. Bavinck who speaks of the non-sacrosanct language of Chalcedon but still maintains the lasting value of its two-natures doctrine which, somewhat hastily we suggest, he argues Dorner has, in effect, abandoned, Bavinck, *Reformed Dogmatics*, Vol. 3, p. 237.

it was without redemption, and yet capable of redemption. The new and concluding revelation has been realized by the manifestation of Jesus Christ, the Son of God and of man, in the fulness of times and in the form conditioned by sin, and realized in such a way that in His Person the Divine justice and love, as they have their eternal *union* in God, have also come, in spite of sin, to perfect revelation and mutual interpenetration in the world.[9]

We have then in this statement, a determination to display the connectedness (and appropriateness) of the divine response to sin with the original divine purposes for the world. While Dorner is careful to describe the occurrence of evil as occasioning a *reaction* from God – characterized as punitive – he seeks to depict the content of this reaction as consistent with the intentions for which the world is eternally destined – the perfecting of revelation and the mutual interpenetration of justice and love, *crucially*, realized in the God-man. While the response is reactive, it is not *restricted* by the freedom of the world (to become sinful). The punitive reaction to evil, which is derived from the ethical constitution of God's being, does not *exclude* but, rather, tends towards the redemption and restoration of the world. What we see depicted in these preparations for the doctrine of Christology is a mapping on to the divine economy of salvation the key features of his doctrine of God. Dorner seeks to depict the immanent relations existing in such a way as to show intra-trinitarian love expressed as the *free obedience to the good*. In this way, God is *holy* Love, since He is in free conformity with Himself (which, simultaneously, of course, is free conformity with the Good). This *theo*logical insight manifests itself in the above statement concerning the connection between sin and Christ, since the punitive *response* to sin is also the *perfecting* – loving – conclusion of the divine intentions for the world, to be actualized in the *unio* of God and man in the God-man.

Dorner is seeking to demonstrate that God's *proper* response to the sinful world is the incarnation (just as he had in the first part of his system sought to demonstrate that the God-man was the appropriate divine intention for the world as the 'perfecting of revelation'[10]). He represents his immediate task as 'seeing how the divine justice itself stretches beyond its exhibition as punitive',[11] which leads him to conclude that only in the incarnation can *both* 'satisfaction...be given to legislative and redistributory justice' *and* the 'destiny of man'[12] be maintained. This linking of the demonstration of justice, the revelation of love, and the realization of the ideal God-man brings

[9] *SCD*, III, p. 133.
[10] Ibid. p. 141.
[11] Ibid.
[12] Ibid.

Dorner to his formal consideration of the doctrine of Christ. We will turn to this exposition shortly. Before we do this, however, we will attend briefly to the nature and significance of his historical investigation of Christology which he gives in the *System* as a much condensed form of his *magnum opus* the *History of the Development of the Person of Christ* (published first in 1839[13] and then much revised and expanded in 1845–1856[14]). We do not wish to offer a detailed analysis of this work but want to acknowledge certain aspects of its composition and the way in which it is informed by dogmatic principles which come to full expression in the much later *System of Christian Doctrine* (1879–1881) which forms the focus of the present study.[15]

II. The History of the Development of the Person of Christ

The preparation for the multi-volume historical survey of Christology begins for Dorner with his earliest published essay (in two parts), 'Über die Entwicklungsgeschichte der Christologie, besonders in den neuern

---

[13] Isaak Dorner, *Entwicklungsgeschichte der Lehre von der Person Christi von den ältesten Zeiten bis auf die neuesten* (Stuttgart: S. G. Leisching, 1839).

[14] Isaak Dorner, *Entwicklungsgeschichte der Lehre von der Person Christi von den ältesten Zeiten bis auf die neuesten*, Zweite, stark vermehrte Auflage in zwei Theilen (Stuttgart: S. G. Liesching, 1845/Berlin: Gustav Schlawitz, 1856). As one reviewer of this second publication remarks, the first publication came during the furore caused by the Straussian critique – impressive more for the scandal of its claims than its proof of them – and was marked by a concern to lay out carefully the outline of the development of doctrine; and this strategy is continued in the second publication, with greater detail added to the exposition, Book Review by H. Reuter, in *Allgemeines Repertorium für die theologische Literatur und kirchliche Statistik*, Zweiundfunfzigster Band, (Berlin: Herbig, 1846), pp. 13–14. It is the second, revised work which forms the basis of the redoubtable English translations undertaken between 1861–1884.

[15] The question of whether Dorner's Christology is different in the *History* from its final form in the *System* has been ably resolved by Thomas Koppehl. Koppehl argues against Rothermundt (Rothermundt, *Synthese*, p. 223) who argues (as had W. F. Geß in his late work *Das Dogma von Christi Person und Werk*, p. 342.) that Dorner can be read as advocating in the 1856 *History* a doctrine of the Logos as in Himself personal. This is a position which he, crucially, no longer holds in the *System*. Koppehl argues, however, that Dorner has already given the kernel of his doctrine of the Logos as a *moment* of the eternal personality of God in a letter to Martensen on August 5, 1843 (Koppehl, *Standpunkt*, p. 165) – a point also made by Axt-Piscalar (Axt-Piscalar, *Grund*, p. 221) – and as such in the *History* is merely advancing a general view or 'Konsens' of the contemporary forms of Christology, rather than giving his own definitive view (Koppehl, p. 181). We suggest that by acknowledging the distinctive purposes of the *History*, we need not infer a major shift in Dorner's theory.

Zeiten'.[16] In this study, Dorner lays out the conditions in which the study of Christology and its doctrinal development has taken place during the 'long struggle between Christendom and Reason' (my translation).[17] This is a struggle which has taken as its focal point – *Mittelpunkt* – the Person of Christ. Various strategies have been developed in order to overcome the conflict, not least among them being the decision of some theologies to advance in separation from the philosophical tradition. However, Dorner insists that for those who regard Christendom as wholly *reasonable* ('Allervernünftigste'[18]) – by which he means that it provides the 'key to the history of the world' – there must be an intentional involvement in the speculative activity of philosophy. Since the focal point of the conflict, the Person of Christ, is the focal point of Christendom – the 'innerstes Wesen des Christenthums'[19] – the development of the doctrine of Christ will function as the touchstone for the wider debate, and, for Dorner, also be the source of its resolution. This leads him to lay out in the essay the threefold division of the historical development of Christology which he will go on to use in his later historical survey:

  I. Die Periode des Bewußtwerdens, daß Christus sowhol Gott als Mensch sei...Vorausgesetste, oder unmittelbare *unio Personalis.*
  II. Periode des einseitigen Hervorkehrens des einen oder des andern Elementes in der *unio.*
  III. Die Zeit der Versuche, das Göttliche und das Menschliche als gleichberechtigt, in Einheit zu betrachten.[20]

This interpretative matrix depicts the history of doctrinal development as following a distinct pattern. The first period (following the apostolic testimony to A.D. 381), is seen as having established the two sides ('natures') of the Person of Christ. The second period (A.D. to the end of the eighteenth century) is characterized by its mostly vain attempts to seek the unity of the Person without paying due attention to the way in which the two sides meet, leading to one side being abridged by the other. The third period (from 1800 onwards), however, is seen as having the possibility for the representation of the Person of Christ as *theanthropic,* that is (as he comments in his *System*), 'actually and truly human and Divine at once', since the divine and human

---

[16] Isaak Dorner, *Tübinger Zeitschrift für Theologie*, 1835, Vol. 4, pp. 81–204 & 1836, Vol. 1, pp. 96–240.

[17] Ibid. 1835, p. 81.

[18] Ibid. p. 83.

[19] 'Es muß zwar mit Recht in der christlichen Kirche als Mittelpunkt und innerstes Wesen des Christenthums festgestalten werden, daß in Christo das göttliche und das menchliche Leben Eins geworden sei', Ibid. p. 84.

[20] Ibid. p. 93.

sides are recognized in their 'equality of authority'.[21] The survey portrays the history of ecclesial doctrine as an *advancement* towards a positive account of that which had been prefigured only negatively by the very first stage in its configuration of the apostolic testimony.

However, for Dorner, unlike his colleague F. C. Baur,[22] the development of the doctrine of Christ does not represent the immanent development of God in the processes of thought towards a completion in the *universal union* of God and man.[23] Rather, a progression towards more adequate representations of the primitive confession of the *verus Deus-verus homo*, first of all apprehended by the primary Apostolic Church,[24] and then subsequently developed by the Church to a more 'comprehensive', though not 'more complete'[25] state.

Therefore, when he comes to the composition of his *History*, Dorner displays a noticeable *charity* towards the efforts of his predecessors in the tradition, as befits their status as seekers after the best means of developing the decisive apostolic confession concerning the Person of Christ. Dorner's

[21] *SCD*, III, p. 197.

[22] Thomas Koppehl argues that Dorner's Christological thought was fixed early on in response to his more famous colleague F. C. Baur at Tübingen, *Standpunkt*, pp. 21–22, n. 4.

[23] 'Auf dem objektiven Standpunkte der Hegelschen Philosophie ist das Christentum, seinem wesentlichen Inhalte nach, die sich explizierende absolute Idee selbst. Die absolute Idee ist Gott als der absolute, in dem Prozesse des Denkens sich mit sich selbst vermittelnde Geist. Das Christentum ist daher wesentliche dieser Prozess selbst, der im Denken als der Natur des Geistes, sich explizierende Lebensprozess Gottes', F. C. Baur, *Lehrbuch der Dogmengeschichte* (Darmstadt: Wissenschaftliche Buchgesellschaft, 1974, unaltered publication of 3rd reprint Leipzig: Becher, 1867), p. 355; and, 'shall the God-man...be the general man...[or] identical with a certain particular individual' (my translation), *Die christliche Lehre von der Versöhnung in ihrer geschichtlichen Entwicklung*, (Tübingen: C. F. Osiander, 1838), p. 732 f. The fundamental difference between Baur and Dorner's approach to the development of doctrine may be seen in the different titles given to the historical investigations of Christology. As Koppehl observes, the title of Baur's three volume work *Die christliche Lehre von der Dreieinigkeit und Menschwerdung Gottes in ihrer geschichtlichen Entwicklung* (Tübingen: C. F. Osiander, 1841–1843) points to Baur's doctrine of immanent development in its linking or fusing ('Zusammenschau') of 'Dreieinigkeit' and 'Menschwerdung Gottes'; while Dorner's title *Entwicklungsgeschichte der Lehre von der Person Christi*'(1845–1856), indicates the specific focus on the thought of the central individual as the specific character of the 'Christologischen Personbegriffs', Koppehl, p. 69, n. 91.

[24] *SCD*, III, p. 196. Dorner surveys the biblical material and concludes that while there are 'considerable differences' between the way in which the N. T. sources conceive of the Person and work of Christ, the differences represent 'only various stages in the development of the *common faith*' (my italics) which he has earlier characterized as including a recognition of Jesus as the 'Son of God' (p. 156).

[25] Ibid. p. 196.

understanding of the tradition – and his own place in it – is that doctrinal development does not manifest a development in the immanent activity or becoming of God. Rather, it is the development of the capacity of the Church[26] to properly formulate the dogmatic account of the reality of the Person of Jesus Christ. For this reason, his threefold structure reflects both a recognition of an *originary* truth from which the earliest – as well as all subsequent – dogmaticians formulated the doctrinal representation of the belief in Jesus Christ's God-manhood. All ecclesial renderings, therefore, are *consequent* endeavours to depict this primary reality in greater degrees of sophistication and accuracy. Even though Dorner contends that the epochal divisions of the tradition have conformed to a developing pattern – within which there have taken place different stages and types of imbalancing in the formulation of doctrine (which we will note below), and which have led up to the present possibility of bringing together the divine and human elements of the basic Christological affirmations in a distinctively assured manner – *because* the development is not itself *constitutive* of the object of dogma (i.e. God-manhood) the construction of doctrine is to be marked out as *subsequent* and informed by its object.[27]

What we see displayed in this procedure is the outworking of Dorner's understanding of the relation between Christian faith and constructive dogmatics. The mode of dogmatic explication is intended to depict with scientific certitude the object which is given *in*, though not determined *by* faith. As such, his historical survey of the development of doctrine reflects an interest in representing the succession of proposals as indebted both to the *objective* content of faith (or faith's 'objective contents'[28]), and the constructive *response*[29] of scientific verification of that content. This means that he may conceive of the sequence of doctrinal proposals as a *development*, progressing towards an ever more appropriate rendition, without needing to regard the earlier proposals as without merit or, indeed, coherency, since the same content of faith has been available and in action

---

[26] Dorner's historical survey demonstrates an interest in the Church (a point noted by Reuter, *Repertorium*, Band 25, p. 15) as both the appropriate and legitimate place in which the formulation of ideas about the truth concerning Jesus take place.

[27] This *subsequence* determines also the criteria for distinguishing between true and false doctrine; and conforms to Dorner's insistence that faith's object is ethically determined as that which brings the Christian into a relationship of non-coerced obedience to God via the redemptive activity of faith's object, Jesus Christ. Dorner contends that any Christological doctrine which excludes the 'fundamental fact of redemption by Christ' are to be considered 'antagonists', *SCD*, III, p. 283.

[28] *SCD*, I, p. 168.

[29] This *responsive* posture of doctrinal development itself mirrors the account of *faith* Dorner earlier provided as that which is an *active*, though not the primarily *constitutive*, partner in the *union* of God and man, cf. *SCD*, II, p. 201 ff. In our earlier discussion of this dynamic we noted Dorner's keen sense of this relation as *ethical* in its nature.

149

(as 'the guidance and stimulus of the Spirit of God and of the Word of the canon'[30]) throughout the history of development.[31] What characterizes Dorner's history, therefore, (apart from its obvious qualities of breadth and catholicity[32]) is the way in which it depicts the history of doctrine as *living*, without being endlessly *restless*. It is an account which has a transparent narrative, leading as it does towards the decisive climax of the possibilities afforded, as he sees it, to modern theology by the advancement towards a non-competitive account of God and humanity. Yet this advancement is seen as both culminative *and* cumulative, so that there is an unbroken connection with the early creedal formulations and their authoritative sources, the apostolic witnesses.[33] This point is evidenced in Dorner's estimation, contra Baur, of an early ecclesial consensus – though not without controversy – regarding the Person and nature of Christ. He speaks of an '*essentially Christian doctrine* – that of the true manhood of Christ and his divine pre-existent being' as having been 'about the middle of the second century, the prevalent doctrine in the leading churches' (my italics).[34] With such an early dating of dogmatic agreement, Dorner intends to display a consistent line of conformity to an essential core of belief in the God-manhood of Christ reaching back to the earliest periods of doctrinal rumination (including the apostolic period), to which all subsequent doctrinal development is both subject and enabled. This means that in Dorner's account of the history of Christology he is seeking to depict an advancement towards the constructive possibilities of modern theology. Yet it is also possible to identify in the historical narrative particular theologians (and philosophers) who have made contributions which Dorner has identified as offering moments of advancement which he will himself utilize. Most obvious among these are: Irenaeus (and the doctrine of the necessity of the incarnation[35] and his theory of recapitulation); Theodore of Mopsuestia (and his theory of a moral development in the incarnation[36]); Anselm (and his linking of incarnation

---

[30] *SCD*, III, p. 197.
[31] This common *availability* has also been matched by a persisting tradition of the *reception* of the object by faith which has been accompanied by a readiness to allow 'new momenta' to discern 'what the faith contains', *History of Development*, Div. I, Vol. I, p. 223. This is, of course, the tradition into which Dorner places himself.
[32] Dorner's History is still unparalleled in its range and coverage, Colin Brown, *Jesus in European Protestant Thought 1778–1860* (Grand Rapids: Baker, 1985), p. 267.
[33] *History of Development*, Div. I, Vol. I, p. 48.
[34] Ibid. p. 142. Dorner comes to this conclusion on the basis of his reading of Hegesippus who, he argues, may be seen to demonstrate that the Church had not, as was being suggested, been 'virtually taken over' by ebiontism (Ibid. p. 138).
[35] *History of Development*, Div. II, Vol. I, p. 364.
[36] Dorner displays a sympathy for Mopsuestia not least in his assessment of the shortcomings, as he sees them, of Cyril's anti-Nestorian polemics, according to which he fails because he does not properly acknowledge 'the laws of a true human [moral]

and redemption[37]); Martin Luther (for his 'tendency' to 'effect a real, vital *union* between'[38] the divine and human in Christ) and Lutheranism (for its decisive, new, and fundamental Christological idea, that – 'Finitum capax infiniti'[39]); and Schelling (for discerning that 'it is not right to conceive subject and object as mutually exclusive...but that the essential unity of the two must be taken as the principle of all philosophy'[40]). In identifying these figures, we do not wish to offer a reconstruction of the genetic history of Dorner's thought, but rather to observe the extent to which in Dorner's *own* reconstruction of the history of Christological development, we may see clear traces of *insight* and apprehension which he identifies as prefiguring and preparing for the resolution which comes with the nineteenth-century doctrinal advancement. When he comes to his own Dogmatic Exposition (§99), Dorner is reticent to assume either that he will provide the *decisive* account of the 'mystery'[41] of the incarnation of God or be *unable to advance* the development of the doctrine. While he is duly phlegmatic about the possibility of ever providing a definitive account, the development of doctrine through the ages has delivered certain conclusions – 'a manifold augmentation of knowledge'[42] – of which he and the modern epoch are the beneficiaries and which provide the basis of this noteworthy period of ecclesial doctrinal advance. This legacy has immediate import for Dorner and the structure of his exposition. We turn now to his opening remarks regarding the ordering of his treatment.

III. The Person and Work of Christ

We must endeavour to avoid the evils in the customary arrangement of the Christological material, in order to gain as simple and consistent an image of Christ as possible.[43]

Dorner opens his exposition by eschewing what he describes as the 'customary mode of treatment'[44] which divides Christology into the Person

---

development' (Ibid. p. 70). With this comment he betrays his predilection for this element in the offerings of Cyril's disputant. This sympathy is not surprising given Dorner's research on Mopsuestia, I. A. Dorner, *Inest Theodori Mopsuesteni doctrina de Imagine Dei exposita* (Regiomonti: Hartungianis, 1844).

[37] *History of Development*, Div. II, Vol. I, p. 321.
[38] *History of Development*, Div. II, Vol. II, p. 78.
[39] Ibid. p. 263.
[40] *History of Development*, Div. II, Vol. III, p. 100.
[41] *SCD*, III, p. 281.
[42] Ibid. p. 282.
[43] Ibid. p. 279.
[44] Ibid.

and Work of Christ.[45] For the purposes of our exposition, we will treat the *details* of Christ's work as it pertains to his salvific activity in the next chapter. However, Dorner argues that a formal distinction obviates the notion that Christ is 'Himself...the centre of His gifts to humanity, as the highest good of the world.'[46] It is a move which does not intend a depreciation in the priority of ontological judgements;[47] and neither is it made with an invocation of Melancthon's oft used dictum: 'This is to know Christ...to know his benefits.'[48] Rather, it proceeds from Dorner's representation of Christ as the God-man who brings to the created order definitive perfection via redemption in the manner of his life of free obedience to God. In speaking of Christ as the 'highest good of the world',[49] Dorner is recalling an insight which he holds to be available to faith and scientifically verifiable to dogmatic investigation: the divine purpose for the world is the consummated *union* of God and man perfected in the God-man and mediated through him to the rest of creation. While it is not explicitly stated, Dorner's uncoupling of Person and Work evinces his fundamental concern to display the verifiable truthfulness of Jesus as the *necessary* God-man for the sake of the divine intentions and the world's good. In this way, it coheres with the preparatory intent of the Fundamental account of doctrine according to which the ideal God-man *Himself* is accounted as the *telos* of the created order. Dorner gives the following, additional qualification for his proposed conflation, that:

> [Christ's] Personal perfection extends through His official life, so that it is evident that the doctrine of His Person cannot be brought to an end of itself, and apart from His work.[50]

---

[45] Pannenberg identifies Schleiermacher as the instigator of the shift away from a seventeenth-century Protestant separation of Person and Work, W. Pannenberg, *Jesus, God and Man* (London: SCM, 1968), p. 208.

[46] *SCD*, III, p. 280.

[47] C.f. A. Ritschl's conclusion that the 'solution' to the 'problem of Christ's divinity' lies in an 'analysis of what He has done for the salvation of mankind in the form of His community', *The Christian Doctrine of Justification and Reconciliation*, trans. H. R. Mackintosh & A. Macaulay (Edinburgh: T & T Clark, 1900), p. 417.

[48] Phillip Melancthon, *The Loci Communes of Phillip Melancthon*, trans. C. L. Hill (Boston: Meader Publishing Co., 1944), p. 68. A. Ritschl makes full use of Melancthon's dictum in the development of his Christological account which seeks to define Christ's Godhead (heavily qualified) only *after* and as a *function* of 'His saving influence' (Ritschl, *Justification*, p. 398). C. Schwöbel identifies this usage as part of a tradition which forces a 'disjunction of being and meaning' and became a 'dominant theme' in the 'Christological conceptions' of Ritschl, 'Christology and Trinitarian Thought', in *Trinitarian Theology Today*, ed. Christoph Schwöbel (Edinburgh: T & T Clark, 1995), p. 118.

[49] *SCD*, III, p. 280.

[50] Ibid.

In other words, the identity of the God-man may not be properly accounted *dogmatically* if His behaviour is treated apart from His Person. This linking of the perfection of Christ's Person with the enacting of His official work means, of course, that Dorner is making formal arrangements for an exposition which will seek to articulate the realization of the God-man as that which occurred not merely ontically but *actually*. His Christological project will display the incarnation as that which is initiated by the 'divine side',[51] occasioning an '*essential*'[52] relation to the humanity of Jesus (also describable as 'creature' or 'effect'[53]), but is yet the instantiation of a *unio* of *actively* participant natures. In all this, what Dorner is proposing is a Christological model which mirrors the processes which he has earlier delineated as pertaining to the uncreated, eternal, and perfect triunity of the divine Personality. Indeed, as we will go on to outline in more detail now, his fundamental proposition regarding the incarnation as the unity of the Person of Christ *resulting* from the *unio* of the Logos and humanity is indebted to his doctrine of God. As Absolute Personality God is the 'eternal *result* of the eternal Self-discrimination of God from Himself' (my italics).[54] For Dorner, the doctrine of God as triune is normative for the proper depiction of the doctrine of Christ, and for this reason its connection is plainly acknowledged early on in his dogmatic exposition.

a. The Connection between Christology and the Doctrine of the Trinity

We have already rehearsed (in Chapter 1) the questions relating to the relationship between the doctrine of the Trinity and Christ concerning the fundament of the Christian faith. There we observed a connection which identified the doctrine of God as necessary to the proper construction of the doctrine of Jesus Christ. The certainty and form of the divine economic operation is displayed by its manifestation in the God-man who demonstrates complete conformity with the immanent divine essence. While it is with the revelation of Christ as the God-man that the Christian idea of God is *given*, this idea is taken to be the 'supreme basis of Christianity'.[55]

Here, however, we wish to observe the way in which Dorner, whom we already know sees the doctrine of the Trinity as the necessary precondition and control of a Christologically oriented dogmatics, invokes the major components of his doctrine of God. He does this in order to lay out the *grounds* for an account of the realized God-man as the appropriate and

---

[51] Ibid. p. 217.
[52] Ibid. p. 324.
[53] Ibid. p. 304.
[54] *SCD*, I, p. 412.
[55] Ibid. p. 170.

coherent manifestation of the divine economic activity. (We will see later in our discussion of Christ as the Second Adam the specific *form* this account takes.) Thus, he argues:

> There answers to the Divine in Christ a distinction of God Himself in His eternal being, and consequently the centre of the Christian religion is established in the eternal essence of God Himself, as it corresponds with its absolute character, which simple faith already perceives in its fashion. The absolute God-man is not a transient Divine manifestation, as the old Sabellianism taught, which has no simultaneous Trinity; nor does he introduce a change in God Himself which has first entered in time, but what is supposed to accrue to the Deity only in time apparently, is really an eternal predisposition of Himself, to reveal which belonged to His purpose of love from the beginning.[56]

We find, therefore, a solicitation of the idea of immanent trinitarian distinction as that which renders economic activity consonant both with the divine perfection and a permanent, though free, relationship with the created order, up to and including even unity with a man. All of this is said to be discernible in primitive form by the perception of pre-scientific *simple faith*. Yet there is needed a doctrinal explication which would link together Christ and God so as to secure: (i) the *priority* of God in incarnation (otherwise 'God Himself would be mutable, and the incarnation simply something contingent to Him'[57]); (ii) His *freedom* to act according to His own being ('the being of God in Christ [is] essentially different from the presence of God in the world generally'[58]); and (iii) the *correspondence* of the economic divine identity with the immanent ('there corresponds to the peculiar and permanent being of God in Christ an eternal determination of the Divine essence'[59]). Dorner contends that the *recognition* (not devising[60]) of immanent divine distinction is capable alone of guaranteeing this, and as such appears in connection with the doctrine of Christ as that which *harmonizes* the idea of an eternal God with the most exalted form of economic activity: incarnation.[61] The doctrine of the Trinity is integral to the proper depiction of the Person and Work of Christ because it guarantees the full scope and

---

[56] *SCD*, III, p. 289.

[57] Ibid. p. 285.

[58] Ibid.

[59] Ibid. p. 286.

[60] The doctrine of the Trinity is not to be seen as, for Schleiermacher, the 'coping-stone' (*The Christian Faith*, p. 739) of Christian doctrine, but instead its co-ordinating and indispensable *Realprinzip*.

[61] Of course, the way in which Dorner links the doctrines of God and Christ means that they serve each other.

demeanour of the God-man, and ultimately is the decisive means of *identifying* the economic activity of God as corresponding to the immanent divine identity. It is as God is triune that He is capable of becoming man without detriment either to His own being or the being of man;[62] and it is as this God is in full *possession* of Himself as triune that He acts in creation, preservation and incarnation. Thus, at the entrance to his Christological exposition Dorner brings into play that distinction which he has previously volunteered as the decisive principle at work in determining the relation between God and world: divine aseity.

> *All...depends* on the fundamental truth, that the Divine and human, little as their difference may be ignored, must not be thought as foreign and self-exclusive. And these two requisites are manifestly fulfilled at the same time, when the distinctions are so thought that the very thing which distinguishes the Divine nature and the human from one another, becomes at the same time that which unites the two. The last and inextinguishable distinction between God and man is then, that to God alone pertains self-existence or aseity....He alone has of Himself absolute fulness of life....man, on the contrary, made by God, is absolutely dependent on God, is therefore without aseity, but is at the same time, according to Divine love, destined to godlike participation in the Divine attributes. His difference from God shapes itself therefore into need of God, into receptiveness for God, which longs for His self-communication. (my italics)[63]

This is, we suggest, Dorner's pre-eminent dogmatic contribution since it is this which means that his appeal to the mutuality of divine and human natures (indebted, so he argues elsewhere, to the decisive insights of Luther[64] and Schelling[65]) is not endangered by pantheism[66] or an abandonment of

---

[62] 'The possibility of the incarnation of God would have to be denied if God were simply the abstractly simple Monad, for in that case He could not be master of Himself, and therefore could not complete the act, by means of which, without losing or changing Himself, in accordance with an eternal purpose, He gives Himself a being in unity with humanity', *SCD*, III, p. 290. The significance for his Christology of his doctrine of the triune modes of being is noted early on by Dorner in his correspondence with Hans Martensen, *Briefwechsel I*, p. 121.

[63] *SCD*, III, p. 306.

[64] Ibid. p. 224.

[65] '[T]he gain of the more recent science since Schelling, the knowledge that finite and infinite do not exclude each other has become demonstrable', Ibid. p. 253. Dorner's appropriation of this principle does not also extend to Schelling's (or Hegel's) idea of the incarnation of God which 'manifestly dissipated' the historical importance of Jesus, Ibid. p. 270.

[66] Ibid. p. 307.

the divine priority or completeness[67] in or by its economic activity. Indeed, it is the very fact of the distinction which grounds and makes possible the relation: *because* God sustains man's being (and man does not add to or perfect God), man *may* participate in God's attributes (apart from His aseity). God is God and the human is human even when both are united: 'The creaturely element of the humanity of Christ, however high it be, remains secured by the fact that it has not eternally to reckon the Divine its original being, but only through receiving it.'[68] This is the means by which Dorner is finally excused from the accusation of effecting a divinizing theology (see Chapter 3).[69] It is not enough, as we shall see, to immunize him from other criticisms.

However, while this is the means by which Dorner hopes to *secure* the creaturely element, it remains to be seen how this security is maintained within the *sui generis* unity of the God-man. Dorner needs to demonstrate the way in which *this* creature is at the same time Creator, the 'cause...at the same time its effect'.[70] He does this with appeal to two considerable propositions. First, he foregrounds the significance of the Son of God as the *Mode of Being* in which God becomes man. Second, he sets out the grounds on which he argues the humanity of Christ need not be reckoned *impersonal*. Both of these ideas lead on to a heavy appeal to the illuminating power of the idea of Christ as the Second Adam, a 'side of Christology...hitherto a treasure but little realized'.[71] We will look in turn at each, concluding with the Adam concept.

IV. Jesus Christ: The Son of God and Son of Man

a. The Incarnation of the Son of God

In determining the way in which God became man, and in accordance with his theory of divine *Personality* as that which pertains not to the constituting hypostases (as Persons) but to the *result* of their relations as *modes of being*, Dorner contends that God 'does not become man' in all of these modes of being, but it is 'only the Deity *as Logos* that becomes incarnate' (my italics).[72] This highly significant specification is not accompanied by an explicit assertion of the *impossibility* of Father or Spirit becoming incarnate; but Dorner justifies the move by referring to the connection between

---

[67] 'God does not need in himself incarnation in order to His self-realisation', SCD, III, p. 293.

[68] Ibid.

[69] Cf. Barth's critique, *Church Dogmatics*, Vol. III, Pt. I, p. 47.

[70] SCD, III, p. 304.

[71] Ibid. p. 320.

[72] Ibid. p. 293.

Logos and creation as the act of the divine mode of being through whom
God brings into existence a 'different, relative, self-dependent being' which
nonetheless 'reckons upon a consummation'.[73] Since it is through the Logos
or Son of God that the world came into existence as *both* distinct *and* yet
distinctly inclined towards God as the originator and sustainer of *its* being
(see again the importance of God's aseity), it will be the Logos who becomes
man in order for this arrangement to *retain* this relation of distinction *and*
persistent connection, while manifesting a decisive advance in the specific
form in which this relation occurs; towards a non-identifiable *unity* of originator and originated and conserver and conserved.[74] It will – *must*[75] – be the
Logos who becomes man because it is the Logos who, as the obedient Son
to the Father is *always* the very manifestation of *distinction* without *disjunction* within the Godhead, since he is the 'eternal principle of freedom'.[76] The
unity which characterizes the immanent distinctions is that which will be
replicated in the incarnation; and since the way in which this is instantiated
in the Absolute Personality is through the *specific* order of each Mode of
Being, the incarnation of the Logos *throws light on* the 'special character
of this Person within the divine nature'.[77] With this, Dorner is seeking to

---

[73] Ibid. p. 294.
[74] Carl Theodor Albert Liebner observes that the connection which Dorner makes
between the doctrines of Christ and Trinity has its focal point in the doctrine of the two
Adams, according to which Christ, as the 'Haupt der geistigen Schöpfung', has metaphysical significance which links Christ with the Logos through whom all things are
created (according to the Johannine Prologue), *Die christliche Dogmatik*, Erster Band,
1st Afl., Bd. I (Göttingen: Vandenhoek und Ruprecht, 1849), p. 38.
[75] This is not to imply a necessity on the part of God, which Dorner distinctly rejects
(*SCD*, III, p. 293).
[76] Ibid. p. 292.
[77] This is in apparent contradiction to the post-Augustinian tradition identified by Karl
Rahner as agreeing that 'each of the divine Persons [if it were only freely willed by
God] could become man', K. Rahner, 'Remarks on the Dogmatic Treatise "De Trini-
tate"', in *Theological Investigations* IV (London: Darton, Longman & Todd, 1966),
p. 80. We wonder if Rahner's accompanying insistence that the Trinity is that which
'takes place in us, and as such does not first reach us in the form of statements communicated by revelation' (Ibid. p. 98) – echoing as it does Dorner's own position on the
doctrine's relationship to faith in Christ – provides a useful means of situating Dorner
within a line of dogmaticians for whom the task of seeking a conciliation of God's
being *in* and *ad extra* lies in the depiction of God's modes of being as 'determined by
God himself through appropriation', Eberhard Jüngel, *God's Being Is In Becoming*,
trans. John Webster (Edinburgh: T & T Clark, 2001), p. 52. n. 151, without rendering
this determination as arbitrary or anterior to the instantiation. Like Rahner, Dorner's
proposal is not 'disputing the utterly free act of God in sending the Son and the Spirit
into the world…Rather, he is arguing that the revelation of the Son and the Spirit in
the divine economy reveal that God is indeed triune in the divine being itself, and this
in such a manner that is conceptually consistent', Ralph Del Colle, *Christ and the Spirit*
(Oxford: OUP, 1994), p. 13. Dorner's configuration of aseity is an attempt to do this.

furnish the ecclesial dogma of Christ with a configuration which offers the grounds for a *positive* account of the relation of the two natures, which he argues has been scarcely displayed in the history of the doctrine. For this reason, Dorner's reconstruction of the Chalcedon and post-Chalcedon doctrinal development is vital to the proper accounting of his own doctrine.

b. Chalcedon and After: The Personal Humanity of Christ[78]

First, he awards his imprimatur to the formulators of the Creed on the grounds that they successfully opposed the doctrines of 'mutation or commingling as well as Nestorianism'.[79] What was confirmed was the rejection of identification or division in favour of unity; and even though the Definition did not provide a 'positive description of [the two natures'] relation', vis-à-vis the way in which they might be said to relate as Creator to created, it did offer a constructive proposition regarding the 'result of their *union*',[80] that is, of the *unio hypostatica* or *Personalis*. The *unity* of the Person of Christ was depicted as the result of the *unio*. However, in subsequent doctrinal development, Dorner suggests that the sobriety of the Council's deliberations is lost as the unity of the Divine-human Person is begun to be predicated of the hypostasis of the Son.[81] The unity of the Person of Christ is depicted as the *result* of the hypostasis of the Son constituting the Person:

> Thus resulted the doctrine that the *Unio* Personalis arises because the Person of the Logos assumes a human nature, in order to be therein the Ego or the Personality. But thus Christ is only the Personal Logos, who has a human 'nature' in itself, in relation to which, as well as in relation to Himself, He is the Ego.[82]

---

[78] We note, here, a difference between Dorner's *use* of Chalcedon in his *System* and his detailed analysis of it in his *History of Development*. That is to say, he is much more circumspect in his evaluation of the Creed in the latter, and even differing in his conclusions, e.g. according to *SCD*, III, p. 216, Chalcedon mitigates against commingling, but according to *History of Development*, Div. II, Vol. I, p. 116, Chalcedon 'did not form a deep enough estimate of the distinction...that the two, when they meet, commingle'.

[79] *SCD*, III, p. 216.

[80] Ibid.

[81] Dorner's account of Chalcedon clearly represents it as *not* implying Christ's impersonal humanity. This is, of course, a matter of contention. What is of interest, however, is the way in which Dorner's concern to display the Personality of the humanity as the key to the proper representation of his humanity does not, as it does for others, issue forth in an anti-Chalcedon analysis, cf. Anthony Hanson, *Grace and Truth* (London: SPCK, 1975), pp. 2–3. Dorner's reading of Chalcedon is critical, but not wholly dismissive.

[82] *SCD*, III, p. 218.

This development entails an inappropriate and unchalcedonian abridgment of the humanity of Jesus, since the *anhypostasia* or impersonality
of the human nature, which excluded the possibility of this humanity
having its own Personality (described as 'self-consciousness and self-
determination'[83]) renders inevitable the idea of the Divine Ego taking
'the place of the human',[84] a view which Dorner contends leads back to
Doceticism. Crucially, according to this reading, it is the ancient Church's
doctrine of God which holds the key to these misguided Christological
developments;[85] and it will be with a depiction of the divine tri-unity
as capable of bearing its distinctions and its unity, without detriment to
either, that the negative determinations concerning Christ's *unio hypostatica* delivered by Chalcedon can be cultivated into a positive statement
of the relation of the two natures. It is into this breach that Dorner commends his doctrine of God as Absolute Personality – or holy Love – as
that which insists on the incarnation of the Logos as a mode or 'factor'[86]
in God's eternal triune constitution. With this, what is anticipated is the
enabling of an account which serves both the depiction of a *unity* with
distinction and *unio* without confusion in a representation of Christ's
God-manhood which diminishes neither 'the humanity or the Deity'.[87]
Accordingly, Dorner insists that for this to be successful, the apprehension of a Personal living unity hangs on the methodological recognition of
its being the result of the *union* of the 'Divine and human side in him',[88]
rather than predicating this unity of either the human or Divine side. The
latter is a concern, since anthropocentric Christologies either threaten the
idea of the 'perfection of the Logos' by suggesting that the Logos is *made*
'Personal'[89] through the humanity or make the Divine a 'contingent'[90] factor in the human Personality.[91]

c. Human Ego and Human Nature

This drive to 'begin with the *union* of the natures instead of with the Ego,
Divine or human' appeals heavily to the axiom that the natures have a 'direct

---

[83] Ibid.
[84] Ibid. p. 219.
[85] Koppehl correctly identifies as the key question the central importance of the classical
      doctrine of the Trinity (by which he means the creedal doctrine) to the development of
      Christology, Koppehl, *Standpunkt*, p. 107.
[86] *SCD*, III, p. 318.
[87] Ibid. p. 308.
[88] Ibid.
[89] Ibid. p. 318.
[90] Ibid. p. 311.
[91] This twofold danger reflects, of course, Dorner's persistent concern to avoid pantheis-
      tic and dualist tendencies, cf. *SCD*, II, p. 22.

reference to one another',[92] but also hangs on a particularized definition of the human Ego (specified as self-consciousness and self-determination) as nothing more than the human 'nature itself'.[93] Dorner proposes a non-substantive account of Ego, and instead posits it as the 'actuality [of] conscious and willing'[94] nature. Such a move is, of course, highly significant, and is indicative of his concern to depict the incarnation as having its reality in a gradual, dynamic process. Furthermore, it mirrors again his depiction of God's triune being as Absolute Personality and not Absolute Substance.[95]

On these grounds alone, he argues, is it possible to draw a *positive* outline of the way in which God-human living unity may occur, since the *self* of this unity will be nothing more than the 'contents of the self-consciousness'[96] constituted by the two distinct natures? As such will it be *God-human being*, having knowledge of itself as God-man. This means that the contents of the Divine and human knowledge is God-human; and the explanatory feature central to this idea is the conception of the specific and complementary characteristics of each side of the *unio*: divine 'communication' and creaturely 'appropriation'.[97] The *distinctness* of each nature is instantiated in their *connectedness*: 'as the Divine side is for the human the *complementum* of receptiveness, the human in relation to the Divine is the *complementum* or fulfilling for its love'.[98]

This definition of distinct, though corresponding, characteristics is the way in which Dorner holds it possible to secure the content of the self-consciousness and self-determination of the God-man as embracing a 'Divine self-knowing and willing' without this involving an *identification* of this Divine knowledge and volition with that of the human knowledge and volition. The *complementum* schema follows the definite order given with the 'idea of both', according to which the 'initiative must issue from the Divine side' and the 'human side must maintain itself in receptive attitude'.[99] Thus, the *way* in which the Person of Jesus Christ is the God-man is *as* perfect creaturely receptivity for the full divine self-communication; and since this is the content of his Self-knowing, he knows himself God-man

---

[92] *SCD*, III, p. 313.

[93] Ibid. p. 314.

[94] Ibid. The appropriateness of using 'nature' as a way of expressing both the divine and the human had, of course, come under considerable strain following Schleiermacher's analysis of Christology in which he questions whether 'divine and human [can] be brought together under any single conception' (*The Christian Faith* §96, p. 392) and Dorner's attempts at solving the *problem* of Christ's Person stand under the spotlight of this earlier critique (as Axt-Piscalar helpfully observes, *Grund*, p. 252).

[95] *SCD*, I, p. 419.

[96] Ibid. p. 314.

[97] Ibid. p. 316.

[98] Ibid.

[99] Ibid.

without needing those sides to be identified. Such an identification, after all, would lead to him ceasing to be God-man, since it would signal a loss either of the mode of communication or receptivity. Thus, the Personality of Christ is 'nothing else than the God-humanity',[100] according to which Christ knows Himself as God-man in the manner of His appropriation of the divine Self-communication on the basis of His identity as the incarnate Logos:

> Thus, then, God as the Logos or as the revealing principle thinks the Divine thoughts, which are to be revealed to the God-man, on the ground and by virtue of the original *Unio*, so to speak, in Him. And the God-man sees or perceives what God shows him'[101]

This is the basis for Dorner's developmental Christology, according to which the distinction is made between the *unio* and the unity in order to predicate of the incarnation a process of growth in the humanity of Christ:

> The Personality of Christ is therefore nothing else than the God-humanity, reflected, conceived, and willed in itself, which by virtue of the *Unio* is already initially the real God-human totality, but which must now also become in knowledge and will God-human.[102]

In configuring the Personality of Christ in this way, as the result of acts of consciousness and will (it embraces both *noesis* and volition), Dorner displays his interest in defining the constitutive elements of Christ's God-manhood *dynamically*. It is an arrangement indebted to the dogmatically prior exposition of God's triunity in terms of Absolute Personality or Life, since it requires the depiction of (in this case, Christ's) Personality as that which is the result of a *process* which is yet not indeterminate or absolutely free. Christ is *already*, *initially* the God-human *totality*, since *this* man is 'from the beginning'[103] created and maintained by the Logos. Yet this auspicious beginning awaits completion because a function of *proper* human nature is its plain, mature apprehension of itself: 'The self-consciousness of this man only being true and perfect inasmuch as he knows and thinks his own being as it is.'[104] Since, therefore, the not-yet perfected humanity belongs to the stage of temporal succession (which we noted in a previous chapter is part of a two-part definition of how the creation is also eternal[105]),

[100] Ibid. p. 317.
[101] Ibid. p. 316.
[102] Ibid.
[103] Ibid. p. 318.
[104] Ibid. pp. 314–315.
[105] *SCD*, I, p. 32.

161

its realization will occur in obedience to the particularities of that environment (e.g. spatial and temporal). Furthermore, the way in which these activities of self-consciousness and self-determination will be defined has an ethical character.

This conceptualization means, of course, that Dorner must work hard to represent the incarnation as not *contingent* on creaturely activity (since it is a process which involves the efficacious receptivity of the humanity). Or indeed, as endangering the *unio* (during the period of the incompleteness of its unity), or jeopardizing the *distinction* (by predicating the unity of the resulting Personality). Axt-Piscalar has provided the most extensive analysis of the attendant problems (incorporating the main concerns of Dorner's chief critics), to which we now turn. It is, perhaps, worth noting here that Dorner places himself in the curious position of displaying elements of Christological thinking from across the ecclesial lines, and thereby exposes himself to more than one confrontation. As well as investing in axioms common to the Lutheran tradition (e.g. *finitum capax infiniti*), his handling of them is such that he has been thought to be a Reformed theologian (in seeking the *union* without an immediate communication of attributes).[106]

d. Christine Axt-Piscalar:
The Problem of the God-manhood in Christ

Axt-Piscalar, in a thorough and detailed analysis, focuses on the problems which accompany Dorner's solution to what she identifies as the prevailing question of nineteenth-century theology concerning how the second Person of the Trinity 'mit dem Menschen Jesus eins werden kann unter Wahrung der vollen Menschheit Christi'.[107]Tracing the historical development of Dorner's doctrine, she suggests that Dorner's doctrine of God as Absolute Personality and its concomitant notion of the hypostases as Modes of Being, while trying hard to overcome the dangers of proposing a doctrine of the double Personality of Christ, too often falls into doing so, both because of Dorner's inconsistency of expression, and also on account of his heavy investment in the traditional idea of *perichoresis*. Thus, although Dorner, at an early stage (borrowing the idea from Martensen[108]) speaks of the hypostases as 'bloßer Ichpunkte'[109] – that is,

---

[106] Dorner is described (with Cremer) as a Reformed theologian in *The Immutability of God in the Theology of Hans Urs von Balthasar*, Gerard F. O'Hanlon (Cambridge: CUP, 1990), p. 2. Gottfried Thomasius accuses Dorner of being 'no Lutheran theologian', *Christi Person und Werk*, II (Erlangen: Bläsing, 1857), p. 196.

[107] Axt-Piscalar, *Grund*, p. 221.

[108] Martensen comes to refer to the *hypostases* as 'momenta' (p. 102) or 'Ego-centres' (p. 108) in his *Christian Dogmatics*.

[109] Axt-Piscalar, *Grund*, p. 225. The 'bloß' is Axt-Piscalar's addition.

centres of the '*Urichs*'[110] – Axt-Piscalar suggests that because Dorner holds to the doctrine of perichoresis, according to which each hypostasis immanently participates in the Absolute Personality and as such are actually not *un*personal, the problem remains. If Dorner were able to hold to the conception of the sheer impersonality of the Logos, the difficulty of the double Personality would be eradicated, since the Person of Christ would be the result of two natures which only *together* form a *unio personalis*. However, she argues, this is not secured[111] by Dorner, and there is a series of contradictions in the account concerning the actual role of each side in the realization of the *unio*.

Axt-Piscalar argues that, in spite of his desire to ensure that neither side dominates at the expense of the other, Dorner is unable to offer a stable representation of such an arrangement.[112] His interest in declaring the Logos as the 'principle which forms this person from the beginning',[113] while intended to preserve the divine initiative of the incarnation, is taken to compromise the other claim that the *unio* is 'confirmed and established by the perfection of the humanity, namely by the self-conscious and self-determination of the same'.[114] There is, then, a problem with the way in which the two natures are said to *relate* in mediating the God-man Personality.

Furthermore, the uncertainty surrounding Dorner's attempts to define the Logos as impersonal brings additional problems. If the Logos is *only* an impersonal moment of the Absolute Personality, and as such is itself alone the enactor of the incarnation (with Father and Son merely 'dwelling'[115] in the God-man), then the problem arises that Jesus Christ stands apart from (gegenüber) the Absolute Personality, since his personality is not the product of that Absolute Personality, but of the unification of one Mode of Being with a human nature.[116] This is the problem of the abridgment of the Divine side.

Axt-Piscalar also notes, as we mentioned above, that Dorner's investment in the doctrine of perichoresis brings with it a contrary implication.

---

[110] *Briefwechsel*, I, p. 121.

[111] As previously noted, Axt-Piscalar does not suggest that Dorner's doctrine of God ever formally proposed the personality of the individual hypostases in and for themselves. This is a much more satisfactory summation than that offered by E. Günther who refers to a 'definite' difference between the early and later Dorner, Günther, *Die Entwicklung*, p. 240.

[112] Axt-Piscalar, *Grund*, p. 249.

[113] *SCD*, III, p. 318.

[114] Ibid. p. 314.

[115] Ibid. p. 316, fn. 1.

[116] This is the basis of E. Hirsch's critique which he adjoins to his observations concerning Dorner's 'deviation' from traditional Church dogma concerning the doctrines of the impersonality of the human nature of Christ and the personhood of Jesus Christ residing in the Logos who assumed human nature, Hirsch, *Geschichte*, pp. 381–382.

Although the incarnation is held out as the act of the Logos, since the Father and Spirit are also the points of mediation in the production of Divine self-knowledge, if Christ is said to have knowledge of himself as God, it is not clear ('bleibt freilich erwägen'[117]) if the personal being of God is in Christ since such self-knowledge is a characteristic not of *each* hypostasis in and for themselves but in and for each other. The problem arises of a *perichoretically* personal Logos again being introduced to the Godhumanity. This is the problem of the abridgement of the humanity of Christ.

Dorner is said to have traces of both an underpersonalized or overpersonalized account of the Logos. The first leads to the abridgement of the divinity of Christ, the second to the abridgement of his humanity. Problems which, of course, Dorner had sought to avoid.

We concur with Axt-Piscalar that Dorner's arrangement is left exposed on these points, not least because of some infelicitous expressions. However, we think that there are some aspects of the account which provide ways of, at least, demonstrating a coherency amidst the apparent confusion. We suggest that a firmer grasp of Dorner's doctrine of aseity will give us the grounds for seeing how he is able to posit the relation between natures as non-competitive, and as a result avoid the slippage identified between the divine and human sides. Furthermore, with regard to the question of the personal or impersonal status of the Logos – and the attendant problem of the double personality of Christ[118] – we suggest that reference to what we might describe as the teleological structure of the *points* of personality (both the 'Ego' points of the divine hypostases and the 'Ego' point of Jesus' humanity) may give us an insight into how Dorner holds his position to be tenable. We want to add, however, that we are not here *defending* Dorner's particular delineation of the way in which the two sides of Jesus Christ do come to *union*. Or the notion that this *union* is the *result* of a process of unification. Or indeed that *Personality* is an appropriate means of describing or defining the hypostatic *union*. We will come later to our conclusions regarding these issues. Rather, we wish only to suggest that an explanation of Dorner's positing *both* Christ's Divinity *and* humanity as involved in the perfection of the incarnation can be found in the way in which he relates God's aseity to creatureliness, and in particular creaturely freedom as that which is consonant with dependence on or (if ethically stated) obedience to God. His account of the Logos as 'not *per se* an individual personality' may be seen to be consistent with his being the principle of Christ's personal existence and the mediator of the divine nature without the 'absolute

---

[117] Axt-Piscalar, *Grund*, p. 240.
[118] The implication that Dorner is proposing two personal egos pervades Geß's early response to his early anti-kenotic Christology, *Die Lehre von der Person Christi* (Basel: Bahnmaier, 1856), compare p. 289 and p. 292.

Divine personality, i.e. the Triune God, [being] represented as incarnated in Christ'.[119]

1. Aseity and the Relation of the Natures

Axt-Piscalar acknowledges that Dorner gives as the characteristic definition of the divine nature its 'Durchsichsein, ihre Aseität', and yet suggests that he is unable to stay with this because it does not give sufficient grounds for positing God's 'Bezogenheit auf Anderes'.[120] Instead, as she sees it, he makes a *shift* by referring to self-sufficiency as *forming itself into* 'actual volition of community with the world'.[121]

We suggest, however, that this is a misrepresentation of Dorner's account of God's aseity and its significance for divine economic activity. God's aseity is not that which renders his relation to an *other* problematic (which Axt-Piscalar sees as problematic presumably because it does not give an account of the *cause* of this relation), but instead is precisely the ground on which God does and is *continually* related to that other. The self-sufficiency of God is that which both prompts and preserves the positing of an other which, having been posited by the only self-existent being, is 'absolutely dependent on God', and as such distinct from God, but 'destined to godlike participation in the Divine attributes'.[122] It is posited as capable of *union* with God. God's aseity is not the limit of His freedom, but the very basis of it. Man's difference from God is therefore not inimical to but consonant with, indeed manifest in, his very capacity for God: '[Man's] difference from God shapes itself therefore into need of God, into receptiveness for God, which longs for His self-communication.'[123]

Dorner's delineation of the cause (God's self-sufficiency), form (positing a *different* other) and end (community) of the relation between God and man provides sufficient grounds, therefore, for his account of the way in which the Logos may be said to be the forming principle *and* that the *unio* of natures is 'confirmed and established by the perfection of the humanity'.[124] The humanity of Christ operates properly and in accord with its structure, as that which does not have aseity, when it acts in conformity with its divinely originated and maintained being by *tending* towards the Divine side to which it is essentially bound: 'His dependence upon God is at the same time unity with God.'[125] At the level of volition (on which Dorner has, we

---

[119] *SCD*, III, p. 318.
[120] Axt-Piscalar, *Grund*, p. 237.
[121] *SCD*, III, p. 306.
[122] Ibid.
[123] Ibid.
[124] Ibid. p. 314.
[125] Ibid.

think unfairly, been accused of Samosaticism[126]), what is proposed is that Jesus wills himself at every stage only ever in conformity with his identity as God-man: 'there is no self-volition without a willing of Himself as originally united with God, as the humanity already is in itself.'[127] Jesus displays his proper creatureliness *in* his conformity to his original designation as the *unio* of Logos and humanity. The order and manner of his self-volition indicates the way in which it is uniquely related to the Logos because it has its origination and persistence in dependence on the Logos (who as a *momenta* of the Divine Personality is *a se*) as the principle of its formation. What we see depicted is, once again, a non-competitive account of God and man even in the freedom of the humanity of Jesus and the divine union with this humanity.

2. The Logos as Ego Point

As we have seen, the conclusion that it is the Logos who has initiated the formation of the person of Christ need not be interpreted to imply the abridgement of Christ's humanity, since such an activity involves the enabling of the humanity to conform to its own nature by maintaining its freedom to receive the 'absolute self-communication'.[128] Jesus is not *catching up* with the Logos in his self-determination, but his humanity is being upheld by the Logos to freely correspond with his being as God-man. Jesus does not wake up to *discover* who he is. He acts in conformity to who he is:

> The self-consciousness of this man [is] only true and perfect inasmuch as he knows and thinks his own being as it is, and this being happening to be of the kind that it does not merely have the Divine outside of itself but received into its own property.[129]

---

[126] Among Gottfried Thomasius' criticisms of Dorner's Christology is the accusation of being 'somehow related to Paul of Samosta' because of the manner of the distinction between the two natures which he sees in Dorner, *Christi*, p. 195. Geß also sees a 'samosatic' doctrine at play, *Dogma*, p. 316. This ascription coalesces with Geß's criticism that Dorner's approach sees the incarnation as the free realization of humanity in that it sees Paul's impulse in securing a *union* of wills as indicative of a concern, discerned in Dorner, to identify Christ's humanity as that which is a mediating factor in the perfecting of the *union*. While both Thomasius and Geß see something Paul-*like* in Dorner, rather than an exact replica, the point at stake is, of course, the extent to which the humanity is conceived as not *essentially* related to the Logos and as such a relatively independent agent in the realization of a *union* of equal or mutual complicity.

[127] *SCD*, III, p. 315.

[128] Ibid. p. 318.

[129] Ibid. p. 315.

We suggest, therefore, that the capacity of Dorner's doctrine of divine aseity has been underplayed by Axt-Piscalar, at the expense of seeing how God is related to the created humanity of Christ.

Furthermore, Axt-Piscalar argues that Dorner's designation of the Logos as personal or impersonal is seriously flawed. We suggest, however, that Dorner's description of the Logos as not an 'individual personality' while also being the person forming principle of the God-man has a consistency when its relation to the human nature is considered in terms of the ethically defined *teleology* of both the divine Absolute Personality and the Godhumanity of Christ. Since the Logos is accounted a Mode of Being insofar as He, the Son, exists in a state of free eternal obedience to the Father in and by the enabling of the Spirit, He is defined as personal by the way in which he relates to the other hypostases according to the *telos* of the divine being: God as *holy* Love. God as triune fully coheres with the necessary conditions of his being.[130] The Logos is personal insofar as he reaches the *end* to which he, as a divine mode of being, is eternally posited.

When this arrangement is applied to the *unio* with a man, the same teleological structure is in play. While the Logos is eternally secure in his being prior to the incarnation, in the act of becoming a man, the manner of his becoming includes the positing of a human nature with which he is essentially related, which is upheld by the same Logos to be *for* a specific end. This end will be the *temporally located* demonstration of Jesus Christ as God's Son in his continual, though not endless, activity[131] of free obedience to the 'will of the Father, the ethically necessary'.[132] While the humanity of Christ is of the order of created being, through its acceptance of the Divine ends for which it was created[133] it coheres with its self-identity as belonging uniquely to God through the essential *unio* with the Logos. On these grounds, this 'man will be God-human'.[134] Furthermore, the Logos, as a Mode of Being, mediates his participation with God as the uncreated Absolute Personality without denuding his distinction as a created nature because of the persistent upholding of Christ's human dependency on God.

Crucial to this position is Dorner's heavy investment in the idea of Christ as the Second Adam, since the health of the argument hangs on the careful depiction of the *uniqueness* of Christ's humanity. This is an aspect which we

---

[130] *SCD*, I, p. 138.

[131] Dorner describes the *unio* itself not as a 'rigid and motionless whole, but as *a whole which is in process* of realization', *SCD*, III, p. 334. The intention is to depict the incarnation as living without being indeterminate.

[132] Ibid. p. 317.

[133] 'God as Logos produces the Divine contents, the Divine ends to be realized as the definite impulse in the God-man, and He accepts them livingly and realizes them. To these ends belong pre-eminently the perfect actual being of God in Christ', Ibid.

[134] Ibid. p. 315.

suggest is underexplored in Axt-Piscalar's account (thorough though it is). It is to this that we now turn before concluding our chapter.

V. Christ: The Central Individual as the Second Adam[135]

Dorner foregrounds the idea of Christ as the Second Adam[136] since it marks, for him, a crucial way of representing the incarnation (a *becoming* and not mere *influencing*[137]). It brings to the project the means of explicating his developmental Christology, and linking it with his wider ambition to delineate the incarnation as connected with the *teleologically* defined first creation: the *telos* being the Second Creation. The specification of the Logos as the concrete divine Mode of Being who becomes man is connected to the doctrine of the Creation *and* the new or second Creation. It is *through* the mediating Logos that the persisting distinction between Creator and creation has purchase[138] and the future orientation of creation is posited[139] *and* realized.[140] It is as the Logos that God becomes man in a *new*, though not arbitrary, creative act,[141] and this God-man becomes the instantiation of a

---

[135] While Dorner makes full use of this N. T. idea in his dogmatic exposition, he does not discuss it in any detail in his investigation of Paul's contribution to Christology, apart from interpreting the *grasping* motif in Phil. 2.6 as representing a parallel to the disobedience of Adam, Ibid. p. 183. Furthermore, while he does on occasion refer to the 'second Adam' as the 'last Adam' (cf. *SCD*, III, p. 319), he does not give an account of the reason for his making more use of the former title. This is of particular importance given the fact that Paul only ever refers to the 'last Adam' (1 Cor. 15.45).

[136] What is interesting, though unsurprising, in Dorner's use of this idea is that he still privileges the *becoming* of John 1.14 over the *becoming* of 1 Cor. 15.45b, in that the latter is by itself an insufficient account of the incarnation. It does, however, provide an essential explanatory function.

[137] Dorner refuses all designations for the 'divine act affecting humanity in the Person of Christ' (Ibid. p. 300) which imply either a change in the Logos or the appearance of God *in* a man or as a 'theophany in human form' (Ibid. p. 303.)

[138] 'God as Logos constitutes man in an existence independent of Himself, and distinguishes Himself from him', Ibid. p. 304.

[139] '[C]reation from the beginning reckons upon a consummation.' Ibid. p. 294. 'The Logos creates even the historical preparation for His manifestation', Ibid. p. 295.

[140] 'The New Testament shows the Divine likeness to have become real through the Son, the Divine image.' Ibid. p. 294.

[141] Dorner does not find convincing any appeal to the uniqueness of Christ's creation as a basis for His God-manhood, 'If He were a new creation simply, He would manifestly be no more than a creature', Ibid. p. 301. However, Christ is the result of a specific, unique creative act of creation in which the 'unifying of the Divine and human was never preceded by a time of their mere separation', Ibid. p. 305. Yet this second or new creation is consonant with the first creation, and the conservation of this creation, and

'new higher humanity than the Adamitic'[142] (of which we 'become His cop-ies'[143] by faith). Thus:

> The Christological problem, then, does not require the abrogation of the distinction between the human and Divine; it leaves its rights to the first creation. But Christ is also the second Adam, the second crea-tion, and the idea of this suffices to form a bridge between creation, by means of which man is placed outside of God in an independent exist-ence, and incarnation, inasmuch as in Christ, as in Christians a *union* of the two is found without detriment to the permanent distinction between the Divine and creaturely.[144]

The idea of Christ as the second Adam functions, therefore, as a link between the first creation (enjoying also its principle of distinction) and the incarnation (as the principle of *union*), since it is the biblical trope which brings together the distinction and pneumatological telos of creation with the God-man.[145] It does this by providing a concept through which the idea of incarnation may be approved as the means by which creation is brought to its fulfilment (as the divine image bearer[146]): by God *Himself* becoming united with that creation, or giving 'Himself to humanity as a property'.[147] With this notion in place, Dorner holds it possible to present and apprehend how in the idea of incarnation: 'not an identity of the Divine and human, but unity is posited in difference, inasmuch as the idea of creation is not destroyed in that of incarnation, but is preserved.'[148]

However, further to this use of the Second Adam concept, which seeks to provide a *link* between the doctrines of Creation, Logos and Incarnation, Dorner identifies the concept as enabling an account of Christ's humanity which defines it as neither *impersonal* nor requiring the kind of ontological contortionism which he sees in 'modern Kenotic theories'.[149] This is because Dorner holds that the doctrine of the second Adam enables a depiction of

---

as such represents a decisively *new* act but not a *discrete* new act, 'The Logos has not entered abruptly, or from without, into humanity; but He was ever in the world; indeed the Divine centre of the world, which after all had been made in order to reveal Himself therein progressively', Ibid. p. 342.

[142] Ibid. p. 305.
[143] Ibid.
[144] Ibid.
[145] Second creation 'turns out to be an intermediate idea between incarnation and the first creation, together with conservation, seeing that it holds both distinct, but is also destined to unite them', Ibid. p. 304.
[146] *SCD*, II, pp. 9, 15, 27, 47.
[147] *SCD*, III, p. 305.
[148] Ibid. p. 307.
[149] Ibid. p. 320.

the humanity of Christ as 'receptive of the fulness of the Divine Essence of the Logos'[150] on the basis of a particular and distinct operation of the Logos in setting apart this man as having a receptiveness 'adequate to Him'.[151] Yet this receptivity is such that it identifies Christ as *both* unique – as alone being united with the Logos – *and* universal – as bringing to perfection the 'idea of humanity'[152] as that destined for 'communion'[153] with God. The key to all this lies in Dorner's conception of Christ's adamic or representative status as bearing an *'ethico-religious character'*.[154] Christ is related to all humanity by virtue of his particular, 'individual'[155] constitution as the element from within humanity with the 'receptiveness adequate'[156] to God's purposes of absolute self-communication. As such he is the *central individual*. This means he is universally related to humanity not merely on the basis of the Divine side of his identity, but on the basis of the capacity of his humanity to *receive* God; and, as we have already seen (but which in this place Dorner is frustratingly inexplicit) creaturely reception is an ethical *activity*.[157] All this, of course, sees Dorner committing himself to a model of the hypostatic *union* which, while acknowledging that the human nature does not subsist of itself ('the Logos forms the permanent basis of this Person; He is its centre'[158]), seeks to avoid the depersonalizing gloss (as he sees it[159]) of post-Chalcedon revisionism which seeks to identify the Logos as the 'real principle and prototype of all'.[160] This means that Christ's universal relation to humanity is derived from the Logos Himself alone since human nature 'in general'[161] has been assumed. What Dorner intends is to depict a relation of natures according to which the *priority* of the divine constitution does not preclude the active engagement of the humanity in

[150] *SCD*, III, p. 320.
[151] Ibid. p. 321.
[152] Ibid. p. 322.
[153] Ibid. p. 323.
[154] Ibid. p. 321.
[155] Ibid.
[156] Ibid.
[157] Cf. *SCD*, II, p. 124.
[158] *SCD*, III, p. 318.
[159] This reading sees the anhypostasis/enhypostasis doctrine as the unfortunate consequence of the solution of Chalcedon which, while providing a means to secure the divine and human constitution of Christ, failed to do much more than this. Hendrikus Berkhof describes it as leaving open the question whether the one Person of Christ is 'to be regarded as standing on the side of the divine or of the human nature', Berkhof, *Christian Faith*, p. 288. Dorner agrees that Chalcedon succeeded in opposing the doctrines of 'mutation or commingling' and fixing the limits of the relation of the two natures, but a 'positive description of their relation is not yet found', *SCD*, III, p. 216.
[160] Ibid. p. 320.
[161] Ibid.

bringing this *Unio Personalis* to effect.[162] The execution of these intentions, however, occasionally betrays (as noted above) the difficulty he has in managing such an arrangement without indicating that the incarnation is, as an early critique of Dorner suggests, in some sense finally the 'free realization of humanity'.[163] We see in the following passage the tensions at work in seeking to depict this relationship:

> God first *creates* for Himself within humanity the adequate place for His self-revelation and communication in Him, in whom the pure central receptiveness of human nature has been constituted by the creative efficiency of God. Therefore He could not arise in the way of mere natural generation. But just by the fact that God, namely as Logos, as the Divine centre of the world, *finds* in the humanity of Jesus the place for His central self-revelation, and appropriates the receptiveness of this man, this man becomes the creaturely centre, primarily of humanity as the source of redeeming, perfecting life, and according to the indications of Scripture even beyond humanity. (my italics)[164]

It is, of course, the weight of the divine *finding* which poses certain problems. Of course, Dorner has set about by defining this *found* humanity as already constituted or posited as capable of being found by *God's* creative activity. Accordingly, we could merely harmonize these two verbs as simply the expressions appropriate to the relation which obtains between these two natures. God *creates* a humanity which is capable of receiving Him, and therefore this humanity is *found* to be capable of receiving Him. Yet, even here, we miss the significance of the active form of the verb: it is not man who is found, but God who *finds*.[165] With this slightest of expressions there is encapsulated the problem in Dorner's conception. In order to depict Christ's humanity as co-operative (albeit subsequent to the divine constitution) in the production of the God-man Personality, Dorner on occasion tends towards the suggestion of an incarnational immanentism which belies the priority of the Logos in his account. However, while we acknowledge the tensions at play even in the articulation of the account (as we have noted above in our interaction with Axt-Piscalar), we hold the accusation made by Geß (and others) as flawed when it concludes of Dorner's doctrine that it sees the incarnation as merely the free realization of humanity. Rather, we

---

[162] We see in this, of course, the non-competitive theme which has dominated his dogmatic venture, cf. *SCD*, II, p. 45.

[163] W. F. Geß, *Lehre*, p. 290.

[164] *SCD*, III, p. 324–325.

[165] The English translation is correct. The German original is, 'Gott, nämlich als Logos, als das gpöttliche Centrum der Welt, in Jesu Menscheit den Ort für seine centrale Selbstoffenbarung *findet*' (my italics), *SCG*, II.i., p. 428.

suggest Dorner does enough to confirm an *essential* relation between the Logos and the assumed humanity (providing an explication of the relation between Creator and creation in which their activities and interests are not mutually exclusive) so as to obviate the danger of seeing the incarnation as merely indicative of creaturely possibility rather than as the act in which the Logos became 'what he was not'[166] and as such embraced a particular humanity which was created capable of receiving Him: '*this* individual is constituted for becoming' (my italics).[167] Crucially, while Dorner's interest is in seeking to relinquish the tradition's doctrine of Christ's impersonal humanity, it does not come merely by using the *humanity* of Christ as the 'regulative principle'[168] of Christology. Rather, it is *Christ's* humanity as the incarnate Logos which occupies centre stage. In seeking a depiction of the God-man in which the humanity is not seen as a mere addendum to the divine activity, his regulative principle might adequately be described as the *particular humanity* of the Logos.

Conclusion

Dorner's arrangement of material seeks to posit the incarnation as the result of the union of natures. We have suggested that the problems associated with this doctrine (double personality, externality of God to Jesus, incarnation as a consequence of human possibility) can be resolved with a fuller recognition of the place of aseity and teleology in the wider project. However, as we noted above, such resolution is not intended as a defence of the doctrine, but rather an effort to ensure that *all* Dorner's store of arguments are acknowledged in order to see how he himself conceived it as coherent.

We suggest in conclusion, however, that Dorner's account suffers from an underplaying of the role of the *Spirit* in the continual upholding of this humanity for its telos. This is evidenced most obviously in the absence of the Spirit from the discussion, but even on the occasions when Dorner lays out the relation of the Spirit to the incarnation, he minimizes the Spirit's position with regard to the forming, supporting, sanctifying and preserving

---

[166] *SCD*, III, p. 303.

[167] Ibid. p. 321.

[168] This is how Donald Macleod describes John Knox's use of the humanity of Christ in his doctrinal reconstruction, *The Person of Christ* (Leicester: IVP, 1998), p. 65. Knox's position is far removed from Dorner's, even though both share an interest in a proper depiction of Christ's humanity. For the former, this involves removing all appeals to 'some peculiarity of his nature', *The Humanity and Divinity of Christ* (Cambridge: CUP, 1967), p. 113. For the latter, it is *because* of the peculiarity of his nature that he is related to all humanity: 'Christianity … ventures the claim, that the true idea of man is to be formed, not after the totality of empirical men, but after Christ alone. It opposes Him to all others as *the* man,' *SCD*, III, p. 322.

of the human nature. While he sees Christ as 'pneumatic humanity', it is on account of his being posited as such by the Logos:

> [T]he human soul of Jesus, constituted by the Logos, and at the same time united with Him, therefore a pneumatic soul.[169]

Furthermore, while the Holy Spirit is described as preparing 'for Himself in humanity...receptiveness for the Messiah', focused in the *faith* 'wrought in Mary by the Spirit of God', it is again emphasized that it is God 'as Logos who makes the pure soul of this man, and imparts to it by His own assumption or appropriation the power at the same time to reject all that is impure'.[170] Again, Dorner argues, the guarantee for the 'natural holiness of the child Jesus [lies] only in the Divine power of the pneumatic man united with the Logos, which effects a correct, and not a perverted coalescence of the elements from Mary, in order that all the stages of life may be normally run through by Jesus'.[171] According to these explanations, Jesus is sustained in his capacity for perfection by the Logos alone. The Holy Spirit appears submissive to the determinations of the Logos to the point of absorption, even though in foregrounding Christ's status as the pneumatic man might be thought the occasion for a detailed account of the Spirit's ongoing role in the particularizing of this man.[172] While the Holy Spirit is earlier acknowledged, as the 'divine principle of union' and as himself *passing* 'from the Logos to the humanity of Christ himself',[173] the quality and persistent character of this passage is entirely underplayed while the agency of the Logos alone is highlighted. This, we suggest, weakens his ambitions to see the full creatureliness of Christ as contributing to the complete realization of the God-man.

We suggest, however, that there is benefit in his positing the doctrine of Christ as the Second Adam in its capacity to lay out his humanity as particular, and as *normative* humanity, without at the same time being disunited from the rest of humanity. We also suggest that in his doctrine of aseity, trinitarianly configured, lies the basis for an account of the way in which the two natures of Christ can be conceived as being united without competition.

---

[169] *SCD*, III, p. 341.

[170] Ibid. p. 343.

[171] Ibid. p. 344.

[172] We feel about Dorner's appropriation (or lack thereof) of the Holy Spirit in the depiction of the authentic creatureliness of Christ Robert Jenson's confusion that the Holy Spirit simply disappears 'from theology's description of God's triune action, often just when he might be expected to have a leading role,' *Systematic Theology, Vol. 1, The Triune God* (Oxford: OUP, 1997), p. 153.

[173] *SCD*, III, p. 292.

6

THE DOCTRINES OF
THE ATONEMENT AND
JUSTIFICATION BY FAITH

Introduction

Dorner holds to the inseparability of Christ's person and work, and he depicts the *perfection* of this personage as coterminous with his activity: '[Christ's] Personal perfection extends through His official life, so that it is evident that the doctrine of His Person cannot be brought to an end of itself, and apart from His work.'[1] As he continues his investigation of the doctrine of Christ, we are reminded that the subsequent exposition of, first, the three offices (§109–113) and, second, the doctrine of the atonement (§114–123), are offered both as the means of laying out the grounds on which Christ may be designated saviour of the world, and also as the way to depict Christ's own progress towards personal fulfilment. What Dorner seeks to do is present an account of the doctrine of atonement not isolated from the wider interests of the doctrine of Christ. This *local* connection to Christ is itself explicitly related to the doctrine of God: 'the concept formed of man and sin on one side and of Christology on the other, depends in the last resort on the definition of the doctrine of God'.[2] We arrive, therefore, at the doctrine of atonement as it pertains not only to the specific *mechanics* of the act of reconciliation (e.g. the ideas of judgement, substitution, representation, expiation) but also to its central place in the uninterrupted delineation of the *way* in which Jesus is the fulfilment of God's purposes for the world in and through his own personal realization. The key to this lies in the repeated emphasis on the significance of Christ's own *attitude* towards his death. By this Dorner seeks to account for the event as that which achieves

[1] *SCD*, III, p. 280.
[2] *SCD*, IV, p. 6.

its reconciling purpose through Christ acting in free conformity with his unique, though universal, identity as God-man. This he does by freely submitting to the rightfulness of the divine displeasure with sin (and with this absorbing the weight of this displeasure). By virtue of his unique status this disposition is taken as meeting the demands of this just displeasure[3] (since he is himself of unparalleled 'high dignity' according to his 'divine human person'[4]). Because this disposition has its origins in Christ's love for humanity, of which he is its 'Head and Representative',[5] God is happy to confer on it 'life and blessedness'.[6]

This is an account like those of Dorner's milieu, yet with some significant differences. For example, the emphasis on Christ's own attitude, sometimes represented as 'feeling',[7] bears the impress of Schleiermacher's turn towards Christ's sympathy[8] (together with his reinvigoration of the high-priestly office[9]) as the key to explicating his redeeming power, since it has 'the power of drawing us into the communion of Christ's holiness and blessedness'.[10] However, while Dorner's approach displays the influence of this move (described by Bavinck as the 'mystical theory'[11] of atonement), it is marked by a concern for the place of the 'divine justice in relation to the work of atonement',[12] on which Dorner (and others[13]) suggest Schleiermacher and his dependents[14] have less interest. Dorner's investment in the place of divine justice emerges from the idea of God whom he conceives as *holy* Love. Because of this it is possible to say that 'justice and the necessity of punishment are grounded in *God's essence*'.[15] While Dorner's position reflects some of the characteristics of the era, his handling of the material displays a doctrinal consistency in its use of the doctrine of God, ethically conceived,

---

[3] The *demonstration* of divine Justice (cf. Rom. 3.25) is explicitly connected to the instantiation of divine Love. Dorner describes Christ's self-offering as originating out of 'love to the divine Justice', Ibid. p. 116.

[4] Ibid. p. 105.

[5] Ibid. p. 117.

[6] Ibid. p. 116.

[7] Ibid. p. 31.

[8] Cf. Schleiermacher, *The Christian Faith*, pp. 407, 436, 447.

[9] Schleiermacher insists that it is in the high priestly office that Christ's 'union with us' is most evidenced (in contrast to the prophetic office). It is central to faith's affirmations concerning human salvation and 'recognized by God as absolute and eternal', Ibid. p. 455.

[10] *SCD*, IV, p. 52.

[11] Herman Bavinck, *Reformed Dogmatics*, Vol. 3, p. 353.

[12] *SCD*, IV, p. 51.

[13] Cf. Gunther Wenz on Schleiermacher and Abelardianism in *Geschichte der Versöhnungslehre in der evangelischen Theologie der Neuzeit*, Band I, (München: Kaiser Verlag, 1984), p. 372. Hereafter *Versöhnungslehre*.

[14] Dorner identifies J. C. K. Hofmann as indebted to Schleiermacher, *SCD*, IV, p. 55.

[15] Ibid. p. 60.

to make possible a way of explicating the event of atonement as manifesting both divine justice and love. We suggest, however, that Dorner's account comes close consistently to synergism, and finally, because of the terms of his supralapsarian schema, threatens the atonement as merely an incidental feature to the divine purposes realized in the God-man. We will analyse the terms of these problems during the course of the chapter.

We will follow the order which Dorner himself lays out. Following a brief analysis of his treatment and arrangement of the three offices of Christ, we will turn to the question of the need of atonement and God's eternal purpose of atonement; we will then address the substitutionary status of Christ; and close with the depiction of the substitutionary satisfaction of Christ.

I. The Official Godhumanity of Jesus Christ

Dorner holds the threefold division of Christ's official activity as 'justifiable both historically and in itself'.[16] Its value lies in the extent to which it can aid[17] the depiction of Christ's work as indicative of God's definitive and comprehensive purposes for the world, which embraces *both* the formation of the 'new personality'[18] – the 'godlike personality of the sons of God [with] the conscious union of the free with the ethically necessary as the absolutely worthy and deserving of love'[19] – *and* its concomitant, the personal revelation to the world of God Himself. The *munus triplex* assists the proper dogmatic representation of the correlation between Christ's work and his person as they, together, bring to realization the divine ambitions for the world. Dorner is prepared even to use the scheme as a means of evaluating the propriety of other theological accounts:

> [T]he threefold office of Christ is…the pure mirror of the perfect idea of God. For in His living personal activity or office Christ is also the Divine-human, historically realized image of God, and restores that image in us through illumination, justification, and sanctification. Hence there must always be essential defects in the fundamental apprehension of Christianity, where this union of the three offices in Christ

[16] *SCD*, III, p. 381. Dorner contends that the ancients' use of the word Χριστός is 'early referred to His being King, Prophet, Priest'. Furthermore, the New Testament supports the triple division since it sees in Christ the consummation of the three offices of the old covenant, Ibid. p. 387.

[17] Dorner partially accepts J. A. Ernesti's influential critique that prophet, priest, king can *either* lack clear definition and overlap in their meaning, thereby reducing their connotative value, *or* if granted definite meaning, disrupt the unity of the work of salvation, *SCD*, IV, p. 384.

[18] Ibid. p. 385.

[19] *SCD*, I, p. 446.

is not acknowledged, where His individual words, acts, sufferings, are not considered from the viewpoint of this unity, where they are rather severed from each other, or even one only is neglected. Hence a touchstone for the integrity for Christianity, or the completeness of a system, is to be seen in the attitude taken to Christ's threefold office.[20]

The attitude taken to the offices stands, therefore, as a decisive feature in Dorner's vision.[21] However, it is not merely the deployment of this scheme which holds significance (though Dorner is clearly on the side of those who *do* maintain its place in Christology), but the way in which it is handled. In both the definition of the relationship of the different offices as distinct without being disconnected, and the specific ordering of the offices, Dorner contends for the importance of expositional precision.

a. The Relationship between the Three Offices of Christ

[I]n Christ – this is the meaning of the triple division – the threefold office was united, not merely in the way of addition, externally, as in a triple crown, but inwardly, or in such a way that they mutually interpenetrate, and each one of the three, rightly understood, carries the two others in itself, but in its own fashion.[22]

Dorner signals his intentions to treat the offices as complete and determinable only in so far as they are explicated with reference to each other. This means that each office does not *lose* (vis-à-vis Ernesti) but rather *finds* its distinctiveness in association with the others. This is because it is *as* each office pertains to the 'one collective activity'[23] of Christ's personality that the possibility of each is instantiated. As each office is predicated of Christ's person, his *one* person is demonstrated to have the '*capacity* for all three'[24] securing the place and integrity of each particular office. Dorner suggests, therefore, that the neglect of the three offices comes at the expense of the unity of Christ's person.

It is worth noting at this point that while Dorner's interest in displaying both the distinctiveness and interconnectedness of the offices hangs on the same principle which he employs in his doctrine of the *perichoretic* triunity of God, and that his insistence on the three offices give 'three fundamental

---

[20] *SCD*, III, p. 389.
[21] Note should be taken again at this point, however, of the way in which Dorner includes the doctrine of the offices within the wider doctrine of Christ's Person, and not as a separate division, Ibid. p. 386.
[22] Ibid. p. 388.
[23] Ibid.
[24] Ibid.

definitions of God's revelation of Himself'[25] he does not extrapolate from this a specific connection between each of the offices and the particular persons or *modes of being* of God (e.g. in the manner recently envisaged by Robert Sherman in *King, Priest, and Prophet*[26]). This appears to be because he takes each of the three offices as '*points of view*' of the one collective activity.[27] The immediate significance of this probably lies in the fact that he wants to emphasize the *unity* of Christ's official activity as the revelation of God's triunity, and is not anxious (as Sherman appears to be) that the unity (and consequent expansive import) of this activity is endangered if, as Dorner does, the three offices are said to centre in – though not be exhausted by – Christ's priestly role. For Dorner, the identification of the offices with the three *modes of being* would imply either that there is not *one* final aim of Christ's official activity (since each mode of being would have particular interest in His own achievement of Christ) or that the mutual relationality of the offices precludes one – namely, the priestly – being that which requires particular dogmatic emphasis. Ultimately, the discussion rests on whether the depiction of *final aims* of God in Christ is enhanced or inhibited by the foregrounding of one office. Dorner holds the former.

Neglecting all three offices is, he suggests, a problem for those theological accounts which hold to only one or even two of the offices. The route taken by the Socinians and Rationalists of predicating of Christ only the *prophetic* office means that, rather than securing this capacity, it is endangered since it has no need of the doctrine of incarnation (since all that is required of the world is 'more powerful knowledge of truth'[28]) and consequently the confidence that Christ is speaking God's truth – as the God-man – is reduced. The authority of his prophetic ministry would therefore be jeopardized. The same precariousness is attributed to those solely emphasizing the high-priestly office (generating either a quietism or antinomianism), or the kingly office (leading to an insecure practicalism or activism). The decisive reason, therefore, for embracing all three offices (apart from the biblical support he finds for them) resides in the extent to which *together* they contribute to the *fullness* of Christ's person and work by safeguarding the integrity and rightfulness of each office and therefore the comprehensiveness of God's economic activity.

This *fullness* – as befits Dorner's efforts to bring together person and work – pertains to the breadth of Christ's personal capacity to complete the divine purposes for the world as his personal activity corresponds to the soteriological needs of the sinful world. Dorner sees in the offices a way of delivering clarity to the exposition of Christ's fittedness for the task of

---

[25] *SCD*, III, p. 389.
[26] Robert Sherman in *King, Priest, and Prophet* (London: T & T Clark, 2004), p. 9.
[27] *SCD*, III, p. 388.
[28] *SCD*, III, p. 389.

'healing and...imparting full health' to humanity in its 'state of spiritual darkness';[29] and in this fittedness, Christ is himself designated as the focal point in the account. The offices are, therefore, not merely the means of explicating the way in which Christ meets the needs of the world. They are intended to contribute to the identification of Christ *himself* as the centre of this mission (recalling his earlier statement that Christ is 'Himself...the centre of His gifts to humanity, as the highest good of the world'[30]). In his description of the mutual co-ordination of the offices, Dorner seeks to show that Christ meets the threefold need of the world:

1. By 'teaching and example'[31] being equipped to respond to the spiritual error in which the world stands – the *prophetic* office;
2. By abolishing 'guilt and punishment'[32] which attend the entrance of sin – the *high-priestly* function;
3. By having power to give to the world the principles of 'regeneration, sanctification, and the new life'[33] – the *kingly* office.

However, this representation of the suitability of Christ's capacities for the world's needs is incomplete if it is not also accompanied by an apprehension of how these capacities are *interpenetrative* and indicative of the comprehensiveness of Christ's person. In response, therefore, to those who refer Christ's *kingly* office primarily to his post-resurrection and ascension state,[34] Dorner speaks of this office as properly attributable to Christ *before* his death. Only then can the 'greatness of His condescension even to death, and its inner value, [be] rightly perceived'.[35] Furthermore, his high-priestly role is not applicable only to Christ's last days but is 'exercised in labour, prayer and blessing',[36] while conversely his prophetic ministry is active also in his 'exaltation'.[37] In all this, what Dorner is outlining is the pervasiveness (and mutual dependence) of the three offices in order to prevent the work of Christ becoming detached from his person.[38] Detached either by the *focus*

---

[29] Ibid. p. 388.

[30] Ibid. p. 280.

[31] Ibid. p. 388.

[32] Ibid.

[33] Ibid.

[34] Dorner is probably referring here to Socinians. Cf. R. S. Franks, *The Work of Christ* (Edinburgh: Thomas Nelson, 1962), p. 373.

[35] *SCD*, III, p. 391.

[36] Ibid.

[37] Ibid.

[38] It is perhaps worth noting that while Dorner's position sees him seeking a unification of Christ's person and work, the sheer capaciousness of his *History of Development* dwarfs his treatment on the details of Christ's work *qua* Saviour. This is a point which is observed by Sydney Cave in *The Doctrine of the Work of Christ* (London: Hodder &

of attention residing in how each office meets the particular needs of the world (though this is not excluded), but also by demonstrating that Christ enacts his person without his person being subsumed by his acts. In the coalescence of his threefold official activity he temporally instantiates the completeness of his person and as he does this he meets the soteriological needs of the world: he acts with power (as *king*), wisdom (as *prophet*), and suffering (as *priest*). It is an arrangement which prevents the doctrine of the gradual incarnation, outlined earlier, from being (over)interpreted as irrevocably rupturing the ontological union of Christ's God-manhood. As such it is an underacknowledged facet of the wider ambitions of Dorner's theological contribution.

b. The Ordering of the Offices

Dorner's appeal to the interdependence and 'mutual conditionality'[39] of the three offices does not mean that he is ambivalent about their particular order of treatment, or that this mutuality excludes a sequence of consequence. He contends with those who argue that 'the work of atonement alone is the central work…which the high-priestly office specifically subserves',[40] but is still minded to describe that office as the 'fundamental and central one'.[41] It is a distinction which befits the overall march of his project which, beginning with the appeal of Fundamental doctrine to the necessity of a God-man for the completion of the divine purposes for the world, seeks to represent the actual and historical God-man as attaining this necessary end according to the terms set by the non-necessary entrance of sin and guilt to the world. While the high-priestly role is *central* and *fundamental* it is not exhaustive of the divine purposes because those purposes are not *necessarily* defined as reaching their fulfilment via the God-man *as Saviour*. Rather, the 'founding of the new personality' and the 'new common life'[42] more definitively

Stoughton, 1937), in which he records the significant contribution of Dorner to the theology of the Person of Christ, of which 'we should have to speak at length', compared to the 'less distinctive' contribution on the doctrine of Christ's work, (p. 199). We suspect that this remark is a little unfair, given that Dorner was, with the first work, seeking to respond to what he saw as an unnecessary historical revisionism at play in some recent theology concerning the *unio personalis*. Furthermore, Gunther Wenz's summation of Dorner's doctrine of salvation as bearing a more conservative tendency than his more original Christology misses the significant use Dorner makes of his innovative doctrine of divine immutability to depict the twofold effect of reconciliation (according to which *both* God and man are reconciled to each other), Wenz, *Versöhnungslehre*, I, p. 24.

[39] *SCD*, III, p. 385.
[40] Ibid.
[41] Ibid.
[42] Ibid.

describe the end for which the world was created. The sacerdotal act of the God-man is 'subservient'[43] to this end since it is not in the soteriological act itself for which the world was created. While it is the means by which this end is attained, because it is not the end itself, it need not monopolize the place and significance of the God-man.

The high-priestly office remains, though, for the purposes of expositing *Christology* as the Specific doctrine *sine qua non*, the focal point and controlling lens through which Dorner explicates the way in which Christ is properly represented as Saviour of the world.[44] It is the division in which he lays out his doctrine of atonement, so he does not treat the high-priestly office *before* he formally considers that doctrine.[45] This means that his sequence is: King (§110), Prophet (§111), Priest (§112–123). We will proceed swiftly to the last since it contains the atonement doctrine. However, we ought here to note the significance of Dorner's particular placing of King and Prophet.

1. Christ the King

He gives as his reason for reversing the normal order (in which King is treated last):

> [T]he revelation of [Christ's] kingly position, must find place on earth, because otherwise history would not supply the fitting attestation, that He is Head of God's kingdom.[46]

The way in which this kingship is revealed is precisely in the 'unlimited'[47] revelation of His love and the *limitation* of the revelation of His regal power. It is *in*, and not merely subsequent to, Christ's redemptive display of love that is revealed the 'power of His person'.[48] In this depiction Dorner defines Christ's kingship as bearing an 'ethical impress'[49] since its display 'will not

---

[43] Ibid.

[44] As such, he treats it, as R. S. Franks correctly observes, with 'special fullness', Franks, *The Work of Christ*, p. 583.

[45] This decision, of course, is contiguous with his collapsing of the distinction between Person and Work.

[46] *SCD*, III, p. 393.

[47] Ibid.

[48] Ibid. p. 394. In this linking of power with the display of love Dorner is making a move which coheres with his representation of the ethical structure of God's power, according to which, as *holy* Love, God is necessarily in control of Himself. It is also a means of portraying the humiliation of the God-man without requiring the *self*-humiliation or emptying of the Logos – in the manner of modern Kenosis theories – since the full power of the true Messianic King is in the *possession* of Christ on account of his origination as the God-man, and is not taken up again only at his glorification.

[49] Ibid. p. 396.

181

and cannot *at once* exhibit'[50] his εξουσία as the simple grounds on which to command obedience. Rather it is in the gradual unfolding of his teaching and his person that his kingship will be discerned as that of a 'King who dies for His people'.[51] This handling of the *munus regium* means Dorner is seeking a depiction in which 'something eternal is revealed'[52] of Christ's historically temporal existence; the 'Divine might' is placed at the service of his 'redeeming action'[53] (a point on which Dorner also seeks to secure the necessity of this action, since it is as King of men – and not subject to them – that Jesus enters and completes his mission).

2. Christ the Prophet

His similarly brief description of the prophetic office seeks to trace its focus as resting on Christ himself:

> The proper and ultimate object or content of His teaching and expo-
> sition in His prophetic activity is necessarily Himself, and that as
> regards the totality of His being, in which is contained the very truth
> of the Divine and the human, the highest good for men. The teaching
> of Christ in the last resort is always teaching about Christ.[54]

It is unsurprising that this should be Dorner's description of the prophetic office. He speaks of the offices as pertaining not merely to particular stages in the life of Jesus[55] but to the 'history of His entire life'[56] since, in this case, Christ is prophet in the extent to which his words, his acts, his miracles, sufferings, death and resurrection all 'teach somewhat of His person'.[57] This is not to be taken as *excluding* the educative and exemplary content of Christ's prophetic activity – he is the *Way* – but rather to ensure that the 'acknowledgement of Him as Pattern' leads 'to the acknowledgement of His absolute dignity'.[58]

---

[50] *SCD*, III, p. 396.

[51] Ibid. p. 397.

[52] Ibid. p. 392.

[53] Ibid. p. 394.

[54] Ibid. p. 399.

[55] This point is, of course, not unique to Dorner. Carl Nitzsch, for example, had earlier expressed the same scepticism about the division of these offices or functions 'chronologically', Nitzsch, *System*, p. 260, n. 1.

[56] *SCD*, III, p. 399.

[57] Ibid. Dorner is not blind to what he calls a 'progressiveness of development' in the form of Christ's teaching, according to which there is a gradual unfolding of Christ himself as the centre of his teaching about God's law, love, kingdom, righteousness, Ibid. p. 399.

[58] Ibid. p. 398.

Dorner is carefully limiting the extent to which Christ may be taken as the first and supreme instigator – as *revealer* of God's will – of a moral community which itself will instantiate what he himself alone is, namely, the personal unity of God and man.

Although unspecified, Dorner's efforts to define the prophetic office as indicative of an essential *difference* between Christ and Church, is clearly aimed at opposing those ecclesial or semi-ecclesial traditions which he has identified as representing Christ as mere archetype of a humanity reconcilable to God. In its modern Kantian form, the historical Jesus is seen as *accidental* to the moral restoration found in the ethical community.[59] This anti-metaphysical account of Christ's personal relationship to the community which succeeds him is, of course, also a feature for Ritschl whom Dorner describes as defining Christ's significance as lying not in 'His person, but conversely His person is to be apprehended from His work.'[60] For Ritschl, Christ reveals God as a *prophet* in so far as he acts in accordance with his own vocation.[61]

Yet for Dorner there can be 'no objective perfectibility of Christianity' since the Church is merely the *reflection* of that unity which is 'given perfectly in Him'.[62] The prophetic office of Christ is principally related to the 'revelation of the wealth enclosed in His Person',[63] of which the world is invited to enjoy. Crucially, it is *'through* penal…visitations' (my italics)[64] that this wealth is secured, connecting both the offices of prophet and priest, and also providing the link with the subsequent exposition of that final office and its place as the location of the doctrine of the atonement, to which we now turn.

II. Christ the High Priest

a. The Need of Atonement and God's Eternal Purpose of Atonement

Consistent with his normal method, Dorner prefaces his account of the doctrine of atonement with an extended survey of the ecclesiastical history of the doctrine (§114–118). During the course of this review, he identifies two

---

[59] *History of Development*, Div. II, Vol. III, p. 34.
[60] *SCD*, III, p. 275.
[61] Albrecht Ritschl, *The Christian Doctrine of Justification and Reconciliation* (Clifton, NJ: Reference Book, 1966), p. 436.
[62] *SCD*, III, p. 400.
[63] Ibid. p. 401.
[64] Ibid.

principles on which the Church is united in all ages:

> I. [R]edemption must not be effected by sheer might or in the way of violence, but in the way of *suffering and dying love*;[65]
> II. The *necessity of mortal suffering* is always brought in some way, directly or indirectly, *into connection with the divine justice.* (my italics)[66]

Having extrapolated these principles, Dorner proceeds to offer a sustained critique of those theories which seek *either* to conceptualize the redemptive act in a way which *relativizes* the place of justice in the divine essence and, by implication remove or reduce its significance to the doctrine of atonement (as in his analysis of Duns Scotus and Thomas[67]), *or* question the necessity of expiation[68] (as in his sustained critique of Ritschl[69]). It is a framework which sees him identify Anselm's theory as that which 'deserves unceasing acknowledgement'[70] for the way in which it demonstrates that the atonement by the incarnate Christ is *necessary* on account of the maintenance of God's honour:

> It would be inconceivable, as well as unworthy of God, that He should will anything opposed to justice. In this way God's power and plenary authority are placed beneath, not above, His justice. In His character of justice He must require righteousness or obedience to His righteous will from rational beings.[71]

---

[65] *SCD*, IV, p. 9.

[66] Ibid.

[67] On Thomas, 'no special place is left by Aquinas in God's eternal essence for the justice of God in particular. On the contrary, God's absolute plenitude of authority now gains most essential influence. But in this case, God might just as well accept (*acceptare*) a mere finite worth as satisfaction as that infinite worth which dwells in Christ, and which transcends the amount required by Justice.' On Scotus, 'The necessity of atonement by Christ is to him altogether immaterial, because to him God in His innermost essence is nothing but free plenary authority,' Ibid. p. 18.

[68] The word for which the translators give 'expiation' is most often 'Sühne' (e.g. 'Die göttliche Gerechtigkeit fordert Sühne', *SCG*, II.i., p. 612). For a clear description of the various differences between the use of 'expiation' (describing God's act in putting forward Christ as being directed towards sinners) and 'propitiation' (describing that act as directed towards God Himself) see John Ziesler, *Paul's Letter to the Romans* (London: SCM, 1989), p. 112–113.

[69] Wenz identifies Dorner more than once, with Kähler and Geß, as presenting the most significant objection to Ritschl and his school, Wenz, *Versöhnungslehre*, Bd. II, pp. 124, 183–184.

[70] *SCD*, IV, p. 16.

[71] Ibid. p. 14 ff.

Anselm represents the key figure for Dorner in this ecclesiastical reconstruction, and for two reasons. First, with his identification of justice (even if differently conceived) as the key to the atonement he provides theological relief to the idea that divine justice need not be seen in *competition* with divine love.[72] Secondly, Anselm's proposition that atonement can be made only from *within* humanity but yet cannot be made alone *by* humanity offers the space for an account of a necessary incarnation. We will look at the latter of these two propositions when we address Dorner's understanding of the substitutionary satisfaction of Christ. We want here, however, to lay out Dorner's configuration of the necessity of expiation which sees him echoing Anselm's move in bringing the atonement 'into direct relation to God and to His justice'.[73] It is here that the consequences of his ethical conceptualization of the triune Godhead are once again called upon.

In the first article of his dogmatic investigation into the need of atonement, Dorner affirms the following:

> The divine justice demands expiation, and without it humanity, unable to make it out of its own resources, is exposed to God's retributive displeasure, or to punishment, which fills with dread of destruction and death. The sin and guilt of the world, which call forth retributive justice, stand therefore as a barrier in the way of God's loving purpose, which created the world for perfection in holiness and blessedness. But as Justice and Love exist eternally in *God* in harmonious interpenetration, so God wills the *world* to be the scene of the combined revelation of the two so long and so far as the world is still capable of redemption.[74]

Dorner connects the link between sin and judgement – characterized as *retributive displeasure* ('vergeltenden Ungnade'[75]) – to the essential constitution of God[76], and, crucially, he relates the manifestation of this displeasure in the expiatory event (of Christ's death) to the *revelation* of God to the world. The atonement therefore becomes the scene of the *correspondence* between God's immanent and economic being and not merely an *exchange*

---

[72] Dorner argues that God does only what He allows Himself to do according to His self-sustaining ethical character: 'God's ethical essence co-ordinates the power which is even above omnipotence and its works', Ibid. p. 83.

[73] Ibid. p. 16.

[74] Ibid. p. 79.

[75] SCG, II.ii., p. 612.

[76] An early reader of Dorner eloquently describes him as seeing in punitive justice an 'amiable attribute, worthy of God, and indispensable to the moral welfare of mankind', George Smeaton, *The Doctrine of the Atonement* (Edinburgh: T & T Clark, 1868), p. 366.

of some kind between God and humanity (although this remains integral to the arrangement). By affirming the eternal harmony of Justice and Love, he is recalling his definition of the triune God as holy Love. God – in His threefoldness – is the instantiation of free obedience to the necessary good and, as such, is Love (since love is defined as 'the unity of ethical necessity and freedom because it wills [with] absolute desire'[77]). By allocating to the atonement the resources of God's own essentially ethical being, Dorner is seeking to depict the doctrine as accommodating the ideas of human sin as bringing and warranting divine displeasure. But with this *active* divine displeasure (as *holy* Love), also engaging the fullness of the divine Absolute Personality (as holy *Love*) and thereby bringing holiness and blessedness to the world.

Just as he sees no disjunction between Justice and Love in the Godhead, he sees none in the atonement. Rather, it is in those accounts which, he suggests, have no room for the necessity of judgement – the 'satisfaction of justice'[78] – that leave unanswered the question of how God's love, if offered 'without condition and expiation',[79] is able to offer the world security in its enjoyment of God's 'unchiding'[80] fatherliness. What is lacking is provision of the 'morally satisfactory means for bridging over the distance between the empirical condition and the ideal world'.[81] Dorner is seeking to establish the atonement as that which reveals God's essence. It is on these grounds – with the appeal to God's nature – that unethical behaviour (which is, by implication, unloving) *necessitates* expiation.

We shall comment in the next section on the precise meaning of this expiation. For now we wish to refer to the way in which he uses his argument about the correspondence between God's essential ethical being and the atonement to advance the claim that the necessity of expiation refers not only to the world being reconciled to God but also God being reconciled to the world. He lays out how the particular manifestation of God's justice as wrath is the pre-condition of the manifestation of God's 'acts of grace'[82] (and even *ratified* by their appearance). In all of this, the focal point is God's ethical immutability.

b. The Atonement and Divine Immutability

The satisfaction of justice is the negative pre-condition of the revelation of love as self-communication. God must therefore make the

---

[77] *SCD*, I, p. 437.
[78] *SCD*, IV, p. 83.
[79] Ibid. p. 77.
[80] Ibid.
[81] Ibid. p. 78.
[82] Ibid. p. 82.

maintenance of His ethical glory and unchangeableness, the satisfaction
of His justice which is necessarily angry and displeased with sin, the
indispensable condition of His loving fellowship and favour.[83]

For Dorner there is a causal relationship between sin and judgement because
of the divine ethical essence. God cannot allow unpunished unethical behaviour which fails to cohere with the divine essence and the divine purpose
for the world: the establishment of a perfect communion between God and
humanity which will be characterized by a life of *'holy* love'.[84] What is certain, then, for Dorner is that sinful humanity represents a *personal* affront to
God and is a state of affairs which requires resolution in order for the divine
purposes to be realized. While for Anselm the key was God's honour which,
when violated, requires punishment in order for the honour to maintain
itself ('it would be against God's honour to forgive sin without satisfaction'[85]), the locus for Dorner is God's *ethical glory*, which is maintained as
the basis of God's self-communication.

These are the grounds on which Dorner rejects accounts which argue that
'we only need to be reconciled with God, but no need exists for *God* to be
reconciled *with us*, or what is the same, no need exists of an expiation for
us'.[86] A false view of God's immutability leads, he argues, to this error. There
is required a conceptual reorientation according to which the 'distinctions
in the world and its history are not indifferent to God, and therefore value-
less in themselves, [but] that rather God is, above all, immutable in ethical
vitality'.[87] God is immutable in His ethical expectations and standards, and
as such, He allows Himself to be affected (though not arbitrarily) by the
ethical life of the creature: 'It is His own essence…and own volition by
which He allows Himself to be determined to modify His sympathy with
the world.'[88] This notion of divine ethical immutability does not *exclude*
but rather *assumes* the capacity to be affected by creaturely ethical activity.
The two are not mutually exclusive, but rather ethical immutability *presupposes* the possibility of change in relation to the new ethical being created as
destined to bear the divine image. This is the corresponding implication of
Dorner's account of a progressive incarnation, according to which God 'as
Logos' is said to *seize* and *appropriate* the 'new sides which are generated

---

[83] Ibid. p. 83.
[84] Ibid. p. 87.
[85] Ibid. p. 15.
[86] Ibid. p. 80.
[87] Ibid. Dorner is joined in this connection of a revised doctrine of divine immutability
with God Himself requiring reconciliation by Hans Martensen who also argues that 'it
is not merely man, but God Himself, who is to be reconciled' in accord with a 'living
idea of God's unchangeableness', Martensen, *Christian Dogmatics*, p. 204.
[88] *SCD*, IV, p. 81.

by the true human development'[89] of Christ Jesus. As there is a responsiveness from the Logos to the human development of Christ, so too is there a responsiveness of God to the world in its creaturely development. This is not to imply an imperfection in the essence of the Logos. It speaks of the capacity of the Logos to respond to the creaturely development of Jesus in correspondence *both* with Himself as uniquely united with this man *and* cohering with the ethical nature of the God-man's essential being. As a temporally located creature, it is instantiated in the gradual unfolding of His official life. Dorner describes God's response to sinful humanity in the following terms:

> [God] accompanies the history of men with His sympathy, which modifies itself, moment by moment, according to the actual character of men, [which] implies no passive dependence of God on the world; but it is His own essence, abiding eternally the same, and His own volition, by which He allows Himself to be determined to modify His sympathy with the world.[90]

While God's mode of relation to the world is personal and active (the original German given here as 'sympathy' is 'Theilnahme',[91] perhaps better rendered as 'participation'), this does not violate the capacity of the *character of men* to be and remain distinct from such divine immanence (recalling here the distinction Dorner makes early on between the world's absolute ontic dependence on God and God's continual upholding of its relatively independent moral integrity and freedom). Since the divine inclination is both *towards* and *for* the world (in its status as that which is destined to bear the divine image) the character of this inclination is altered by the manner in which the world responds to the divine participation (and the ethical constitution and teleology of the world). The 'question of sin and guilt is so serious a thing, that it occasions a change even in God's disposition towards man',[92] and this change in God is a *displeasure* which abolishes the 'state of peace between God and man'.[93] That God Himself needs to be reconciled to man is indicative, therefore, of the ethical mode of His being:

> God's holy essence cannot look otherwise than with disfavour and holy displeasure at sinners as such, and at the evil present in them and done by them. In Himself He *cannot* be eternally reconciled to evil; in Him is neither moral indifference nor caprice.[94]

[89] *SCD*, III, p. 328.
[90] *SCD*, IV, p. 81.
[91] *SCG*, II.ii., p. 613.
[92] *SCD*, IV, p. 85.
[93] Ibid. p. 84.
[94] Ibid. p. 83.

This doctrine of God seeks to resolve what Dorner sees as the 'unavoidable problem'[95] of how God's unchanging goodness is consistent with the divine capacity to change for the purposes of salvation. As such, it is the resource for depicting the atonement as that which pertains to the effect *on God* of humanity's sin without the abandonment of God's purposiveness.

However, while this account demonstrates an ethical constancy in the divine response to sin and guilt, the *gratuitousness* of God's action is not adequately conveyed. In Dorner's subsequent explanation of the way in which God's eternal purposes are focused towards reconciliation and not mere annihilation, there is a significant inattention to the details of how these purposes may be depicted as acts of *mercy* or *grace*. We will see now how this manifests itself.

c. God's Purposes of Reconciliation

Attending the account of God's ethical immutability – as the *basis* of the 'change in God's disposition'[96] – is the assertion of humanity's inability to save itself from the divine displeasure. There is an 'incapacity to furnish the potency of reconciliation'[97] (which, as we shall see, does not mean that humanity is itself devoid of what Dorner calls *powers* of atonement). Yet as he sets out the grounds on which peace is re-establishable only on the basis of *God's* strength and wisdom, Dorner appeals to what he calls the 'eternal counsel of (God's) mercy'[98] as that which not only requires expiation but also gives humanity the 'possibility of reconciliation'.[99] The character and origin of this mercy ('Barmherzigkeit'[100]) is itself not delineated in much detail, to the detriment of the account. Instead, Dorner proceeds to lay out how divine Justice and the will of Love, while objectively *distinctive*, have yet an 'inner mutual relation and indissoluble interconnection'.[101] This means that he is able to explicate God's saving activity as neither contrary to the divine Justice nor merely an act of divine Love, since as holy Love God displays His anger *as* the One who 'bestows on humanity the possibility of expiation'.[102] Dorner fails, however, to explain this divine activity in terms of mercy or grace (both terms to which he refers only fleetingly). This has the disadvantage of neglecting

---

[95] Robert Williams, 'I. A. Dorner: The Ethical Immutability of God', p. 722.
[96] *SCD*, IV, p. 85.
[97] Ibid. p. 86.
[98] Ibid.
[99] Ibid.
[100] *SCG*, II.ii., p. 619.
[101] *SCD*, IV, p. 88.
[102] Ibid. p. 89.

the 'sheer freedom'[103] of God's atoning purposes. Dorner's account of the relation of Love and Justice means that there is not a subordination of one to the other – so that 'freedom is subordinate to necessity'[104] – but rather a mutual *co-ordination*. Yet the manner of his exposition is so heavily ordered towards the depiction of the divine act of atonement as fully co-ordinated (in order to preserve the ethical vitality of God and the world), without what we might call the *relief* of the biblical concepts of grace and mercy, it loses its capacity to display God's atoning purposes as *unnecessary* for the maintenance of His own essential goodness. Dorner consistently fails to articulate the constancy of the divine action in terms of the *graciousness* of God in reconciliation.[105]

In spite of this weakness, however, Dorner comes to the end of his account of the necessity of expiation for reconciliation having made a substantial connection with the essence of the divine personality. In the process of this exposition, passing reference is made to the idea that *suffering* is the 'physically and ethically necessary consequence'[106] of sin. This does not mean

---

[103] This is the way in which T. F. Torrance explains the divine creation of fellowship between himself and others, T. F. Torrance, *The Christian Doctrine of God*, p. 244. This is, of course, intended to display the extent to which God's definitive economic acts are to be identified as indicative of nothing apart from God Himself, 'there is no reason for God's love apart from his love', Ibid. The reference to the sheerness of God's freedom follows a treatment of the doctrine of divine immutability which, via Karl Barth (cf. *Church Dogmatics*, Vol. II, The Doctrine of God, Part I, [Edinburgh: T & T Clark, 1957], p. 493), displays an indebtedness to Dorner's own account. However, what distinguishes the two is the latter's reluctance to frame the ethical invariability in terms which explicate the divine act of atonement as *gracious*.

[104] Williams, 'I. A. Dorner: The Ethical Immutability of God', p. 737. We suggest, contra Williams, that Dorner does not subordinate freedom to necessity, since the necessary good is that which is itself only such when freely embraced, just as freedom is only such when ordered according to the necessary good. There is not subordination, but complementarity.

[105] This, we suspect, lies near to the heart of Matthias Gockel's account of the key difference between Dorner's and Barth's doctrines of reconciliation. According to Gockel, Barth's view is that God's 'love and not merely God's righteousness is "satisfied" in Christ's death', Matthias Gockel, p. 505, a view which he sees as contrary to Dorner's view which was concerned to display the satisfaction of justice as the condition of the revelation of His love. Barth, of course, invested heavily in the doctrine of covenantal election to display God's reconciling activity as essentially gracious (something which is wholly missing from Dorner) and as such Barth 'interprets God's will as the definite expression of God's essence' (Ibid.). However, we disagree with Gockel when he suggests that Dorner's doctrine of God as ethical personality means that God's will is secondary to God's essence. Rather, God's will is instantiated in and with his essence as ethical, and as such, is the reason that the reconciliation in Christ is, even if first the guarantor of righteousness, a constantly loving act. It is the scarcity of Dorner's reference to grace that we suggest presents the major problem in untangling his argument.

[106] *SCD*, IV, p. 83.

that suffering is, in itself, pleasing to God. Dorner criticizes Anselm on this point.[107] Rather, the central point is the extent to which mortal suffering is connected 'with divine justice'.[108] However, it is not merely this connection *per se* which is of significance, since suffering can be germane to divine justice only when it has the power to be satisfactory, and this is resolutely *not* in the possession of humanity in general:

> [T]he rendering of *expiation* to God is utterly out of our power....Just as little is the satisfaction, which our action cannot furnish, to be found in our suffering, or in our willingness to bear as just punishment the divine displeasure with all the effects that may flow from it.[109]

This powerlessness does not mean an incapacity in humanity *for* reconciliation, since in the incarnation of the God-man Dorner sees humanity being itself 'enabled'[110] to present atonement. This brings us to Dorner's understanding of the place and significance of this capacity for redemption as instantiated in the personal work of Christ. We will see how Jesus is fit to be humanity's *substitute* (and how Dorner unifies substitution and representation), how his sufferings and death provide satisfaction for sin, and how this schema relates to the divine idea of a union between God and man which Dorner proposes as the end for which God created the world.

III. The Substitutionary Status of Jesus Christ

Dorner opens his account of the development of ecclesiastical doctrine (§114–118) by identifying atonement as that which addresses 'man's first moral problem [since without a] solution....man's entire existence would be destitute of foundation and assured worth, because an existence without God'.[111] With this diagnosis, we hear the central significance to Dorner of the ontological *distinction* between God and humanity which is also the very basis of their moral relationship. With the entrance of sin (earlier defined as 'opposition to God and his holy precepts'[112]) and evil (as 'defect of that which ought to exist'[113]) an alteration occurs in the kind of ontic dependence in which the creature stands – with its ethical import – which endangers

---

[107] According to Dorner, Anselm attributed to the 'spontaneous [non-obligatory] suffering the character of a good work, meritorious because non-obligatory', Ibid. p. 16.

[108] Ibid. p. 9.

[109] Ibid. p. 85.

[110] Ibid. p. 87.

[111] Ibid. p. 3.

[112] *SCD*, II, p. 313.

[113] Ibid. p. 363.

both the ethico-existential future of humanity and the divine intentions for the world. What this leads to is the necessity of an expiation of sin, and, as we observed in connection with the second principle gathered from Anselm, this can be made only from within humanity yet cannot be made alone by humanity. Here we arrive at Dorner's account of how Jesus uniquely offers substitutionary satisfaction as the sufficient means of expiation.

He begins his exposition by detailing what he calls the 'general' evidence for substitutionary and satisfying forces in the world:

> Atonement is only possible through the fact that there are *substitutionary* forces at work for the good of humanity and receptiveness in humanity for those forces. As the second Adam, or Representative of humanity before God, Christ is the Substitute for humanity outside Him, so far as humanity is defective in religious personality.[114]

There is in Dorner's account, cohering with his overall apologetic intentions (to display the Christian faith as that which uniquely explicates the universal problem of sin and evil[115] and its overcoming, thereby demonstrating the certainty of Jesus Christ's God-manhood), an interest in laying out the grounds in which substitution is an immanent property or characteristic of the created realm.[116] It is not inimical to the maintenance of proper order and flourishing of its being. He suggests *all* 'culture is conditioned by substitution'.[117] Dorner is seeking to excavate the grounds on which substitution may be recovered for the depiction of Christ's death as expiatory. However, he is also keen to challenge ideas of substitution which tend to exclude or diminish the freedom (as responsibility) of the sinful subject in the efficaciousness of the genus' substitute. Returning to the nexus of ideas which permeated his ponerology, Dorner appeals to the uniqueness and universality of Christ as the key to explicating the way in which he may be properly represented as, in some way, standing in the place (passive), or acting on behalf (active) of humanity without precluding the 'peculiarity and freedom'[118] of this humanity. This is possible because Christ stands in relation to humanity as its completion and, as such, he is *proper* humanity. He stands in relation to God as both unique recipient of His favour – as perfect man – and also, as God-man, the divine communication to humanity:

> [Christ] is the centre and reality of our genus. Consequently, His personality cannot absorb our individual peculiarity and freedom;

---

[114] *SCD*, IV, p. 89.
[115] Cf. Dorner's ponerology, *SCD*, III, p. 11.
[116] Cf. 'engrafting', *SCD*, IV, p. 90.
[117] *SCD*, IV, p. 91.
[118] Ibid. p. 93.

but if we have natural receptiveness for God, we have in a special degree receptiveness for Him in whom both true humanity and the absolute revelation of God are given. Since, therefore, receptiveness is directed to Him, both the receptiveness for the genus with its substitutionary forces and the receptiveness for God find their satisfaction in Him. Receptiveness for the genus and its substitutionary forces, directing itself to Christ, is in an eminent sense well-pleasing to God, because it is also receptiveness for God. This is the meaning of *believing* in Him.[119]

Since Christ is uniquely related both to the genus and to God (we are, after all, still addressing this subject within the section on the *mediatorial* office of Christ as High Priest) he stands both *as* humanity to God (as the *reality of our genus*) – and thereby his substitutionary actions *complete* or fulfil humanity rather than negate it – and the presence of God to humanity (as the *absolute revelation of God*) – thereby his substitutionary actions may be embraced by humanity as pertaining to its own completion because they bear the approval of God. Humanity can have a substitute because humanity is constituted as that which finds its proper completion in the God-man who, standing both as humanity before God and as God before humanity, is uniquely capable of acting on behalf of the sinful genus. Dorner's arrangement hangs on the particular relations in which Jesus Christ stands:

> The possibility of salvation is restored by this, that humanity in some way carries within itself a saving, personal force of universal significance side by side with its common sin and guilt, whose effect is a common punishment. This saving force is able to answer for the whole, because God Himself lives in it, as conversely every individual has receptiveness for it. And this power to make satisfaction in the name of the genus to God's punitive justice, which has reference to the genus, is conferred on the genus by the Son whom God's love vouchsafes to it. He through the act of divine Incarnation has divine power to answer for humanity, while He also became a true scion of humanity as the Son of Man, having universal relation to humanity.[120]

Here is an account which posits Christ as the Saviour on the basis of his status as the central individual. Since the focus is fixed firmly on the status of Christ as God-man, and not, for example on the ethics of transference (although this is covered by his proposals), Dorner has merged

[119] Ibid. pp. 93–94.
[120] Ibid. p. 98.

together substitutionary and representational dynamics in his account.[121] While substitution is the terminology employed to account for Christ's saving significance, the paragraph above contains examples of language which evoke more his representational status: 'the saving force is *able to answer for the whole*'; or 'to make satisfaction *in the name of* the genus'; or 'He…has divine power *to answer for humanity.*' Of course, it is not unusual for representation and substitution to be taken as mutually inclusive categories, particularly when Christ's status as Second Adam is prioritized.[122] Yet, what is surprising is the extent to which Dorner is much less likely to use more substitutionary language, e.g. 'in the place of'; or, 'instead of'. This is the consequence of Dorner's concern to depict the atonement as taking place with the *active* participation of humanity, since it is Jesus Christ as the (central) and *true* man who acts. The God-man acts on behalf of humanity, and because it is he and not humanity who acts, he may be said to be acting instead of them. Yet, conversely, since he is acting instead of humanity *because* he is acting on their behalf, humanity may be said to be included in the act. While humanity may not be said to *contribute* to the reconciling activity it need not also be abstracted or isolated from it because Christ is related to humanity. Dorner is seeking to depict an account of substitutionary atonement which allows for the singularity of Christ's personal work while acknowledging the inseparability of this work from those to whom it pertains. In this connectedness and distinction, we suggest Dorner manages to avoid, though rather narrowly, the synergist pitfalls which attend other models of substitution which tend to foreground the 'inclusive'[123] nature of Christ's activity. While Christ's personal work is that of '*humanity* in Him' (my italics),[124] it is he alone who is 'able to effect'[125] this and as such it is 'unsubstitutable work'.[126] *Narrowly* avoided, though, because his exposition appears sometimes to suggest that reconciliation – of which substitution is a part – is an

---

[121] Such a strategy has been described as seeing substitution and representation as 'correlative' and not 'opposed' concepts, Colin E. Gunton, *The Actuality of Atonement* (Edinburgh: T & T Clark, 1988), p. 166.

[122] For example, John Owen in *The Works of John Owen*, Vol. 10 (Edinburgh: The Banner of Truth Trust, 1967), p. 598.

[123] We use 'inclusive' here to refer to those models of atonement which argue that the union of Christ with us means that Christ *includes us* when he takes our place rather than merely standing *in the place of* sinful human being. Karl P. Donfried refers to its more recent advocates who *contrast* inclusive substitution with exclusive substitution, Karl P. Donfried, 'Paul and the Revisionists: Did Luther Really Get it All Wrong?', in *Dialog: A Journal of Theology*, Vol. 46, No. 1, Spring 2007, p. 36.

[124] *SCD*, IV, p. 98.

[125] Ibid.

[126] Otto Weber, *Foundations of Dogmatics*, Vol. 2, trans. Darrell L. Guder (Grand Rapids: Eerdmans, 1983), p. 207.

immanent *possession* of humanity. We have, therefore, the proposition, 'humanity…*carries* within itself a saving, personal force' (my italics).[127] Of course, this is swiftly delineated as divinely posited, ('God Himself lives in it'[128]) and yet the sense of strain remains. What is noticeable by its absence in Dorner's account is reference to the place of the Holy Spirit in the saving constitution of Christ's humanity. It is an aporia in the exposition which, if addressed, might have offered greater relief to the problem of synergism since, as has elsewhere been argued, the recognition of the Spirit's agency in the 'power of Christ's sacrifice' means that the atonement may be seen as 'genuinely the work of God…but taking shape within the autonomous human life'[129] (given by the Spirit). Were the Spirit's role in the maintenance and direction of Christ's humanity to have been more explicitly acknowledged by Dorner he would, arguably, have had greater resources not to underplay that same humanity in the mediation of salvation endangering its divine priority.

We come now to the question of how this Christ as Representative and Substitute fulfils the eternal purpose of atonement, for which he alone is appointed and capable. We turn, then, to Dorner's account of how Christ *satisfies* the ethical demands of the divine essence in judgement.

a. The Substitutionary Satisfaction of Jesus Christ

At the beginning of the chapter, we saw how Dorner lays out his doctrine of atonement within the confines of his description of Jesus Christ as High Priest, and it is in this role that he provides atoning efficaciousness. Dorner holds that the occasions of sin and guilt produce the divine response of displeasure and require expiation in order for the relation between God and humanity to be restored. It is *to* God that such expiation is to be made, and the righteous displeasure towards sin needs to find its proper telos both for God to remain faithful to Himself and, consistent with the purposes of atonement, effectual for the reconciliation of this *satisfied* God with the world. Central to Dorner's depiction of how this twofold effect will be achieved is in the *attitude* towards the rectitude of the punitive divine posture towards the fallen world:

> [E]xpiation consists not primarily in righteousness of life, but in voluntary subjection to that law of the divine justice which imposes just sufferings on sin and guilt, the centre of which is the divine displeasure.[130]

---

[127] *SCD*, IV, p. 98.
[128] Ibid.
[129] Gunton, *Atonement*, p. 136.
[130] *SCD*, IV, p. 99.

In defining expiation as that which is instantiated by the substitute's conduct in relation to the divine position, we hear, of course, the structure of ethical being which Dorner has maintained throughout his dogmatic project. Just as the triune God is conceived as holy Love according to the way in which He – within and as Himself – freely obeys the good, so too is the expiation for sin and guilt attained by *voluntary subjection* to the divine justice which, according to its ethical immutability, is now changed to impose *just sufferings*. We have the beginnings of Dorner's exposition of how Jesus' salvific activity coincides with his progression towards incarnational perfection. The move towards defining satisfaction as that manifest in free *attitudinal* submission to God's just displeasure marks the continued outworking of Dorner's developmental Christology. In the representation of expiation as that which is realized only in 'unconditional and willing submission'[131] Dorner is seeking to depict the reconciling activity of Christ as the further instantiation of his necessary Godhumanity. It is the mark of one who is *both* properly human *and* uniquely intimate with the divine will (which is Dorner's reconstruction of Anselm's two-sided definition of the sufficient atonement). What this does is produce a definition of satisfaction which pertains to the way in which the divine absolute Personality is related to the world and how the world is eternally purposed to be: the scene of free creaturely obedience to the holy God:

> [W]herever…unconditional and willing submission to the divine judgement is found, there God's just displeasure is propitiated, there God may forgive and again impart His favour to man; for therewith the inviolable holiness of the divine justice is again established in its rights among men, and the unreserved submission to its judgement in thought, feeling, and will is an expiatory satisfaction to it. But all this is impossible to humanity before Christ.[132]

When the divine justice is *established* in its rights among men, satisfaction is guaranteed. While this is impossible to man, it is possible for the 'divine-human Mediator' to represent 'to God the expiatory power of humanity'.[133] It is a proposal which suits Dorner's concern to maintain the creaturely sphere as abidingly ethical, since the satisfaction for its sin and guilt – though provided by the divinely instituted incarnation – is realized together with the resources of this God-man's humanity. The responsibilities of humanity – even the feeling and bearing of the *'penal desert of sin'*[134] – are met within its own sphere by its divinely appointed eternal *telos*.

---

[131] *SCD*, IV, p. 106.
[132] Ibid.
[133] Ibid.
[134] Ibid.

This account of expiation, though finding efficaciousness in its mode of free submission, is connected to the particular manner of Christ's death. It is as Jesus identifies his 'own sense of suffering'[135] with the suffering which comes with the divine response to the sin and guilt of humanity, that substitutionary satisfaction is complete. Dorner lays out the way in which this suffering of Christ in the crucifixion is claimed by Christ himself and God as expiatory in the first section of a two-part chapter (on the '*Subjective Aspect*' of the substitutionary satisfaction, [§122a]), in which the second part looks at the *effect* of this suffering (on the '*Objective Aspect*' of Christ's substitutionary satisfaction, [§122b]). We will lay out the key features, before closing with an examination of the doctrines of justification and sanctification concerning the way in which Dorner handles how the expiated life of the believer is maintained with and subsequent to the resurrection of Christ.

1. Subjective Aspect

Dorner locates the crucial centre of expiation in the suffering willing obedience of the God-man. Indeed, in a brief excursus, Dorner suggests that his arrangement is an advance on the debate surrounding the place of Christ's passive and/or active obedience. It means that the two elements of suffering and Christ's disposition are immediately related to, respectively, expiation and satisfaction:

> In reference to the atonement of sin and guilt, – sins of commission and omission, – Christ's *suffering* comes first into consideration as a special act indispensable to expiation, although, in order to making satisfaction, it must be grounded in the strength of the positive, holy disposition that enters God's will.[136]

While Dorner's concern is to see Christ's '*loving sympathy*'[137] recognized as central, it is only conceptualized properly when both suffering and disposition are brought together as requisite elements in the fulfilment of Christ's high-priestly role. This is consistent with his wider determination to see Christ's enactment of his identity as the key to a proper accounting of the integrity of his humanity. This means that it is in the particular combination of his historical life (which leads up to mortal *suffering*[138]) and his ethical

---

[135] Ibid. p. 107.
[136] Ibid. p. 109.
[137] Ibid. p. 106.
[138] Dorner sees a substantive difference between the suffering which Christ experienced during the course of his life from that which he experienced at the end, Ibid. p. 112. The point of distinction is that before the passion, Christ's suffering was only *with* the world.

response or, better, appropriation of this life (which includes his *holy disposition* to his own mortal suffering), that the atonement may be exposited as consistent with the three interconnected sites of God's essential being as holy Love, Christ's gradual incarnational perfection and the attainment of the divine purposes for the world.

A consequence of Dorner's interlinking of these features is the way in which it plays into his exposition of Christ's 'relation to the divine penal justice (οργή)'[139] and the question of the inner-trinitarian relation of Father and Son. The event of his expiatory death is that in which Christ is complicit and in which the *actual* suffering and acceptance of Christ in his Godhumanity is essential. He provides a reading of penal substitution different to accounts which are *accused* (not always fairly) of implying an 'artificial enigma or mystery' by bringing Christ 'before the throne of the Father in order to let Him – the Son of His love – be judged and punished by the Father'.[140] His penal account does not bring a personal conflict between Father and Son (although he does not, as we have seen, judge this to exclude a 'God-reconciling suffering for sinners'[141]):

> Certainly…the Son could not be the personal object of the Father's wrath or displeasure. He was and remained well-pleasing to God even in His act of substitution, nay, on account of it. Moreover, in His unselfish surrender, no giving up of His moral personality is to be seen, no confounding of His person with that of men, for even His feeling could contain nothing untrue. The substitution for us can be no *commutatio personarum*. He does not Himself become the sinful personality.[142]

The subjective element of the substitution resides in the extent to which the suffering which Christ endures *through* the hands of sinners is recognized and permitted by him (he is not a passive victim) as coinciding with the suffering which is the necessary consequence of the divine reaction to sin. Yet this act of correspondence is not singularly occupied with the recognition of the divine justice. It is simultaneously the 'inner act of love',[143] since it is with Christ's unique insight – an instantiation of his Godhumanity – into the full depths of human sinfulness (Dorner is not clear whether this insight is most clear in the event of his suffering at the hands of humanity, though we might reasonably assume that he holds this point) that the 'substitutionary disposition'[144] is enlivened in order to see restored 'God's loving relationship to

---

[139] *SCD*, IV, p. 110.
[140] Ibid.
[141] Ibid.
[142] Ibid. p. 111.
[143] Ibid. p. 115.
[144] Ibid.

men'[145] by the offering of his own self in and as he is enduring the suffering which is itself the supreme example of that 'over which God's displeasure hangs':[146] the disobedient rejection of the divine purposes for the world in and as the consummating God-man.

Dorner's account rests on the connection he makes between Christ's official activity and his identity as the central individual, 'representing humanity'[147] even in rendering 'satisfaction to the divine Justice'.[148] There is a consistency in his treatment with what has preceded. However, there remain questions about the precise nature of Christ's death. Dorner leaves unclear precisely how the shedding of blood on a divinely cursed site is essential to the expiation of sin and guilt. Because he does not provide detailed exegesis of the key biblical texts concerning the atonement, he does not marshal the resources which otherwise might have been of help to him. While he provides an assessment of the concept of reconciliation, he singularly fails to consider other biblical models which describe the atonement (e.g. sacrifice, redemption, reconciliation, victory[149]). Dorner fails to do enough to lay out the connection between Christ's blood-shedding death and the necessary meeting of the divine justice. It is something which fails to enter even his description of the objective aspect of the atonement, to which we turn now.

2. Objective Aspect

While Dorner has laid out Christ's own attitude towards his sufferings (as coinciding with the divine penalty for sin), he wants to confirm that God 'also regarded it as Christ would have it'.[150] The connection is secured, he argues, because of the way in which divine justice is disposed to accept the substitutionary value of the loving act of Christ's self-sacrifice:

[I]f it were possible for God's justice to characterize such action on the part of love as worthless, as an essentially futile and impossible aspiration, then love, which yet cannot but do this, would be severed from justice at its highest point. But no justice can exist which could forbid love doing that which it must do, and without which, therefore, Christ's love in particular would not be perfect. Justice is the guard of love, not an interdict upon it. On the contrary, if justice exists for the

---

[145] Ibid.
[146] Ibid.
[147] Ibid.
[148] Ibid.
[149] We see this inattention to the details of the different soteriological metaphors when Dorner refers to 'expiation or ἀντίλυτρον' without any explanation of the way in which each carves out a place in the construction of the doctrine, Ibid. p. 117.
[150] Ibid. p. 116.

purpose of shielding good of essential value, and therefore love, it wills love after its manner. This implies an objective value in Christ's work of love even for God.[151]

In appealing to the complementarity of justice and love within the divine essence, Dorner seeks to demonstrate how the ambitions of Christ, deriving from his sympathetic compassion (which is the enactment of his holy personality), find in the divine justice a sympathetic reception. Justice is not opposed to love, but properly manifest only with their correspondence. Christ's appropriation of the sin and guilt of humanity and the accompanying divine penal judgement are acknowledged as fulfilling the demands of justice – by the feeling of the rightness of the judgement in the moment of his suffering – and in this, since it is *lovingly as substitute* for humanity, it has objective value. *Justice is the guard of love*, and as such, in the death of Christ God's personality as holy Love is upheld: the rightness of His judgement is maintained, even *glorified*,[152] and in the same act His love is demonstrated in forgiving humanity, 'so far as Christ represents it, no longer imputing former guilt'.[153]

Dorner is seeking to depict the atonement as that in which both the divine justice and the divine love are properly accommodated. Accounts of atonement find their propriety *only* when connected with 'the right idea of justice'.[154] While the atonement breaks the 'power of Satan'[155] and abolishes the 'fear of death',[156] it is not the deliverance from these two factors which represents the centre of atonement, but *with* the satisfaction of divine justice are removed the penal character of death and the vulnerability of humanity to the 'perverseness of frivolity or despair'[157] encouraged by the 'power of

---

[151] *SCD*, IV, p. 117.
[152] Ibid. p. 124.
[153] Ibid.
[154] Ibid. p. 123.
[155] Ibid. p. 120.
[156] Ibid. p. 119. Dorner surveys other theories: (1) which locate the centre of the atonement in the restoration of a knowledge or consciousness of humanity's 'true, noble nature' (Ibid. p. 120); (2) those which see Christ as God's symbol of how much He hates sin (Ibid. p. 121); (3) those which see Christ as the principle of redemption, though not having procured 'forgiveness and atonement' (Ibid. p. 122); and (4) those which see Christ's physical sufferings as representing the 'penalties deserved by humanity' (Ibid. p. 123). In all of these theories, Dorner suggests elements of truth, e.g. humanity's reordered consciousness of God *is* central, though only insofar as it is connected to the substitution of Christ 'for us' (Ibid. p. 120). In all of the four examples, it is only as the elements pertain to Christ's expiation of sin and guilt that they have theological purchase.
[157] Ibid. p. 120.

darkness'.[158] The objective recognition of Christ's substitutionary suffering hangs on the proper accounting of the relationship between divine justice and divine love.

Dorner presents an account which brings attention to how the content of expiation conforms to the details of the divine essence, and how Christ's substitutionary suffering operates in the context of his own personal development.[159]

b. The Personal Perfection of Jesus Christ: Death, Resurrection and Ascension

The death of Christ marks both the consummation of his 'own earthly work' and also the establishment of 'His person'.[160] The coincidence of these fundamental elements leads to Christ's person assuming a 'higher state of life, pneumatic in character'[161] which (manifest first in his descent into Hades [§124][162]) consists in his capacity to operate 'independently of space and time'.[163] His resurrection is itself a consequence of the attainment of this 'inner, spiritual perfecting'[164] since the manner of his death demonstrated the ethical perfection of his person, and as such, he instantiates the proper idea of humanity which does not have death as a necessary (end) point ('Death is a hostile power in humanity, the consequence not of its idea, but of its sinfulness'[165]). In Christ's resurrection from the dead, Dorner harmonizes the New Testament's active and passive voices by arguing that *Christ's* active cooperation is commensurate with *God's* activity:

> Through the primarily spiritual consummation of His person in death, it became possible for the *raising* up of His body to become also His own act, a *rising* up and reunion with the body.[166]

The immediate consequence of this investment in the idea of the resurrection as of central importance for the *perfection* of the personality of Christ (rather than, say, in its vindicatory import) lies in Christ's completed capacity

---

[158] Ibid.
[159] Ibid. p. 125.
[160] Ibid.
[161] Ibid. p. 127.
[162] Accordingly, for Dorner, the descent to Hades represents a first step in the state of his exaltation, and not a final step in the state of humiliation.
[163] Ibid.
[164] Ibid. p. 132.
[165] Ibid. p. 135.
[166] Ibid. p. 134.

to evoke the 'consummation of humanity':[167]

> In the power of the indissoluble life, which is His, He can and will now communicate Himself by His spirit to believing humanity.[168]

With the resurrection and ascension, Christ's earthly personality has been transformed into a perfected 'pneumatic personality'[169] which means that the humanity of Jesus has become the 'free, adequate organ of the Logos'.[170] That the consequence of Christ's perfection should be the transition to perfect divine self-communication – 'set free from all earthly burden, all narrowing force of matter, from every, even physical imperfection'[171] – brings to a conclusion Dorner's interest in depicting the incarnation as the means by which God effects the union of Himself with the created order. That it is the God-man himself who is the subject of this divine self-communication, means that Christ's enduring status as the mediator between the world and God is secured. With Christ's exaltation comes the perfection and 'effectual continuance' of his official position as the '*sole* Mediator to His Church'.[172] Dorner concludes that the retention of an understanding of Christ's 'continued working'[173] as exalted Redeemer remains essential to the proper accounting of the basis and maintenance of Christian life.

In the final section of the chapter, we want to consider the way in which this reconciliation is realized in the Christian life. We will use Dorner's treatment of the doctrines of justification and sanctification as examples of how he works out the consequences of his project. Before we turn to this, however, we need to be reminded of the distinction which Dorner made earlier in his treatment of the doctrine of sin, namely, the difference between the forgivable or redeemable and the unforgivable and

[167] *SCD*, IV, p. 137.
[168] Ibid. p. 136.
[169] Ibid. p. 138.
[170] Ibid.
[171] Ibid. p. 139. In speaking of Christ in this way, Dorner is not advocating a particular account of the way in which Christ is present in or to the world. Rather, he seeks to avoid the 'metaphysical questions of space and time' (Ibid. p. 141) which have attended the ecclesial controversies, by advocating 'dogmatic sobriety' (Ibid.) and refusing to lay out a theory of how Christ is present except to say that he is present in such a way as to retain the integrity of the unio (and not its confusion), the identification of the God-man with the Godhead, and the capacity of the God-man to be present in the world in accordance with His appropriation by the world (Ibid. pp. 142–143).
[172] Ibid. p. 150.
[173] Ibid. p. 152.

unredeemable sin:

> God, it is true, on His part, is in Christ reconciled with humanity even before its faith, not through faith; access to God is free, God can now offer Himself to us as a father to his children. But He offers Himself thus, *in order that* we may believe, on our part affirm Christ's fellowship with us, therefore seek fellowship with Him, and in this fellowship not merely have the consciousness of forgiveness, but also find in Him the powers of sanctification. But wherever this atoning, prevenient grace is despised or turned to wantonness, there long-suffering is at an end, and the flame of judgement bursts forth against irremediable wickedness. This very atoning, i.e. absolutely revealing love, must also be absolutely condemning love to those who scorn it. But, first of all, the effect of what has been objectively done and procured by Christ is, that God now regards humanity as atoned for in Christ, that in His heart He has forgiven it for Christ's sake – not merely if or because it believes, but objectively in Himself in free prevenient love *because of the connection of Christ with it*, and therefore can offer forgiveness to it without injury to His justice.[174]

What the atonement brings is a fundamental change in *God's* relation to the world. He moves from a posture of displeasure to peace, since in Christ the divine wrath has been satisfied from within humanity itself by divine action. However, while this has changed God's relation to the world, a complete *rapprochement* hangs on the necessary change in the *world's* relation to God, and it is this change which includes the notion of the 'flame of judgement' attending the rejection of this new relation. The atonement creates the conditions in which fellowship may be consummated between God and humanity, and yet it is also the grounds on which final judgement is assessed.

This is the means by which Dorner finalizes his impulse to centre all things, including the eternal destiny of humanity, on the God-man. Both the divine displeasure with sin – which found its expiation in Christ – and the final divine condemnation of unrepentant humanity – which stems from the rejection of Christ – have this central individual as the dogmatic focal point. It is *fellowship* with Christ which is identified as the central characteristic of the salvation offered to humanity (and its rejection which is the touchstone of divine judgement), through which humanity is reconciled to God. However, as we noted in our conclusion to Dorner's doctrine of sin (and Kierkegaard's critique concerning the implications of the distinction between forgivable and unforgivable sin for the doctrine of atonement), there is a way in which

---

[174] Ibid. p. 118.

this configuration underestimates the extent and weight of the atonement. This arises because that which is forgivable pertains only to that sin and guilt which belongs to the genus, and as such, is not yet *personal* sin and guilt for which there is no satisfaction. Yet the implication of this is that what is condemned in the expiatory sacrifice does not *belong* to the individuals who make up the genus, since they are not yet completely ethically responsible (waiting, as they must, for the arrival of the central individual to instantiate personal identity), and as such, not absolutely responsible for the sin and guilt which is punished in the crucifixion. It is only with the death of Christ that humanity first becomes fully responsible for its sin,[175] and it is this responsibility which will be the occasion of divine rejection when forgiveness is itself rejected. The notion arises, therefore, that Christ's death is germane only to that which is less than *absolutely* wicked, and as such, reduced in its revelation of the absolute graciousness of God. The weight of the sin which is punished, therefore, is lessened, as is the weight of the sacrifice.

Dorner's account of atonement is exposed, furthermore, to the systemic problem associated with all dogmatic efforts to secure the idea of the necessity of the incarnation of the God-man. Although he is intent on displaying the expiation of sin as necessary, since he has already committed himself to the notion that the perfection of the God-man is that to which the world is destined – with the perfection of humanity as its attendant corollary – there remains the problem that this reduces the atonement to what has been described as an 'accidental accompaniment of the incarnation',[176] rather than the secure act of the gracious divine freedom.

If the expiation of generic sin is necessary for the attainment of the eternally desired end of the perfection of the God-man, it leaves open the question of whether the atonement can properly be said to be an absolutely free and generous divine act – as that which *alone* definitively defines the divine relation to the world – since it has to a large extent already been displayed, according to the supralapsarian scheme, as necessary for the attainment of the true end, which is *incarnation*. The atonement, therefore, becomes the necessary means to *this* end, and threatens the extent to which the forgiveness of sin through substitutionary atonement may be seen as an absolutely free divine act (since it is tied to the prior divine commitment to the realization of the God-man). We suggest, however, that Dorner has done enough to depict the atonement as indicative of the *general* divine disposition to the

---

[175] Kierkegaard concludes that Dorner's account cannot make sense of Christ as Saviour, since it implies that it is only with his coming that humanity arrives at *full* ethical responsibility and as such is confronted by a free choice for good or evil only for the first time: 'According to Dorner Christ does not become "the second time" but the "first time"', Kierkegaard, *Journals and Papers*, p. 195.

[176] George Smeaton, *Atonement*, p. 371.

world. That is, while the atonement cannot be seen apart from the wider interest in seeing the end as the realization of Christ's godhumanity, since God's overall ambition for the world is to see it posited, maintained and consummated as the sphere of *free* ethical behaviour and divine-imaging enactment, for which the incarnation is the necessary and appropriate source and norm, the atonement may still be assessed as definitely suggestive of the divine purpose for the world as attaining its end with consistent recognition and adherence to the moral constitution of the world and its creator. Given that the world is created and conserved by God, who is holy Love, it is appropriate that its end should be reached, with the entrance of sin and guilt, with the kind of divine provision instanced by the ethically rigorous sacrifice of Christ. Therefore, the constancy of God's relation to the world is preserved and actually instantiated in the atonement, and its centrality to the divine relation to the world secured.

The end of the doctrine of atonement marks, however, the point of transition to the account of the process by which this fellowship, which includes the 'consciousness of forgiveness' and discovery of the 'powers of sanctification', finds its expression as the entrance to the Christian life. We turn now, in our final section, to the doctrines of justification by faith and sanctification. In these loci we will see the principles which guide the administration of the remainder of Dorner's dogmatic project, containing as they do the excavation of how God and humanity relate in the light of Christ's atonement for the attainment of God's purposes for the world.

IV. Reconciliation and the Doctrine of Justification by Faith

Dorner's exposition of the doctrines of justification and sanctification, as for the whole of his account of the Christian life, is marked by an interest in displaying the new Christian personality as morally engaged. However, just as he had sought in his accounts of the relation between God and world, culminating in his exposition of the way in which the incarnation was perfected through a gradual process of ethical enactment, moral engagement is only ever configured in a way which preserves the freedom and independence of the creature in and with its obedience to, and dependence on, God. Though seeking to maintain the *distinction* between the divine and the human sides in both the production (justification) and maintenance (sanctification) of the new Christian personality, therefore, Dorner displays a concern to demonstrate their *relation* without implying an *identification* of agencies. This issues forth in a two-sided enterprise in the explanation of the doctrine of justification. On the one hand, he seeks to depict the new life of the new Christian personality as having security in the *objective* work of God ('the bottomless compassion and love of God'[177]), rather than finding the locus of its salvation in its subjective *fiduciary* activity (when 'divine forgiveness itself is supposed to be the effect of our conversion and faith'[178]). On the other hand, he seeks to secure the status of *faith* as the appropriate and indispensable human activity for the completion of justification. While the divine side has priority – it alone originates the 'contents of faith'[179] – the human side is not evacuated of ethical vibrancy since it acts – with its 'humbling and shaming'[180] – by *appropriating* the divine. While we will see that the process of sanctification represents a decisively different step in the cooperation of the divine and human in the progress towards the world's consummation, Dorner is keen to display a *correspondence* between divine and human activity even in his treatment of justification. In this, he continues the venture to depict all things, including the origin and sustenance of the new human, as having their bearing in the inner ethical dynamic of the Godhead:

> What else is the godlike personality of the sons of God but the conscious union of the free with the ethically necessary as the absolutely worthy and deserving love?
>
> [God] is, according to His essence, content with nothing less that Self-conscious and free desire after the good, and that He straightaway requires the form of this freedom as the only worthy means of the realization of the good.[181]

The transition, therefore, to the doctrines which surround the origin and preservation of the Church as the community in which Christian life occurs, is scored with the same elements which characterized his foundational insights into the idea of God as the Absolute Personality. It is on these grounds that he describes the new humanity as the *godlike personality*.

a. Justification by Faith: Divine Grace and Human Activity

Dorner comes to his exposition of the doctrine of justification after briefly considering the content of human repentance (§131) which, he argues, is marked by a *'feeling* of personal guilt and penal desert' and a desire for 'divinely given righteousness',[182] and brought about through a 'connection

---

[177] George Smeaton, *Atonement*, p. 227.
[178] Ibid.
[179] Ibid.
[180] *SCD*, I, p. 446.
[181] Ibid.
[182] *SCD*, IV, p. 188. This definition does not represent a prescription of the manner in which repentance and faith will occur (for which he criticizes Methodism here as he

with the word of Christ'.[183] These two dimensions (which Dorner is keen to distinguish in order to preserve the necessity of the *call* to repentance and the 'acknowledgment of the law and its rights'[184]) represent the means of access to the Church ('The Origin of the Church through Faith and Regeneration'[§130]). They are laid out in detail following a lengthy discussion of the consonance of divine grace and human activity in the purposes of salvation. Central to Dorner's conception lies the concern to lay out this activity – specifically, the work of grace – as being indicative of both divine and human engagement, without this implying independent human possession of grace (and its Pelagian or Semi-Pelagian implications). He seeks to achieve this by making a distinction between the 'prevenient *grace of justification*' which 'cannot be an effect of man's action'[185] and the stage subsequent to its reception in which the creature is *enabled* first to approach a 'turning point'[186] in which he is convinced by the atoning significance of Christ (with the attendant intimations of penal desert), and then second, when this conviction has assumed the quality of trust in 'God's unchangeable fidelity'[187] and with this the acceptance[188] of Christ's substitutionary significance, when 'real freedom'[189] is instantiated in the Christian believer. The *reality* of this freedom is thus displayed in its working 'for good'.[190] In Dorner's estimation the work of salvation must be seen to evince the fundamental relations between God and world (union without identification) and the fundamental constitution of the world as represented by humanity (eternally disposed to be the divine image bearer in free obedience to God):

> That the divine and human sides must combine in a vital manner in the work of salvation, as implied generally by the *ethical* character of Christianity. (my italics)[191]

With this supposition we hear once again the refrain continually repeated in Dorner's theological project and which pertains to the non-competitive

had done in *Protestant History*, p. 94), but rather is intended to describe those elements which will variously comprise the attitude of the penitent believer.

[183] *SCD*, IV, p. 189.

[184] Ibid. This acknowledgement of the law is part of Dorner's concern not to lose or abdicate from soteriology the propriety of the goodness of the ethical demands under which the creature stands on account of the essentially ethical constitution of God.

[185] Ibid. p. 165. '[I]n opposition to Synergism, the natural man has not this capacity of free appropriation,' (Ibid. p. 181).

[186] Ibid. p. 183.

[187] Ibid. p. 185.

[188] Dorner describes this as the 'faith of acceptance', Ibid. p. 192.

[189] Ibid. p. 186.

[190] Ibid.

[191] Ibid. p. 177.

agenda which we recalled above. The *ethical character of Christianity* is that which finds its origins and justification in the ethical definition of the divine Absolute Personality; and in the account of salvation as that which must allow for the combination of divine and creaturely elements in the production of the desired ends (with the necessary conditions attached to preserve the constant priority of the divine) we see once again the outworking of the relation between God and world in the distinction between the world's creation and its conservation (see Chapter 2). There we observed how Dorner sought an account which defended the distinction between God and world without obscuring the abiding relation. This had, of course, its *telos* in the incarnation. We will see now how his doctrine of justification seeks to maintain the ethical constitution of his dogmatic project ('Even the receiving of divine grace is a moral act, an obedience of faith'[192]); and how it rests on the decisive notion of God's relation to the world as both transcendent and immanent, intending the production of a world which lives freely in willing dependence on His creative and conserving power. The doctrine of justification does not see the suspension of this relation, but rather its instantiation. Humanity is re-created by God for free obedience to Him.

b. Justification by Faith: Divine Prerogative and Human Correspondence

> On the part of man, there is appropriation of Christ and His righteousness, primarily of propitiating grace or justification, in virtue of which our sin is not reckoned to us by God, but forgiven, and the righteousness of Christ is imputed; and on the part of Christ, real appropriation of man, union of the divine life with the human by the power of the Holy Spirit...the result of this union through the Holy Spirit is a new, living phenomenon, namely a personality after the image of God, which is a reflection of the union of the divine and human in Christ...But the communion instituted by faith between Christ and the soul does not end in participation in reconciliation; but, on the permanent basis of justification in virtue of the same communion, the sanctification, which is the end and fruit of reconciliation, is developed through the Holy Spirit.[193]

Dorner opens his account by defining *justification* as the appropriation of 'propitiating grace'.[194] As such, the believer becomes *associated* (we will look in more detail of this association below) – 'by the power of the Holy Spirit'[195] – with the righteousness which Christ had in and with the act of his atoning death. This means that the righteousness of Christ, appropriated by

---

[192] *SCD*, IV, p. 236.
[193] Ibid. p. 193.
[194] Ibid.
[195] Ibid.

the believer and 'imputed'[196] to the believer, is being defined as that which found its consummation and perfection in Christ's freely willed acknowledgement of the rightfulness of God's displeasure at sin *and* the instantiation of God's love for the world. A consequence of Dorner's interest in bringing together *person* and *work*, it is the righteousness of the *crucified* and *resurrected* Christ: the perfect God-man. Central to Dorner's ambitions for his doctrine of justification, therefore, is the connection between the doctrines of atonement and justification (although not their identification[197]). The importance of this connection is twofold. First, the doctrine of justification functions as the *subjective* side of the *objective* state of affairs brought about by the atonement since it includes the believer's acknowledgement that 'God *has* forgiven sin and guilt' (my italics).[198] Second, a clear connection excludes the inference that it is *faith* which makes God reconciled, since justification is merely (though vitally) the recognition that 'independently of the faith of the world and before it, God has forgiven it'[199] through Christ.

The priority of the 'objective reconciliation of the world by Christ'[200] is further encouraged by the concomitant recognition of the *distinction* which obtains between atonement and justification. The 'peculiar independent meaning'[201] of each preserves the 'independence of the atonement'[202] and the proper status of justifying faith as that which does not *procure* actual reconciliation: '[o]therwise the consequence would be, that faith is a jointly atoning causality.'[203] Rather, it is that which instantiates the 'moral character of the whole saving process'[204] as the exercising of *free* acceptance of God's forgiveness (and the rightfulness of His displeasure). Faith does not 'create'[205] the conditions necessary for forgiveness to occur (which Dorner sees in much Protestant theology[206]), but instead is *enabled*[207] by the divine

---

[196] Ibid.

[197] Ibid. p. 211.

[198] Ibid. p. 209.

[199] Ibid.

[200] Ibid. p. 212.

[201] Ibid. p. 211.

[202] Ibid.

[203] Ibid. p. 212.

[204] Ibid. p. 215.

[205] Ibid. p. 217.

[206] He singles out Methodism as failing on this point, by deriving the 'actuality of forgiveness from penitence and faith as a subjective act', Ibid. p. 212, n. 1.

[207] Dorner argues that both *gratia praeparans* and *gratia praeveniens* are necessary for the creature to be prepared for free response to God's forgiveness. *Gratia praeparans* is the condition, continually upheld by God as a 'natural endowment' (Ibid. p. 181), according to which humanity is ordered towards a *justitia civilis*, yet insufficient to effect a saving awareness. *Gratia praeveniens* is, therefore, the grace which 'renders possible' (Ibid.) the transition to the grace of regeneration. It is the consequence of the

propitiousness towards the world – because of Christ's substitutionary atonement – to *respond* in freedom to God either with 'resistance'[208] or 'to make it our own personal possession'.[209] Central to Dorner's definition of justification, therefore, is an interest in laying out the necessary objectivity of the atonement – and the new state of affairs which it creates – without precluding the corresponding role of the creature in its realization in the life of the believer: 'The doctrine of atonement affirms that *God* is reconciled to the sinful world through Christ, but by no means that the enmity of the *world* to God is abolished.'[210] In both areas we see the persistent concern to see the process of salvation conceived as that which exhibits both the ethical necessity of atonement (for the maintenance of God's holy love) and the freedom of the human's response to this condition (for the generation of our 'moral personality'[211]).

This arrangement is intended to preserve the ethical propriety of Christian salvation. The way in which Dorner conceives the *imputation* of Christ's righteousness to the believer also, therefore, bears this mark. He is keen to maintain a distinction between justification and sanctification or the *actus Dei forensis* and *justitia infusa*, and in order to preserve this position he responds in detail to the following objections:

1. That it implies an 'indifference to the law'[212] (and antinomianism);
2. That it brings into disrepute God's rectitude by proposing he treats 'one who is a sinner as righteous';[213]
3. That an *actus Dei forensis* or *declaratorius* would leave humanity internally unaffected and still without essential righteousness.

The manner of his replies to these objections displays a concern to show how the act of justification and the state of being justified are consonant both with the conservation, indeed are the enactment, of divine rectitude *and* the instantiation of an inward ethical change to the believer (without recourse to the idea of *justitia infusa*). By recalling the connection between justification and atonement, Dorner argues that the law has in fact been upheld in the salvation process by Christ's vicarious atonement; and according to his representation of expiation as dependant on the 'acknowledgement of

new way in which God is related to the world following the atonement: 'This grace on the one hand vivifies the knowledge of sin and guilt and...on the other the longing after moral worth and a salvation coming from above' (*SCD*, IV, p. 182).

[208] Ibid. p. 216.
[209] Ibid. p. 217.
[210] Ibid. p. 209.
[211] Ibid. p. 216.
[212] Ibid. p. 232.
[213] Ibid. p. 233.

the weight and penal character of sin and guilt',[214] he suggests that this is both met and satisfied in Christ and is also a necessary characteristic of the 'man who desires justification [that he] shall recognize his penal liability'[215] (This last dimension implying a contribution by the justified believer *only* in affirming Christ's propitiatory work[216]). Furthermore, in the notion of God pronouncing the sinner righteous, Dorner argues that the declaration includes an affirmation of human 'penal liability':[217]

> Nor does the sentence imply primarily that man is holy and righteous habitually or in himself, but simply affirms the divine favour and pro-pitiousness to the sinner, and indeed not to the sinner in himself...but affirms that the divine justice contemplates and treats man as recon-ciled for the sake of Christ's advocacy and perfect righteousness.[218]

The act of justification is, therefore, not the affirmation of creaturely inno-cence, but rather the *acknowledgement* of guilt and penal desert which have found their expiation instead in Christ. Once again, however, we also have Dorner repeating the importance to the process of the sinful human's *faith* as that by which it enters into 'fellowship with Christ's righteousness'[219] and is, thus, not regarded without faith as righteous and holy for Christ's sake. In responding to the third and final criticism, the principle of Christ's fellowship with the sinner becomes ever more decisive, both in terms of the particular point concerning the externality of the *actus declatorius*, but also in relation to the wider scheme. What this means is that Dorner rejects the accusation of the idea of the *actus Dei forensis* as 'empty [and] outward',[220] because it underplays the extent to which the declaration is made not only by God within Himself but also, because of the fellowship of Christ [as the Central Individual], is a declaration or proclamation of acquittal 'made *to* man' (my italics).[221] This understanding is intended to show that the act of justification is both the prerogative of God alone ('this act or this sentence, which within the divine nature is independent of all human action of a moral kind'[222]) without entailing a discoordination with the human recipient. The

---

[214] Ibid.
[215] Ibid.
[216] The *meagerness* of the human contribution, though necessary, is evidence of the objectivity of the atonement which, he argues elsewhere, means that the affirmation of the forgiveness which follows Christ's atoning sacrifice is neither the production of that forgiveness, and neither is it 'even at once receptive', Ibid.
[217] Ibid. p. 234.
[218] Ibid.
[219] Ibid. p. 235.
[220] Ibid.
[221] Ibid.
[222] Ibid.

appeal to a direct divine *address* to the forgiven sinner seeks to position the justified human as the beneficiary of an independently achieved state of affairs (forgiveness) whose response (of 'implanted'[223] faith) is appropriate to the creature's constitution as that which is indebted to God for its dependent freedom (in both the first and now second creations). With the terms of this doctrine excavated in which the two sides are depicted as corresponding in ways appropriate to their identities, so that there is a *fittedness* to the divine priority and the human receptivity, Dorner is ready to lay out the way in which the new humanity, declared righteous, is prepared to live an ethically appropriate life.

c. Sanctification

The first necessary function of the new man is the preserving of the salvation in possession...Conservation joins on to Creation, as everything living co-operates in its own preservation and seeks food as the means of its preservation....If up to the point of justification man's activity consisted merely in spontaneity of living receptiveness, and the divine activity so predominated that the man is justified, now that the new personality is present, co-operation begins.[224]

While the doctrine of justification by faith saw the accent fall on the divine initiative without abdicating the human side, its corresponding role in appropriating the grace offered, the doctrine of sanctification sees the transition to a state of affairs in which the newly re-created Christian personality is posited as such *in process*. Sanctification is that which is initiated by the act of justification – so that the human is free *from* punishment and free *for* the 'growth in holiness of will'[225] – and ordered towards the consummation of that which is posited by this original creative act. Just as the doctrine of humanity was arranged teleologically,[226] so too is the doctrine of restored humanity:

The state of justification...is again itself an infinite, life-pregnant beginning of a process stretching into eternity, in which that which is already gained undergoes development, and man is shaped into a new personality belonging to and resembling Christ.[227]

Central to Dorner's understanding of sanctification is its relation to justification as that which has initiated a process – at its inception temporal, though

---

[223] *SCD*, IV, p. 235.
[224] Ibid. p. 239.
[225] Ibid.
[226] Ibid. p. 376.
[227] Ibid. pp. 237–238.

having eternal range – which is ordered towards the complete attainment[228] of Christlikeness. Sanctification is, therefore, the process in which the new humanity is itself engaged in order to *enact* its divinely designated identity – originating in its justification – of a humanity brought into union with God, ethically defined, and as such attaining its proper relation to the divine.[229] The process of sanctification is not merely the advance towards personal holiness, but is itself the mode in which humanity comes to the perfection of its essential being in relation to God:

> The state of sanctification relates not merely to growth in holiness of will, but embraces the whole man and the development of his entire personality, and *therefore the preservation and growth of sonship to God* in the regenerate. (my italics)[230]

With this focus on the production, maintenance and fulfilment of a new personality as the instantiation of humanity's proper destiny as being united with God – as *sons* – Dorner is presenting an account of the Christian life which seeks to depict Christian ethical activity as pertaining to this specific end (so that the pursuit of the good for which the new human is now free is also the free obedience to God) *and* opening the grounds for such activity to be indicative not only of the divine life now within the believer but also of the cooperating agency of the believer himself. The accent is now on the new personality, which means that humanity has been freed to obey God in conformity both with the exigencies of the good and for the delight of the Lord.

Together with this focus on the development of the new Christian personality comes an interest in locating the particular sphere in which it occurs. It is not merely as *individuals* that the end is reached, but the personal development is set within and towards the production of an 'intimate communion'[231] with a divinely desired genus:

> [P]ersonal consciousness is perfected in true generic consciousness, in love, just as the world-aim – the divine idea of humanity – is directed to a living, indivisible spirit-kingdom, a real communion of love with God in Christ, and with the brethren. Since, then, in the new personality

---

[228] Before the consummation of all things with the world's end, the believer is both designated and oriented towards complete perfection as a 'new personality' while at the same time still in simultaneous possession of its old humanity, Ibid. p. 240.

[229] This enactment is not, of course, to be separated from God's continual upholding and self-communication. Rather, it is in and with the persistent reception and possession of God's graciousness that such enactment occurs.

[230] Ibid. p. 239.

[231] Ibid. p. 241.

even the generic consciousness is ennobled and attains its reality, the antithesis of the individual and identical is brought to unity in the living communion, the organism of which is the supreme end.[232]

The consummation of the Christian life is found, therefore, only within the fellowship of individuals who together represent the 'aim of regenerating grace'.[233] Yet this is not a mere voluntary co-ordination of individuals to form a community of identical interests, though in the processes of 'giving and taking'[234] relations *are* temporally instantiated by consistent cooperation. Rather it is a community which finds its basis in the 'impulse to exercise the spirit of communion [given]…in [the believer's] regeneration'.[235] This impulse is in place because it is in and with the communal relations that both the individual and the whole will attain their 'perfecting'[236] and at the same time adhere to the *duty* to glorify Christ. The focus of Dorner's doctrine of sanctification rests, therefore, on the creation and maintenance of the Church as the sphere in which the divine purposes for the world find their goal. It could only be such for Dorner, since it is in the ethical life – conceived as holy love – that the divine impression could be properly instantiated; and it is only with the 'movement in giving and taking'[237] which belongs to the fellowship of a true moral *community* that such could be evidenced and enjoyed.

Conclusion

Dorner's intentions for his account of the doctrines of atonement and justification is the representation of salvation as that which corresponds with the ethical constitution of the divine Absolute Personality as holy Love, and as that which brings the 'moral perfecting of man as a member of [God's] kingdom'.[238] This means the positing by God and the attaining by humanity of an ethical existence which is characterized by a continual and active 'surrender to God'[239] both in the acts of justification and sanctification.

What is, however, notably absent from Dorner's account is an extended exposition of the way in which the Holy Spirit is the accompanying and liberating agent in this progress towards essential holiness. While there is

[232] *SCD*, IV, p. 241.
[233] Ibid.
[234] Ibid. p. 242.
[235] Ibid.
[236] Ibid. p. 241.
[237] Ibid. p. 243.
[238] Ibid. p. 236.
[239] Ibid. p. 237.

reference to the Spirit's presence in the new humanity, it continually stops short of detailing how the creaturely ethical activity is specifically upheld and oriented by the Spirit's purposing. For example, Dorner speaks of the Spirit of Christ being 'communicated' to the new life at the moment of apprehension of Christ's 'personal righteousness and love',[240] without an accompanying explanation of what this communication means for the instantiation of the believer's capacity for ethical behaviour. The Spirit is depicted as being to the believer the agent of his new moral capacity ('[The new man] no longer needs an outward law, but is a law to himself by the Holy Spirit'); and yet it appears that while the Spirit directs by *disciplining* the person's character, (this point is expressed in its connection to the individualizing of the person), it is as the *ratifier* of distinctions advanced by the new moral personality that the Spirit is said to act.[241] The sense that this brings is of a divine agency which is subsequent (though involved) to the ethical activity of the creature. We do not propose that Dorner is laying out an account which seeks to relegate the Spirit to *ad hoc* patron of the Christian life. However, we suggest that Dorner's heavy investment in the new personality as one who is posited as engaged in an ethical process towards its final consummation requires a stronger account of the way in which the Spirit specifically works within, without confusion of divine and human agencies, to bring this to its conclusion. What is needed, we suggest, is an exposition which explains how the Spirit is as essential to the ethical life of the believer – in its free obedience to God – as He is to the eternal returning in the ethical life of the triune God.

---

[240] Ibid. p. 236.
[241] Ibid. p. 241.

CONCLUSION

Christian Doctrine has not merely to do with the divine deeds in redemption and restoration, but also with the knowledge of God in Himself and according to His essence. It is not possible that that only should be of value to the pious man which God does for him and for humanity, especially as regards salvation. These deeds already point back to the divine Essence, which is actually revealed in them, and does not remain a mere mystery. If it is said, His deeds point back to His will, to His disposition, but with the knowledge of His disposition there is no knowledge given of His essence, the supposed independent relation between the Divine disposition and essence must make the former precarious, and leave room for thoughts of mutability, because it would not be the heart of God which revealed itself in the deeds, but something still higher would be presupposed (for example, a Supremum arbitrium), by means of which His disposition of love, in its duration and stability, and His deeds in their eternal importance and validity, would be put in question. Further, the opposite view, which excludes all knowledge of God Himself, might possibly leave room for gratitude for the divine favours, but not for the glory and praise of God.[1]

In the course of our analysis of Isaak Dorner's theological project, we have sought to display the extent to which the doctrine of God – as (ethical) Absolute Personality – functions as its orienting principle; and we have endeavoured to trace the way in which the details of that doctrine inform and influence the progression towards the construction of his account of the doctrines of sin and salvation. Along the way we have noted how Dorner's ambitions for the demonstration of the Christian faith *as true* see him make moves (e.g. his commitment to the necessary incarnation) which, at times, appear to threaten the *priority* of the divine interest in the details of the world's salvation (see Chapter 3). For the purposes of exhibiting the certainty of the Christian faith, great systemic appeal is made to the fact that the *actual* incarnation points to the *necessity* of its occurrence for the fulfilment of the eternal divine purposes for the world. This means that the *accent* of Dorner's project falls, we might say, more firmly on Christ's saving *godhumanity* than his *saving* godhumanity (notwithstanding Dorner's

---

[1] *SCD*, I, p. 27.

rejection of the distinction between Christ's person and work [§99[2]]. However, as the extract above indicates, this *emphasis* is one which is not intended to remove from the Christian faith its soteriological import (since Christian doctrine *is* 'to do with the divine deeds in redemption and restoration'[3]), but rather to seek their vital *connection* with the essential being of God which is 'actually revealed'[4] in these saving acts.

What we find in Dorner, therefore, is a theologian whose ambitions for systematic theology extend beyond the desire only to provide *certitude* for the believer (though, of course, he himself prioritizes the apologetic intentions of thetic theology[5]), and much more in its attendant capacity to depict the essential *bond* between God's being and God's acts. He disallows those theological propositions which either deny the relation between the 'Divine disposition and essence' or which exclude 'all knowledge of God Himself'.[6] Rather, it is the capacity of doctrinal exposition to draw a clear line from the immediate insights of faith concerning, first, the saving significance of Jesus Christ and, secondly, the ethical constitution of Christ's God (as instigator of the new ethical personality) to the demonstration of complete correspondence between the experience of forgiveness and sanctification and the essential being of the triune God. According to this scheme, what is advanced is the consistent priority of God in both creation and reconciliation without detriment to the relative freedom or independence of the creature. It is in the heavy appeal, first, to God as Absolute Personality or *holy* Love that Dorner seeks to depict a living and engaged deity – and one who as such is properly denoted triune – and, second, in the realized, historical God-man Jesus Christ that he locates the nexus of the divine purposes to establish a perfect union with the world without prejudicing their distinction.

We have sought to demonstrate the consistency of Dorner's approach, and display what we regard as his underexplored but highly significant investment in the doctrine of the divine *aseity*. In Chapter 2 we suggested that it was the key to his being able to posit the world as free, without falling into the danger of disconnecting God and world (since God relates to the world because he is in himself self-sufficient, and the world is free to relate to God because it depends on God).

God's self-sufficiency is the eternal result of the triune relations, and the instantiation of the divine perfection (to which the world adds nothing). It is central to Dorner's project to preserve the idea of God's triunity as indicative of the divine completeness, and it is to this that appeal is made to preserve the world from being posited as necessary to the divine perfection. However,

---

[2] *SCD*, III, pp. 279–283.
[3] *SCD*, I, p. 27.
[4] Ibid.
[5] *SCD*, I, p. 17 ff.
[6] Ibid. p. 27.

while this is central, Dorner's account suffers, as we have repeatedly noted, from its reluctance to speak of the relation between the self-sufficient God and the dependent world in terms of grace. It is this reluctance which, we suggest, means that he is exposed to the charge of advancing the necessity of creation (see Chapter 2) from which we have sought to defend him. Karl Barth's description of God's perfection in relation to the world displays this dimension more satisfactorily, we suggest, since he describes the world forcefully as the product of grace (though Dorner's commitment to the divine self-sufficiency is no less strident):

> Everything that the creature seems to offer Him – its otherness, its being in – antithesis to Himself and therefore His own existence in co-existence – He has also in Himself as God...Without the creature He has all this originally in Himself, and it is His free grace...if He allows its existence as another, as a counterpart to Himself, and His own co-existence with it. In superfluity – we have to say this because we are in fact dealing with an overflowing, not with a filling up of the perfection of God which needs no filling.'[7]

We saw how the details of this position appear central to his depiction in Chapter 3 of the *idea* of the God-man and in Chapter 5 the *realized* God-man. What appears most inviting in Dorner's explication is the way in which his foundational investment in the concept of God as the 'Organism of the Absolute divine Personality'[8] (with its trinitarian and ethical connotations) means that the relation between God and world, which finds its fulfilment and perfection in the incarnation, may be said to be *maximal*, that is, involve even the personal union of God with a single human without detriment either to His own abiding distinctiveness (since His Self-preservation and Self-communication are functions of His immanent Self-existence) or to the detriment of the relative independence of the creature (since its creatureliness will be guaranteed by God's giving only what is proper to its dependent being). This arrangement means that Dorner may posit the freedom of the creature – in the supreme instance as the incarnate Jesus Christ – as that which finds its bearing and fulfilment in an ordered obedience to God (and not, as has been noted of the 'modern context' as the 'capacity for self-determination'[9] in a 'taking leave of God'[10]). Thus, the divine and human

---

[7] Karl Barth, *Church Dogmatics*, Vol. IV, The Doctrine of Reconciliation, Part 1, (Edinburgh: T & T Clark, 1956), p. 201.

[8] Ibid. p. 412.

[9] Christoph Schwöbel, 'Imago Libertatis: Human and Divine Freedom' in *God and Freedom: Essays in Historical and Systematic Theology*, ed. Colin E. Gunton (Edinburgh: T & T Clark, 1995), p. 62.

[10] Ibid. p. 70.

sides may be represented as non-competitive in bringing to a proper conclusion the divine purposes for the world (without undermining the priority of God in instigating and achieving this end).

Furthermore, this proposal means that there is a *correspondence* between the way in which human personality comes to completion, in its spatio-temporal context, and the way in which the perfect divine personality is always complete as the eternal *result* of its inner-trinitarian relations (see Chapters 1 and 3). In this is given the meaning and significance of the doctrine of *imago dei*: humanity may be said to be an image of God in its ethically constituted temporal correlation with the essential ethical being of God.[11] With it Dorner has made a doctrinal connection between the constitution of God and the constitution of the world which sets the latter's relation to the former as fulfilled in and with its conformity to God's necessary being.

This is not to say that there are not significant oversights in Dorner's account. Alan Spence's *The Promise of Peace: A Unified Theory of Atonement* is a recent attempt to offer a 'particular interpretative model of salvation'[12] with echoes of Dorner's ordering of dogmatic material, using the idea of representation as the unifying means of explication. Spence seeks to identify the proposition that 'Jesus might have acted as man on our behalf towards God'[13] as capable of affirming the 'significance of the human agency of Christ'[14] and 'able to affirm God's saving generosity in the gift of His Son'.[15] However, while there is a similarity with this dimension of Dorner's strategy, Spence displays a consistent interest in laying out the continually active place of the Holy Spirit in both Christ's self-offering[16] (pertaining to Christ's high-priestly office[17]) and in the Christian life.[18] This is not a major part of

---

[11] This obtains even if Dorner's expression of the 'positive value' of divine holiness in the 'realization of the world' on occasion belies its personal nature and threatens the distinction between God and world, see John Webster, *Holiness* (London: SCM, 2003), p. 109.

[12] Alan Spence, *The Promise of Peace: A Unified theory of Atonement* (London: T & T Clark, 2006), p. 19.

[13] Ibid. p. 20.

[14] Ibid. p. 33.

[15] Ibid. p. 52.

[16] Ibid. p. 33.

[17] In contrast to Dorner's account Alan Spence lays out the value to John Owen's account of Christ's high-priestly office of the recognition of the Spirit's 'sanctifying and renewing work' (p. 85) on Christ by calling attention to the fact that it means that while salvation is 'considered, from first to last, as God's gracious and loving initiative...the actual act of atonement must also be seen as an act towards God of one who is man' (p. 86), Alan Spence, 'Christ's Humanity and Ours: John Owen' in *Persons Divine and Human*, eds. Christoph Schwöbel and Colin E. Gunton (Edinburgh: T & T Clark, 1991).

[18] Ibid. p. 100.

219

Dorner's account and represents, we suggest, a key weakness in his project, since the Spirit appears as almost entirely dependent on and subsequent to the determinations of Christ's godhumanity.

We also noted in Chapter 1, for example, that his methodological decision to proceed from the general to the Christian idea of God is attended by an interest in displaying its propriety as a *problem solving* tool. Though he, no doubt, sees this strategy as central to his ambitions to reinvigorate the doctrine of the Trinity as the justifiable foundation for Christian dogmatics, it threatens to obscure the connection which we nevertheless maintain is present in his theology between that doctrine and the soteriological thrust of the Christian faith. It is an aspect which, of course, is part of his interest in demonstrating the truthfulness of that faith's contents, but sees him accused of avoiding a focus on the 'divine work of reconciliation'.[19] This analysis, as we have sought to argue, is only partially correct, in that while the primary focus is on that perfection which is brought by the incarnation only contingently through Christ's saving activity, the *general* divine disposition to the world is such that while God's reconciling activities cannot be separated from His wider vision in seeing the world's fulfilment in the *necessary* God-man, *because* God's purposes for the world are that it become the created space of free ethical conformity to himself, the reconciling activity of Christ is *indicative* of that general divine disposition. It is an approach which seeks to distinguish the different aspects of God's activity through history without indicating a disconnection. It brings to mind Colin Gunton's description of what he sees as Irenaeus' conception of the divine economy as thought together in its 'distinctness, but not separateness, and interrelatedness'.[20] Gunton's interpretation of Irenaeus as giving to created world's time and space their 'distinctive dynamic of interrelatedness by God's creating, upholding, redeeming and perfecting activity'[21] might also be said of Dorner for whom the relative independence of creation is maintained by the divine activity and not abridged by it. Indeed, Dorner's heavy investment in the teleological constitution of the created order which is destined to find its fulfilment in the freely obedient God-man, actualized in and through his sacrificial suffering, finds echoes in Gunton's own concern to see the link between Christ and creation made in the latter's perfection by and with the former's 'perfect offering of himself to the Father'.[22] For these reasons it is perhaps surprising that Dorner does not feature in Gunton's corpus, since the similarities do not end with the link between Christ and creation. We note how Gunton leans

[19] Karl Barth, *Church Dogmatics*, Vol. III, Part I, p. 47.
[20] Colin Gunton, *The One, the Three and the Many: God, Creation and the Culture of Modernity* (Cambridge: CUP, 1993), p. 158.
[21] Ibid. p. 159.
[22] Colin E. Gunton, *Christ and Creation* (Carlisle: The Paternoster Press, 1992), p. 57.

on the testimony of P. T. Forsyth to assist his depiction of Jesus' identity. It is worth quoting the passage which Gunton himself – with qualification – offers as a means of expressing Christ's godhumanity. Its similarities with Dorner are obvious:

> We have within this single increate person the mutual involution of the two personal acts or movements…the one distinctive of man, the other distinctive of God; the one actively productive from the side of Eternal God, the other actively receptive from the side of growing man.[23]

That Forsyth's endeavours find a place in Gunton's theology makes Dorner's absence more notable. Indeed, the help which Gunton finds in Forsyth on Christology extends to the latter's account of God's omnipresence, and once again a position which is found in Dorner's earlier dogmatics. Gunton, indebted to Forsyth, argues that 'God's capacity to be present to and in particular places…is grounded in his omnipresence'.[24] Dorner's contribution to the development of these theological loci is unfortunately absent.

However, what we have sought to propose is that in the material which Dorner has marshalled in his account of the doctrine of God (not least in his innovative treatment of attributes and proofs as finding their combined locus in the idea of God's triunity) he provides himself with the resources to depict the saving significance of Jesus Christ as inimical neither to the ideas of divine justice or love; and in his depiction of the way in which this God-man comes to perfection in the actual obedience *even to death on a cross* Dorner is able to present the supreme *revelation* of God as coterminus with the divine *reconciliation*.[25]

An obvious example of such resources lies in his appeal to the ethical constancy of God – his immutability – as the grounds on which the divine disposition towards the world is *affected* by its descent into sin without this competing with his abiding essential being: God *remains* who he is in and as he reacts to sin in the world, and as such is *able* to meet and

---

[23] P. T. Forsyth, *The Person and Place of Jesus Christ* (London: Independent Press, 1909), pp. 343–344. Quoted in Colin Gunton, *The Christian Faith* (Oxford, Blackwell Publishing, 2002), p. 95.

[24] Gunton, *Christian Faith*, p. 115.

[25] As Christoph Schwöbel has argued, for 'Christian theology the choice between reconciliation and revelation is one that must be rejected' since it is with the revelation that 'the glory of God [is found] in the face of Jesus Christ' that the truth of the reconciling message is disclosed, 'Reconciliation' in *The Theology of Reconciliation*, ed. Colin E. Gunton (London: T & T Clark, 2003), p. 32.

overcome the challenge which has arisen:[26]

> God does not lose but maintains and affirms Himself in all His actions...God has His Immutability absolutely in His ethical essence, from which He cannot and will not fall away.[27]

It is on this account that God's disposition to the world after the advent of sin is able to be described as *anger* without implying a change in his essential being. However, it is due to the definition of God as *holy* Love that we see Dorner able to envisage this ('conditioned'[28]) posture as consistent with the divine intention to bring about a reconciliation. He does not see the need to reduce the place of justice or question the necessity of expiation in order to depict the world's salvation as invoking divine wrath or requiring 'mortal suffering'[29] in order for this wrath to be dealt with. This is because it is not in the overcoming or abandonment of justice that love may be instantiated. Rather, it is in its demonstration and enactment. This is, of course, because in God himself exist 'Justice and Love' in 'harmonious interpenetration' so that in their 'combined revelation'[30] will be the revelation of God's loving purposes for the world in and with his holiness. God's actions in reconciliation will be shown to correspond with his immanent being: 'God, the ethically necessary is, according to His Essence, content with nothing less than Self-conscious and free desire after the good.'[31] Dorner's heavy investment in mapping out the atoning activity of Christ in terms of its coherence with the immanent identity of the triune God means that he, unlike for example Robert Jensen or Wolfhart Pannenberg, feels comfortable picturing God as reconciling *himself* to the world (and not only reconciling the *world* to himself).[32]

In addition to these features of his account, we suggest that in his treatment of dogmatic loci such as the *munus triplex* Dorner displays a capacity to retain elements common to theological tradition (though, as in the case of Christ's offices, often unfashionable in his own period) while ordering them according to the presuppositions of his own agenda. With this he displays

---

[26] Though Dorner does not speak explicitly in these terms, God's ethical immutability is the guarantor of His *power* to act (a feature of the doctrine of immutability or constancy which is explicated by Barth to explain how the *movable* deity is 'able to do everything: everything, that is, which as His possibility is real possibility', *Church Dogmatics*, Vol. II, Part I, p. 522).

[27] *SCD*, I, p. 460.

[28] Ibid. p. 462.

[29] *SCD*, IV, pp. 9, 83.

[30] *SCD*, IV, p. 79.

[31] *SCD*, I, p. 446.

[32] Robert W. Jenson, *Systematic Theology*, Vol. 1, The Triune God (Oxford: OUP, 1997), p. 186; and Wolfhart Pannenberg, *Systematische Theologie*, Vol. 2, (Göttingen: Vandenhoek und Ruprecht, 1988–1992), pp. 447–461.

himself as a theologian committed to the pursuit of *continuity* with ecclesial tradition without gravitating towards mere doctrinal repristination. Thus, while we see his developmental theory of the incarnation as essentially flawed because of its tendency towards depicting the incarnation as the result of the free realization of humanity (though we have sought to correct some of the more excessive complaints against it), we suggest that its motivation (e.g. his reading of what he considered underused biblical data[33] and the desire not to abridge Christ's humanity without abandoning its dependent relation to God[34]) is indicative of a concern to revivify Christian doctrine by meeting both the demands of its sources and norms (Scripture and ecclesial tradition) and conforming to the immediate insights (as he saw them) of basic Christian faith in a considered appeal to the priority of the triune God in creation, conservation, reconciliation and consummation of the world without detriment to the relative freedom and independence of what has been made (and remade). We contend that with this Dorner may comfortably be described as a major dogmatician whose relative obscurity within many retellings of the story of modern theology is ultimately misplaced.[35] We suggest, in closing, that Dorner himself has provided a most suitable description of the kind of theologian he endeavoured to be (when writing of those Church Fathers who he contends had to deal with the rise of Montanism):

> The Church must have had men rich in faith, and love and knowledge, who being gentle and favourable towards what was true in montanism, and along with this attaching great importance to the unity of the Church, had skill to reconcile the mutually repelling and conflicting elements, to appropriate them to the Church, thereby overcoming contradictions, and resolving all into a higher spiritual unity.[36]

---

[33] E.g. Lk. 2.52; Phil. 2.8; esp. Heb. 5.8-9.

[34] While Dorner sought to display Christ as properly human, since it was *Christ's* humanity which is proposed as proper (cf. the Second Adam typology) it is an account which is ultimately defined *Christologically* and not anthropologically *remoto Christi*.

[35] Barth is, of course, an exception to this pattern. While he argues that Dorner's theology contains significant 'source of error' he commends what he sees as Dorner's concern to 'reckon seriously with God as the ground of revelation and faith', a point largely unrecognized by his contemporaries and the subsequent flow of theological history (which had, by the time of the publication of the *System of Christian Faith*, become overwhelmingly influenced by Ritschl and his school), *Protestant Theology in the Nineteenth Century*, p. 563. It is telling that Ritschl himself does not refer to Dorner in his *Christian Doctrine of Justification and Reconciliation*. It is probable that by the time Dorner came to write his final and definitive account, the appetite for dogmatics of that kind had largely disappeared.

[36] *History of Development*, Div. I, Vol. I, p. 256.

BIBLIOGRAPHY

I. Writings of I. A. Dorner

German

Briefwechsel Zwischen H. L. Martensen und I. A. Dorner. 1839–1881. Bande I & II (Berlin: H. Reuter's Verlagsbuchandlung, 1888).

Entwicklungsgeschichte der Lehre von der Person Christi von den ältesten Zeiten bis auf die neuesten (Stuttgart: S. G. Leisching, 1839).

Entwicklungsgeschichte der Lehre von der Person Christi von den ältesten Zeiten bis auf die neuesten dargestellt. Zweite, stark vermehrte Auflage in zwei Theilen (Stuttgart: S. G. Liesching, 1845–1856).

Gesammelte Schriften aus dem Gebiet der Systematischen Theologie, Exegese und Geschichte (Berlin: Willhelm Hertz, 1883).

Geschichte der Protestantischen Theologie, Besonders in Deutschland, nach ihrer Prinzipiellen Bewegung und im Zusammenhang mit dem Religiösen, Sittlichen und Intellektuellen Leben Betrachtet (München: Gotta'schen Buchhandlung, 1867).

Book Review in *H. Reuters Repertorium für Theologische Literatur und Kirchliche Statistik*, Berlin, 1845, Bd. I.

Inest Theodori Mopsuestia doctrina de Imagine Dei exposita (Regiomonti: Hartungianis, 1844).

System der Christlichen Glaubenslehre, Erster Band, Grundlegung oder Apologetik, Zweite Auflage (Berlin: Wilhelm Hertz, 1886).

System der Christlichen Glaubenslehre, Zweiter Band, Specielle Glaubenslehre, I. Hälfte, Zweite Auflage (Berlin: Wilhelm Hertz, 1886).

System der Christlichen Glaubenslehre, Zweiter Band, Specielle Glaubenslehre, II. Hälfte, Zweite Auflage (Berlin: Wilhelm Hertz, 1886).

System der Christlichen Sittenlehre (Berlin: Willhelm Hertz, 1885).

'Über die Entwicklungsgeschichte der Christologie besonders in den neuern Zeiten. Eine historisch-kritische Abhandlung' in *Tübinger Zeitschrift für Theologie*, Vol. 1 (1836): pp. 96–240.

'Über Die Entwicklungsgeschichte der Christologie besonders in den neuern Zeiten. Eine historisch-kritische Abhandlung' in *Tübinger Zeitschrift für Theologie*, Vol. 4 (1835): pp. 81–204.

English Translations

Divine Immutability, trans. Robert R. Williams and Claude Welch (Minneapolis: Fortress Press, 1994).

History of Protestant Theology, Particularly in Germany, trans. G. Robson and S. Taylor (Edinburgh: T & T Clark, 1871).

History of the Development of the Doctrine of the Person of Christ, Division First: First Four Centuries, trans. W. L. Alexander and D. W. Simon. Vol. I (Edinburgh: T & T Clark, 1861).

History of the Development of the Doctrine of the Person of Christ, Division First: First Four Centuries, trans. D. W. Simon. Vol. II (Edinburgh: T & T Clark, 1862).

History of the Development of the Doctrine of the Person of Christ, Division Second: From the End of the Fourth Century to the Present Time, trans. D. W. Simon. Vol. I (Edinburgh: T & T Clark, 1861)

History of the Development of the Doctrine of the Person of Christ, Division Second: From the End of the Fourth Century to the Present Time, trans. D. W. Simon. Vol. II (Edinburgh: T & T Clark, 1862).

History of the Development of the Doctrine of the Person of Christ, Division Second: From the End of the Fourth Century to the Present Time, trans. Patrick Fairnbairn. Vol. III (Edinburgh: T & T Clark, 1884).

A System of Christian Doctrine, trans. Alfred Cave. Vol. I (Edinburgh: T & T Clark, 1880).

A System of Christian Doctrine, trans. J. S. Banks. Vol. II (Edinburgh: T & T Clark, 1881).

A System of Christian Doctrine, trans. Alfred Cave and J. S. Banks. Vol. III (Edinburgh: T & T Clark, 1882).

A System of Christian Doctrine, trans. Alfred Cave and J. S. Banks. Vol. IV (Edinburgh: T & T Clark, 1882).

System of Christian Ethics, trans. C. M. Mead and R. T. Cunningham (Edinburgh: T & T Clark, 1887).

II. Secondary Literature

Anselm, St *Cur Deus Homo?* (Edinburgh: John Grant, 1909).

Axt-Piscalar, Christine. *Der Grund Des Glaubens* (Tübingen: Mohr Siebeck, 1990).

—*Ohnmächtige Freiheit* (Tübingen: Mohr Siebeck, 1996).

Barth, Karl. *Church Dogmatics*, Vol. II, The Doctrine of God, Part I (Edinburgh: T & T Clark, 1957).

—*Church Dogmatics*, Vol. III, The Doctrine of Creation, Part I (Edinburgh: T & T Clark, 1958).

—*Church Dogmatics*, Vol. IV, The Doctrine of Reconciliation, Part I (Edinburgh: T & T Clark, 1956).

—*Die christliche Dogmatik im Entwurf*, Erster Band, Die Lehre Vom Worte Gottes, 1927 (Zürich: Theologischer Verlag, 1982).

—*Protestant Theology in the Nineteenth Century*, New Edition (London: SCM, 2001).

Baur, F. C. *Die christliche Lehre von der Dreieinigkeit und Menschwerdung Gottes in ihrer geschichtlichen Entwicklung* (Tübingen: C. F. Osiander, 1841–1843).

—*Die christliche Lehre von der Versöhnung in ihrer geschichtlichen Entwicklung* (Tübingen: C. F. Osiander, 1838).

—*Ferdinand Christian Baur on the Writing of Church History*, ed. and trans. Peter C. Hodgson (New York: Oxford University Press, 1968).

Baur, F. C. *Lehrbuch der Dogmengeschichte*, Unaltered Publication of 3rd Reprint Leipzig: Becher, 1867 (Darmstadt: Wissenschaftliche Buchgesellschaft, 1974).

Bavinck, Herman. *Reformed Dogmatics: God and Creation*, Vol. 2, ed. John Bolt, trans. John Vriend (Grand Rapids: Eerdmans, 2004).

—*Reformed Dogmatics: Sin and Salvation in Christ*, Vol. 3, ed. John Bolt, trans. John Vriend (Grand Rapids: Baker, 2006).

Benckert, Heinrich. 'Isaak August Dorners "Pisteologie"' in *Zeitschrift für Theologie und Kirche*, Vol. 14 (1933): pp. 257–276.

Berkhof, Hendrikus. *Christian Faith* (Grand Rapids: Eerdmans, 1986).

Berkouwer, G. C. *Man: The Image of God* (Grand Rapids: Eerdmans, 1962).

—*Sin* (Grand Rapids: Eerdmans, 1971).

Blocher, Henri. *Original Sin* (Leicester: Apollos, 1997).

Bobertag, J. *Isaak August Dorner: Sein Leben und seine Lehre, mit besonderer Berücksichtigung seiner bleibenden Bedeutung für Theologie und Kirche* (Gütersloh: G. Bertelsmann, 1906).

Brown, Colin. *Jesus in European Protestant Thought 1778–1860* (Grand Rapids: Baker, 1985).

Brown, Robert F. 'On the Necessary Imperfection of Creation: Irenaeus' Adversus Haereses iv. 38' in *Scottish Journal of Theology*, No. 1 (February 1975): pp. 17–25.

Cave, A. S. *The Doctrine of the Work of Christ* (London: Hodder & Stoughton, 1937).

Chan, Mark. *Christology From Within and Ahead* (Leiden: Brill, 2001).

Clemen, C. *Die Christliche Lehre der Sünde* (Göttingen: Vandenhoek & Ruprecht, 1897).

Coffey, David. *Deus Trinitas: the Doctrine of the Triune God* (Oxford: Oxford University Press, 1999).

Craig, William L. *The Problems of Divine Foreknowledge and Future Contingents from Aristotle to Suarez* (Leiden: E. J. Brill, 1988).

Del Colle, Ralph. *Christ and the Spirit* (Oxford: Oxford University Press, 1994).

Delitzsch, Franz. *Commentar über die Genesis* (Leipzig: Dörffling und Franke, 1872).

Donfried, Karl P. 'Paul and the Revisionists: Did Luther Really Get It All Wrong?' in *Dialog: a Journal of Theology*, Vol. 46, No. 1 (Spring 2007): pp. 31–40.

Dorner, August. 'Dem Andenken von Dr. I. A. Dorner' in *Theologische Studien und Kritiken*, Erster Band (1885): pp. 417–452.

Drews, Andrew. *Die deutsche Spekulation seit Kant mit besonderer Rücksicht auf das Wesen des Absoluten und die Persönlichkeit Gottes* (Berlin: Paul Maeter, 1893).

Drickamer, John M. 'Higher Criticism and the Incarnation in the Thought of I. A. Dorner' in *Concordia Theological Quarterly*, Vol. 43, No. 3 (June 1979): pp. 197–207.

Edmondson, Stephen. *Calvin's Christology* (Cambridge: Cambridge University Press, 2004).

Flückiger, Felix. *Die protestantische Theologie des 19 Jahrhunderts* (Göttingen: Vandenhoek & Ruprecht, 1975).

Forsyth, P. T. *The Person and Place of Jesus Christ* (London: Independent Press, 1909).

Franks, Robert S. *A History of the Doctrine of the Work of Christ*, Vol. II (London: Hodder & Stoughton, 1918).

—*The Work of Christ* (Edinburgh: Thomas Nelson, 1962).

Frei, Hans. *I. A. Dorners Christologie und Trinitätslehre* (Leipzig: Sturm & Koppe, 1930).

Geß, W. F. *Das Dogma von Christi Person und Werk, Entwickelt aus Christi Selbst.* (Basel: Detloff, 1887).

—*Die Lehre von der Person Christi*. (Basel: Bahnmaier, 1856).

Gockel, Matthias. 'On the way from Schleiermacher to Barth: A critical reappraisal of Isaak August Dorner's essay on divine immutability' in *Scottish Journal of Theology*, Vol. 53, No. 4 (2000), pp. 490–510.

Greer, Rowan. *The Captain of Our Salvation* (Tübingen: Mohr Siebeck, 1973).

Greschat, Martin, ed. *Theologen des Protestantismus im 19 und 20 Jahrhunderts*, 2 Vols (Stuttgart: Kohlhammer, 1978).

Günther, E. *Die Entwicklung der Lehre von der Person Christi im XIX Jahrhundert*, (Tübingen: Mohr, 1911).

Gunton, Colin E. *The Actuality of Atonement* (Edinburgh: T & T Clark, 1988).

—*A Brief Theology of Revelation* (Edinburgh: T & T Clark, 1995).

—*Christ and Creation* (Carlisle: The Paternoster Press, 1992).

—*The Christian Faith* (Oxford: Blackwell Publishing, 2002).

—'The End of Causality? The Reformers and Their Predecessors' in *The Doctrine of Creation*, ed. Colin E. Gunton (Edinburgh: T & T Clark, 1997): pp. 63–82.

—ed. *God and Freedom* (Edinburgh: T & T Clark, 1995).

—*The One, the Three and the Many: God, Creation and the Culture of Modernity* (Cambridge: Cambridge University Press, 1993).

—*The Triune Creator* (Edinburgh: Edinburgh University Press, 1998).

Hanson, Anthony. *Grace and Truth* (London: SPCK, 1975).

Harris, Horton. *The Tübingen School* (Oxford: Clarendon Press, 1975).

Hartmann, Eduard Von. *Lotze's Philosophie* (Leipzig: Wilhelm Friedrich, 1888).

Hauck, D. A., ed. *Realencyklopädia für Protestantische Theologie und Kirche* (Leipzig: J. C. Hinrichs, 1898).

Herrmann, Christian. 'Gewissheit durch Differenz und Konkretion: Zum Verhältnis von Schöpfung und Erlösung bei Oswald Bayer' in *Theologische Zeitschrift*, Vol. 58 (2002): pp. 114–139.

Hirsch, Emanuel. *Geschichte der neuern evangelischen Theologie*, Bd. 5 (Gütersloh: C. Bertelsmann Verlag, 1951).

Holte, Ragnar. *Die Vermittlungstheologie: Ihre theologischen Grundbegriffe kritisch untersucht* (Upsalla: Almquist & Wiksells, 1965).

Horton, Michael Scott. *Lord and Servant: A Covenant Christology* (Westminster: John Knox Press, 2005).

Hüttenhoff, Michael. *Erkenntnistheorie und Dogmatik* (Bielfeld: Luther-Verlag, 1991).

Jenson, Robert. *Systematic Theology*, Vol. I, *The Triune God* (Oxford: Oxford University Press, 1997).

Jülicher, Adolf. *Die Religionswissenschaft der Gegenwart in Selbstdarstellung*, ed. Erich Stange (Leipzig: F. Meiner, 1928).

Jüngel, Eberhard. *God's Being is in Becoming*, trans. John Webster (Edinburgh: T & T Clark, 2001).

Kaftan, Julius. *Dogmatik* (Freiburg: Mohr Siebeck, 1897).

—*The Truth of the Christian Religion* (Edinburgh: T & T Clark, 1894).

Kähler, Martin. *Geschichte der Protestantischen Dogmatik im 19. Jahrhundert* (München: Kaiser Verlag, 1962).

Kierkegaard, Søren. *Søren Kierkegaard's Journals and Papers*, F–K, Vol. 2. ed. and trans. Howard V. Hong & Edna H. Hong (Bloomington and London: Indiana University Press, 1970).

Kleinert, P. *Zum Gedächtniß Isaak August Dorner's* (Berlin: Dobberte & Schleiermacher, 1884).

Knox, John. *The Humanity and Divinity of Christ* (Cambridge: Cambridge University Press, 1967).

Koppehl, Thomas. *Der wissenschaftliche Standpunkt der Theologie des Isaak August Dorners* (Berlin: Walter de Gruyter, 1997).

Krause, ed. 'Isaac Dorner' in *Theologische Realenzyklopädie*, Vol. 9 (Berlin: Alter de Gruyter, 1982): pp. 155–158.

Krötke, Wolf. *Gottes Klarheiten* (Tübingen: Mohr Siebeck, 2001).

Krug, W. T. *Pisteologie oder Glaube, Aberglaube und Unglaube sowohl an sich als im Verhältnisse zu Staat und Kirche betrachtet* (Leipzig: Baumgärtner, 1825).

Leith, John, ed. *Creeds of the Churches* (Richmond: John Knox Press, 1973).

Liebner, Carl Theodor Albert. *Die christliche Dogmatik* 1st Afl., Bd. I (Göttingen: Vandenhoek & Ruprecht, 1849).

Luthardt, Ernst. *Kompendium der Dogmatik* (Leipzig: Dörffling und Franke, 1893).

Mackintosh, H. R. *The Christian Experience of Forgiveness* (London: Nisbet and Co., 1934).

Macleod, Donald. *The Person of Christ* (Leicester: IVP, 1998).

Macquarrie, John. *Principles of Christian Theology* (London: SCM, 1977).

Malysz, Piotr J. 'Hegel's Conception of God and its Application by Isaak Dorner to the problem of Divine Immutability' in *Pro Ecclesia*, Vol. XV, No. 4 (Fall 2006): pp. 448–470.

Marheineke, P. *Die Grundlehren der Christlichen Dogmatik als Wissenschaft* (Berlin: Dunker & Humblot, 1827).

Martensen, Hans. *Christian Dogmatics*, trans. William Urwick (Edinburgh: T & T Clark, 1886).

Meessen, Frank. *Unveränderlichkeit und Menschwerdung Gottes* (Freiburg: Herder, 1989).

Melancthon, Phillip. *The Loci Communes of Phillip Melancthon*, trans. C. L. Hill (Boston: Meader Publishing Co., 1944).

Mildenberger, Friedrich. *Geschichte der deutschen evangelischen Theologiei im 19. und 20. Jahrhundert* (Stuttgart: Verlag W. Kohlhammer, 1981).

Müller, Julius. *The Christian Doctrine of Sin*, Vol II, trans. W Pulsford (Edinburgh: T & T Clark, 1853).

—*Die Christliche Lehre von der Sünde*. Bde. I & II (Breslau: Josef Mar, 1844).

—*Die Christliche Lehre von der Sünde*, Bd. I & II, 6th Aufl. (Stuttgart: Stuttgart, 1877).

—*Vom Wesen und Grund der Sünde* (Breslau: Josef Mar, 1839).

Muller, Richard A. 'A Note on "Christocentrism" and the Impudent Use of Such Terminology' in *The Westminster Theological Journal*, Vol. 68, No. 2 (Fall 2006): pp. 253–260.

BIBLIOGRAPHY

Mullins, E. Y. *The Christian Religion in Its Doctrinal Expression* (Philadelphia: The Judson Press, 1917, repr. 1945).

Nitzsch, I. *System of Christian Doctrine*, trans. Robert Montgomery (Edinburgh: T & T Clark, 1849).

O'Collins, Gerald. *Christology* (Oxford: Oxford University Press, 1995).

O'Hanlon, Gerard F. *The Immutability of God in the Theology of Hans Urs von Balthasar*. (Cambridge: Cambridge University Press, 1990).

Owen, John. *The Works of John Owen*, Vol. 10 (Edinburgh: Banner of Truth Trust, 1967).

Pannenberg, Wolfhart. *Anthropology in Theological Perspective* (Edinburgh: T & T Clark, 1985).

—*Jesus-God and Man* (London: SCM, 1968).

—*Systematic Theology*, Vol. I, trans. Geoffrey W. Bromiley (Edinburgh: T & T Clark, 1991).

—*Systematic Theology*, Vol. II, trans. Geoffrey W. Bromiley (Edinburgh: T & T Clark, 1994).

—*Systematische Theologie* (Göttingen: Vandenhoek & Ruprecht, 1988–1992).

Plantinga, Alvin. *The Nature of Necessity* (Oxford: Clarendon Press, 1974).

Rahner, Karl. *Theological Investigations* IV (London: Darton, Longman & Todd, 1966).

Reuter, H. Book Review in *Allgemeines Repertorium für die theologische Literatur und kirchliche Statistik*, Zweiundfunfzigster Band, (Berlin: Herbig, 1846).

Richards, Jay W. *The Untamed God: A Philosophical Exploration of Divine Perfection, Simplicity and Immutability* (Downers Grove: InterVarsity Press, 2003).

Ritschl, Albrecht. *The Christian Doctrine of Justification and Reconciliation*, trans. H. R. Mackintosh and A Macaulay (Edinburgh: T & T Clark, 1900).

—*The Christian Doctrine of Justification and Reconciliation* (Clifton, NJ: Reference Book, 1966.).

Rohls, Jan. *Philosophie und Theologie in Geschichte und Gegenwart* (Tübingen: Mohr Siebeck, 2002).

Rothe, Richard. *Dogmatik*, Bd. I (Heidelberg: J. C. B. Mohr, 1870).

Rothermundt, Jörg. *Personale Synthese: Isaak August Dorners dogmatische Methode* (Göttingen: Vandenhoek & Ruprecht, 1968).

Rössler, D. *Die Vernunft der Religion* (München: Piper, 1976).

Russell, Stanley. 'I. A. Dorner: A Centenary Appreciation' in *Expository Times*, Vol. 96, No. 3 (December 1984): pp. 77–81.

—'Two Nineteenth Century Theologies of Sin – Julius Müller and Søren Kierkegaard' in *Scottish Journal of Theology*, Vol. 40, No. 2 (1987): pp. 231–248.

Sanders, Daniel, ed. *Wörterbuch der Deutschen Sprache* (Leipzig: Otto Wigand, 1860).

Schiller, Friedrich. *Etwas über die erste Menschengesellschaft*, Bd. IX (Haag: Hartmann, 1838).

Schleiermacher, Friedrich. *The Christian Faith*, ed. H. R. Mackintosh and Jonathan S. Stewart (Edinburgh: T & T Clark, 1976).

Schlink, E. *Theology of the Lutheran Confessions*, trans. P Koehneke and H Bouman (St. Louis: Concordia, 1961).

Schweizer, Alexander. *Die Christliche Glaubenslehre* (Leipzig: Hirzel, 1877).

Schwöbel, Christoph. 'Christology and Trinitarian Thought' in *Trinitarian Thought Today*, ed. Christoph Schwöbel (Edinburgh: T & T Clark, 1995): pp. 113–146.

—'Imago Libertatis: Human and Divine Freedom' in *God and Freedom: Essays in Historical and Systematic Theology*, ed. Colin E. Gunton (Edinburgh: T & T Clark, 1995).

—'Reconciliation' in *The Theology of Reconciliation*, ed. Colin E. Gunton (London: T & T Clark, 2003): pp. 13–38.

Shedd, William G. *Dogmatic Theology* (Phillipsburg: Presbyterian and Reformed Company, 3rd edn, 2003).

—*King, Priest, Prophet* (London: T & T Clark, 2004).

Slenczka, Reinhard. *Geschichtlichkeit und Personsein Jesu Christi* (Göttingen: Vandenhoek & Ruprecht, 1967).

Smeaton, George. *The Doctrine of the Atonement* (Edinburgh: T & T Clark, 1868).

Smedes, Lewis B. *The Incarnation: Trends in Modern Anglican Thought* (Amsterdam: Kampen, 1953).

Spence, Alan. 'Christ's Humanity and Ours: John Owen' in *Persons Divine and Human*, eds Christoph Schwöbel and Colin E. Gunton (Edinburgh: T & T Clark, 1991): pp. 74–97.

—*The Promise of Peace: a Unified Theory of Atonement* (London: T & T Clark, 2006).

Spencer, Archibald J. *Clearing a Space for Human Action* (New York: Peter Lang, 2003).

Splett, Jörg. *Die Trinitätslehre G. W. F. Hegels* (Freiburg & München: Verlag Karl Alber, 1965).

Stump, Eleonore. 'Intellect, Will, and the Principle of Alternate Possibilities' in *Christian Theism and the Problems of Philosophy*, ed. M. D. Beaty (Notre Dame: University of Notre Dame, 1990): pp. 254–285.

Tanner, Kathryn. 'Jesus Christ' in *The Cambridge Companion to Christian Doctrine*, ed. Colin E. Gunton (Cambridge: Cambridge University Press, 1997): pp. 245–272.

Tennant, F. R. *The Origin and Propagation of Sin* (Cambridge: Cambridge University Press, 1902).

Tholuck, August. 'Über die Natur der Sünde wider den Heiligen Geist' in *Theologische Studien und Kritiken*, Vol. 9 (1836): pp. 401–416.

Thomasius, Gottfried. *Christi Person und Werk*, Bd. II (Erlangen: Bläsing, 1857).

Tillich, Paul. *Perspectives on 19th and 20th Century Protestant Theology*, ed. C. Braaten. (London: SCM, 1967).

Torrance, Alan. 'Creatio Ex Nihilo and the Spatio-temporal Dimensions, with Special Reference to Jürgen Moltmann and D. C. Williams' in *The Doctrine of Creation*, ed. Colin E. Gunton (Edinburgh: T & T Clark, 1997): pp. 83–104.

Torrance, Thomas F. *The Christian Doctrine of God, One Being Three Persons* (Edinburgh: T & T Clark, 1996).

Wagner, Falk. *Der Gedanke der Persönlichkeit Gottes bei Fichte und Hegel* (Gütersloh: Gütersloher Verlagshaus, 1971).

Warfield, B. B. *The Person and Work of Christ*, ed. Samuel G. Craig (Philadelphia: The Presbyterian and Reformed Company, 1950).

Weber, Otto. *Foundations of Dogmatics*, Vol. I, trans. Darrell L. Guder (Grand Rapids: Eerdmans, 1981).

—*Foundations of Dogmatics*, Vol. II, trans. Darrell L. Guder (Grand Rapids: Eerdmans, 1983).

Webster, John. 'The Divine Perfections', Unpublished.

—*Holiness* (London: SCM, 2003).

Weinandy, Thomas. *Does God Suffer?* (Edinburgh: T & T Clark, 2000).

Welch, Claude. *The Development of Theology in Germany since Kant* (London: S. Sonnenschein, 1890).

—*Protestant Theology in the Nineteenth Century, 1799–1870*, Vol. I (New Haven: Yale, 1972).

Wenz, Gunther. *Geschichte der Versöhnungslehre in der evangelischen Theologie der Neuzeit*, Bd. I (München: Kaiser Verlag, 1984).

—*Geschichte der Versöhnungslehre in der evangelischen Theologie der Neuzeit*, Bd. II (München: Kaiser Verlag, 1986).

—'Vom Unwesen der Sünde' in *Kerygma und Dogma*, Vol. 30 (1984): pp. 298–329.

Wilberforce, Archdeacon. *The Doctrine of the Incarnation of Our Lord Jesus Christ* (London: Walter Smith, 1885).

Williams, Robert R. 'I. A. Dorner: The Ethical Immutability of God' in *Journal of the American Academy of Religion*, Vol. 54, No. 4 (Winter 1986): pp. 721–738.

—. 'Isaak Dorner on Divine Immutability: A Missing Link Between Schleiermacher and Barth' in *The Journal of Religion*, Vol. 77, No. 3 (July 1997): pp. 380–401.

—'Introduction' in *Divine Immutability*, trans. Robert R. Williams and Claude Welch (Minneapolis: Fortress Press, 1994): pp. 12–19.

—'Schelling and Dorner on Divine Immutability' in *Journal of the American Academy of Religion*, Vol. 53, No. 2 (June 1985): pp. 237–249.

Williams, Rowan. 'Barth on the Triune God' in *Karl Barth: Studies in His Theological Method*, ed. S. W. Sykes (Oxford: Clarendon Press, 1979): pp. 147–193.

Yerkes, James. *The Christology of Hegel* (Albany: State University of New York, 1983).

Zeisler, John. *Paul's Letter to the Romans* (London: SCM, 1989).

Zöckler, D. O. *Geschicte der Beziehungen zwischen Theologie und Naturwissenschaft mit besondrer Rücksicht auf Schöpfungsgeschichte* (Gütersloh: Bertelsmann, 1879).

—*Theologia naturalis. Erster Band: Die Prolegomena und die specielle Theologie ehältend* (Frankfurt: Herder & Zimmer, 1860).

INDEX